SENIOR CITIZENSH

Retirement, migration an the European Union

Louise Ackers and Peter Dwyer

The POLICY PRESS

DEDICATION

We would like to dedicate this book to our respective partners,
Eric and Linda.

First published in Great Britain in June 2002 by

The Policy Press
34 Tyndall's Park Road
Bristol BS8 1PY
UK

Tel +44 (0)117 954 6800
Fax +44 (0)117 973 7308
e-mail tpp@bristol.ac.uk
www.policypress.org.uk

British Library Cataloguing in Publication Data
A catalogue record for this book is available from the British Library

ISBN 1 86134 264 0 paperback

Louise Ackers is Jean Monnet Professor in European Law and Director of the Centre for the Study of Law in Europe, and **Peter Dwyer** is a Lecturer in Social Policy at the Department of Sociology and Social Policy, both at the University of Leeds.

Cover design by Qube Design Associates, Bristol.

Printed and bound in Great Britain by Hobbs the Printers Ltd, Southampton.

Contents

List of tables and figures

Tables

Figures

List of acronyms

ADI	Assistenza Donmiciliare Integrata (an integrated system of home nursing, physiotherapy and social care in Italy)
CC	community care
CCS	community care services
CEC	Commission of the European Communities
CMLR	Common Market Law reports
CML Rev	Common Market Law Review
CPAG	Child Poverty Action Group
DSS	Department of Social Security
EC	European Community
ECHR	European Court of Human Rights
ECJ	European Court of Justice
ECR	European Court reports
EEA	European Economic Area
EKAS	pensioners 'social solidarity' benefit (Greece)
ELA	Eurolink Age
EMU	European Monetary Union
EOAOP	European Observatory on Ageing and Older People
ERM	Exchange Rate Mechanism
EU	European Union
GDP	Gross Domestic Product
IAT	Immigration Appeals Tribunal
IC	institutional care
IKA	Institute for Social Security (Greece)
IPNS	National Social Security Institute (Italy)
IRM	International Retirement Migration
KAPI	'open care day centres' (Greece)
LA	local authority
LTRC	long-term residential care
MIG	Minimum Income Guarantee
OAP	old age pensioner
OGA	Agricultural Insurance Organisation (Greece)
ONPTS	Office National des Pensions pour Travailleurs Salaries (France)
PAYG	Pay As You Go
PLM	Paid Labour Market
PRSA	Personal Retirement Saving Accounts (Ireland)
PRSI	Pay-Related Social Insurance (Ireland)
PSS	Personal Social Services
R	Regina
RFV	The National Insurance Board (Sweden)
SERPS	State Earnings Related Pensions
SNS	Servico Nacional de Saúde (Portuguese national health service)

SSN   Sistema Sanitario Nazionale (Italian national health service)
TEU   Treaty on European Union
VAT   Value Added Tax
VHI   Voluntary Health Insurance (Ireland)

List of cases and European Union legislation

Cases

Bettray v Staatssecretaris van Justitie, Case 344/87 [1989] ECR 1621, [1991] 1 CMLR 459

Castelli v ONPTS, Case 261/83 [1984] ECR 3199

Centre public d'aide sociale de Courcelles v Lebon, Case 316/85 [1987] ECR 2811, [1989] 1 CMLR 337

Cristini v Société nationale des chemins de fer français, Case 32/75 [1975] ECR II-1085

de Vos v Bielefeld, Case C-315/94 [1996] ECR 1-1417

Diatta v Land Berlin, Case 267/83 [1985] ECR 567, [1986] 2 CMLR 164

Di Paolo v Office National de L'Emploi, Case 76/76 [1977] ECR I-315

Even, see *Ministere Public v Even & ONPTS*, Case 207/78 [1979] ECR 2019, [1980] 2 CMLR 71

F v Belgian State, Case 7/75 [1975] ECR 679, [1975] 2 CMLR 442

Frascogna v Caisse des Depots et consignations, Case 157/84 [1985] ECR 1739

Kempf v Staatssecretaris van Justitie, Case 139/85 [1986] ECR 1741, [1987] 1 CMLR 101

Konstantinidis v Stadt Altensteig-Standesamt, Case C-168/91 [1993] ECR 1191

Lawrie-Blum v Land Baden-Württemberg, Case 66/85 [1986] ECR 2121, [1987] 3 CMLR 389

Lebon, see *Centre public d'aide sociale de Courcelles v Lebon*, Case 316/85 [1987] ECR 2811, [1989] 1 CMLR 337

Levin v Staatssecretaris van Justitie, Case 53/81 [1982] ECR 1035, [1982] 2 CMLR 454

Luisi and Carbone v Ministero del Tesoro, Cases 286/82 and 26/83 [1984] ECR 377, [1985] 3 CMLR 52

Martinez Sala v Freistaat Bayern, Case C-85/96 (see f/n 27 and 85)/96 [1998] ECR I-2691

Mehment Birden v Stadgemeinde Bremen, Case C-1/97

Ministere Public v Even & ONPTS, Case 207/78 [1979] ECR 2019, [1980] 2 CMLR 71

Netherlands v Reed, Case 59/85 [1986] ECR 1283, [1987] 2 CMLR 448

R v IAT and Surinder Singh ex parte Secretary of State for the Home Department, Case 370/90 [1992] ECR I-4265, [1992] 3 CMLR 358

R v Secretary of State for the Home Department (ex parte Sandhu), [1982] 2 CMLR 553

R v Secretary of State for the Home Department (ex parte Shingara), Joined Cases C-65 and C-111/95 [1997] ECR I-3343, [1997] 3 CMLR 703

Raulin v Minister van Onderwijs en Wetenschappen, Case C-357/89 [1992] ECR I-1027, [1994] 1 CMLR 227

Sandhu, see *R v Secretary of State for the Home Department (ex parte Sandhu)*, [1982] 2 CMLR 553

Schmidt v Belgian State, Case C-310/91 [1993] ECR I-3011

Shingara, see *R v Secretary of State for the Home Department (ex parte Singh Shingara and Abbas Radiom)*, Joined Cases C-65/95 and C-111/95 [1997] ECR I-3343

Skanavi and Chryssanthakopoulos, Case C-193/94 [1996] ECR I-929, [1996] 2 CMLR 372

Snares v Chief Adjudication Officer, Case C-20/96 [1997] ECR I-6057

Steymann v Staatssecretaris van Justitie, Case 196/87 [1988] ECR 6159, [1989] 1 CMLR 449

Stober and Pereira v Bundesanstalt für Arbeit, Joined Cases (C-4 and C-5/95 [1997] ECR I-511

Swaddling v the Adjudication Officer, Case C-90/97 [1999] ECR I-1075

European Union legislation

Council Regulation 1612/68 (Workers' and workers' families rights) Official Journal Special edition 1968, No L257/2, p 475

Council Directive 68/360 (Free movement and residence) Official Journal Special edition 1968, No L257/13, p 485

Council Directive 90/364 (General Right of Residence) Official Journal 1990, No L180/26

Council Directive 90/365 (Residence rights for ex-employees and self-employed) Official Journal 1990, No L180/28

Council Regulation 1408/71 (on the application of social security schemes to employed persons, to self-employed persons and to members of their families moving within the Community) as amended, Official Journal 1997, No L28/1

Acknowledgements

Thanks are due to a number of individuals and organisations that have made the publication of this book possible. Firstly, we would like to acknowledge the support of the Wellcome Trust in funding the research project 'Citizenship and Retirement Migration in the European Union' (project number 048853) on which this book is based. Secondly, we would like to extend our gratitude to our research partners who conducted the interviews with respondents across Europe. They are: Heloisa Perista, Centre for Studies in Social Intervention (CESIS), Lisbon; Martha Blomqvist and Vera Gustaffson, Centre for Feminist Research, University of Uppsala; Simona Berretta, University of Trieste; and Athina Petrogolou, Athens. Liz Morrall, Assistant Director of Eurolink Age has also taken an active interest in the work and provided much interesting material. Thirdly, we would like to extend our thanks to a number of colleagues who have read different parts of the text at various stages of its development. The comments, criticisms and corrections of Kirk Mann, Helen Stalford, Dimitri Papandimitriou and Simon Prideaux have been greatly appreciated. Finally, we would like to record our thanks to all the families and organisations that kindly agreed to be interviewed.

Louise Ackers and Peter Dwyer
November 2001

ONE

Introduction

As a piece of comparative, socio-legal research, this book has three key objectives. First, to describe the development of a framework of formal legal rights for retirement migrants under the free movement of persons' provisions and, in particular, to critically evaluate the concepts of work and family in Community law and their implications for formal entitlement. Second, to develop a comprehensive and 'grounded' understanding of the process and experience of retirement migration as the basis of a more meaningful engagement with European law and policy. Third, to explore the importance of welfare issues in relation to the international migratory movements of retired European citizens who move within the European Union (EU).

The EU itself is not a welfare provider, but rather regulates access to domestic welfare systems. As such, an awareness of comparative social policy and of issues around care and well-being in later life is central to our analysis of the translation of legal rights into material reality and citizenship experience. In order to understand the consequences of a move in retirement (given that the right to freedom of movement is based on a principle of non-discrimination rather than social harmonisation[1]), the book thus considers the social policy context within each of the six member states that were the focus for the fieldwork. These were Greece, Italy, Portugal, the UK, Ireland and Sweden. Chapters Five, Six and Seven outline and discuss the systems of support for senior citizens in these states.

Within social and political science, citizenship remains a much discussed and highly contentious concept, but typically citizenship entails an association between the individual 'citizen' and some form of community. Central in defining the quality of any notion of citizenship is the extent of, and the relationship between, any rights and responsibilities that the status of 'citizenship' involves. In practical terms, this usually translates into a situation whereby a citizen can expect access to certain civil, political and social rights, provided that they in return accept certain communally specified responsibilities. In any book that is exploring the international migratory movement of citizens within the confines of the EU, a consideration of the rights and responsibilities of European Union citizenship as formally laid out in the Treaty on European Union (TEU) is an important initial task; particularly given that freedom of movement has long been central to the very idea of EU citizenship.

'Citizenship of the Union' and mobility

At present EU citizenship, more formally known as 'Citizenship of the Union' (Articles 17-22 EC), is based on nationality and applies to all those persons resident within the EU who are nationals of one of the EU member states[2]. In the context of EU competence, the development of citizenship since the Treaty of Rome has taken place in close connection to the evolution of mobility rights. This relationship between mobility and citizenship was given formal constitutional recognition in the Treaty on European Union (TEU) with the insertion of a new Article declaring the existence of 'Citizenship of the Union':

Citizenship of the Union

Article 17

1. Citizenship of the Union is hereby established. Every person holding the nationality of a Member State shall be a citizen of the Union. Citizenship of the Union shall complement and not replace national citizenship.

2. Citizens of the Union shall enjoy the rights conferred by this Treaty and shall be subject to the duties imposed thereby.

Article 18

1. Every citizen of the Union shall have the right to move and reside freely within the territory of the Member States, subject to the limitations and conditions laid down in this Treaty and by the measures adopted to give it effect.

Article 19

1. Every citizen of the Union residing in a Member State of which he is not a national shall have the right to vote and stand as a candidate at municipal elections in the Member State in which he resides, under the same conditions as nationals of that State.

2. [...] every citizen of the Union residing in a Member State of which he is not a national shall have the right to vote and stand as a candidate in elections to the European Parliament in the Member State in which he resides, under the same conditions as nationals of that State.

This study considers the significance of mobility to the citizenship status of retired migrants in two distinct but linked senses. First, our concept of citizenship goes beyond the evaluation of material status to encompass the ability of persons to exercise choice and agency in the planning of their lives. Second, mobility constitutes a social right of considerable value to well-being and autonomy. Differential ability to move thus reflects an inequality of condition and status in itself. The study considers, therefore, mobility as a right in itself and also as a determinant of social entitlement.

The juxtaposition of the formal establishment of Citizenship of the Union in Article 17 with the rights attached to mobility in Articles 18 and 19 reaffirms the close relationship between citizenship and mobility in Community law[3]. Mobility is thus not only a right in itself but also constitutes the trigger to other forms of social entitlement. Arguably, in the absence of mobility, Citizenship of the Union contributes little to the social status and day-to-day experience of Community nationals (cf Kleinman, 2002).

To the extent that the relationship between citizenship and migration has been subject to analysis, it is usually in the context of drawing a distinction between those migrants who hold community nationality and those who do not (in other words third country nationals), emphasising issues of membership and nationality as the basis of personal entitlement. The concept of 'Citizenship of the Union' is closely linked to notions of membership and inclusivity and implies some form of universal status based on membership of the EU, or at least Community residence or nationality. Referring to the exclusion of non-nationals from the benefits attached to Community citizenship Chalmers and Szyszczak conclude that "Citizenship of the Union has been reserved as an exclusive membership of a club for persons holding nationality of one of the Member States" (1998, p 78). The authors go on to refer to Ward's argument that "law plays a critical role in marginalising certain groups from the full benefits of European integration" (Ward, 1997, p 79). The reference in this last sentence to the full benefits of integration infers a broad equality of status among Community nationals. While nationality doubtless remains the most significant basis of exclusion (and we do not wish to underplay the seriousness of concerns about the status of third country nationals within the EU), it is valid to concentrate on the supposed 'in-group' in order to evaluate the concept of EU citizenship in more detail. In practice, the legal basis of claims determines the scope of personal entitlement. Entitlement is by no means universal nor derived simply from Community nationality, but turns on notions of contribution and family status. As Lister suggests, "It is as 'insiders' also that many women and members of minority groups experience citizenship, in its substantive sense, as exclusion" (1997, p 65). The internal exclusion of certain groups of EU nationals from equal enjoyment of full European citizenship status continues to limit the substantive rights of many who meet the nationality requirement.

At face value Article 18 (1) infers a broad equality of status among Community nationals. The precise wording, however, suggests some caveats, rendering entitlement "subject to the limitations and conditions laid down in this Treaty and by the measures adopted to give it effect". The full implications of this provision and the extent to which the inclusion of Article 18 effectively replaces pre-existing law has not yet been resolved. At present residency rights are provided for under a cluster of Directives specific to different groups of migrants[4].

The research presented in this book reflects an ongoing concern to examine the relationship between citizenship and internal migration within the European Union. Parallel research projects have exposed the tiered nature of EU citizenship with entitlement linked to concepts of dependency, family status and economic contribution via the paid labour market (PLM)[5]. By focusing here on a specific form of intra-Community mobility (of mobile, retired, community nationals) and examining the distinctions in status and social entitlement within this group, this project further exposes a subtle hierarchy of formal entitlement (cf Ackers, 1998) reflecting the legal valuation of different forms of contribution and personal relationships and the consequence of these in terms of the flow of social resources. At the apex of this hierarchy stands the Community migrant worker with full independent entitlement in the host state. In the second tier stand those members of the worker's family with full but derived entitlement. Finally, in the third tier, "a category of citizenship exists which gives rise to very minimal social entitlement, requiring those who claim a right to free movement to demonstrate financial autonomy" (Ackers, 1998, p 314).

In relation to retired EU migrants we initially envisaged a single fundamental status differentiation between two groups; those who moved as workers and then retired, and those who retired and then moved. Unlike the former group, who had full access to host welfare systems, the latter group (referred to in the book as 'post-retirement migrants') are effectively caught by the resources requirement in what became known as the 'playboy directive' (Council Directive 90/365). This requirement to demonstrate financial autonomy specifically underwrites the mobility rights and welfare status of those retired persons who wish to move following cessation of economic activity. The limitations and operational implications of this 'simple' binary logic, based on the presumption of static social groups and classification systems, soon emerged as the research team attempted to define and locate this heterogeneous population. The concepts of 'retirement', 'end of economic activity' and 'migrant' all proved complex and presupposed the ability to identify fixed categories of retirees. In practice, the study of retirement migration, rather than building an additional dimension onto our existing work, presented a complex microcosm of the wider Community citizenship hierarchy.

Pre-existing mobility, pre-retirement work status and the evolution of family relationships (including marital status and the presence and mobility of children) all shape a person's formal legal status in retirement. The highly complex and unpredictable status of this post-retirement group intermeshes with other sources of entitlement and is in constant flux as their lives unfold. In that sense, their rights interconnect and evolve in response to changes in family situation and location. A retired migrant may, for example, be able to base a claim on their own status as a mobile retired person and as the ascendant parent of a migrant worker simultaneously. While it is interesting to examine the distinctiveness of the social groups represented in the three linked projects (that is, men and women of working age, children and retired persons) at least in terms of understanding the kinds of social cleavages generated by Community law, in practice they share many similar experiences and are often part of the same family[6].

To the extent that it is possible to define subgroups with distinctive legal status the research has included the following categories of respondents:

1. Persons who move to another member state for work and then exercise their right to remain (retired community workers).
2. Those who move to another member state for work and then return home on retirement (returning community workers).
3. Persons who retire in the home state and then move (post-retirement migrants).
4. A subgroup of category 3 who move in order to accompany or join their Community migrant children claiming rights as ascendant, dependent, relatives (joiners).
5. A subgroup of category 3 who subsequently return home (returning post-retirement migrants).

The concept of migration or mobility is itself problematic as it typically implies the identification of one significant move perhaps followed by a return move. Migration and retirement often involve a series of moves into and out of work and between different locations. The migration process may commence with extended vacations followed by seasonal moves, a period of 'settled' residence abroad and eventual 'evolving' return. People may retire from their main occupation and then take up part-time, voluntary or self-employed work. Indeed, such movements into and out of work may become increasingly common in the context of labour market shortages and increasing policy emphasis on the importance of delaying retirement and explicitly encouraging retired people to resume paid work. The legal status of respondents is further complicated by the retention of, perhaps seasonal, residences in the home or another member state. Each of these factors impacts on the formal legal status of the person concerned and any accompanying family, irrespective of social need. The retirement migration project has endeavoured to understand the implications of these shifts in status both at the formal level in terms of social and welfare status and in terms of citizenship experience.

Welfare, the 'problems of old age' and EU social policy

A number of significant changes in European society have combined to force the EU to consider the welfare of Europe's senior citizens more closely. A general fall in birth rates, accompanied by a simultaneous increase in life expectancy means that the age structure of Europe's population is undergoing change with significant increases in the number of people aged 65 plus and 80 plus forecast in the next 30 years. Although these demographic changes will affect each member state in different ways and to different degrees, Europe's ageing population has largely been viewed by the EU as problematic in that it represents a challenge to the viability of established national welfare systems. Against this backdrop fears that a decreasing number of paid workers would not be able to meet rising costs required in relation to the pensions, health and social care of the ageing population have dominated debate and influenced policy at both national and EU level (see CEC, 1995, 1999, 2001; Hantrais, 2000; OECD, 2000).

All member states are or have been engaged in reforms designed to contain or reduce the future cost of public pension provision. Another allied development has been a shift in policy with regards to early retirement (OECD, 2000). Recent decades have seen an overall increase in the number of people aged 50 plus who are no longer active in the paid labour market. Indeed, numerous European nations actively encouraged early withdrawal from paid work, in spite of the fact that many members of Europe's retired population are generally healthier and live longer than their own grandparents. This approach has been reversed in recent years with member states now being urged by the Commission (CEC, 1999) to raise official retirement ages and discourage early exit from paid employment. The issue of care in later life also increasingly exercises the minds of European policy makers. As Hantrais reminds us, "rather than disappearing, the problems of disability and frailty associated with biological ageing have been postponed to a later age" (2000, p 149). Increased longevity coupled with higher rates of female activity in the paid labour market have far-reaching implications in terms of the availability of informal familial care of older people in the future.

The social and demographic changes outlined above have moved old age and related issues onto the European social policy agenda in the last decade. The early 1990s saw the establishment of both an Action Programme (to monitor and exchange information about demographic change and its impact on social protection and health systems) and a European Observatory on Ageing and Older People (EOAOP) that was to report to the Commission on the situation in each member state. Subsequently, its communication (CEC, 1999) recommended that member states develop policies to achieve four linked objectives. First, it identified a need to prolong working lives via promotion of lifelong learning/flexibility. Second, it advised the reversal of policies that promoted early retirement. Third, it recommended the commissioning of research into how adequate health and care services could be developed for Europe's senior citizens, and finally, it urged member states to promote policies that combated age discrimination and unemployment and social exclusion among the older population (Hantrais, 2000).

In spite of the Commission's recent interest, issues related to old age and welfare remain peripheral concerns at EU level. Geyer (2000) acknowledges that measures such as the commitment to grant minimum rights to retired workers[7] (CEC, 1990), the setting up of the EOAOP and the introduction of a legal provision prohibiting discrimination on grounds of age (Article 13 EC) are to be applauded. However, he also believes that the rights of Europe's senior citizens remain a secondary concern within the EU, which looks to member states to find their own ways forward. The EU's power to intervene directly in the welfare systems of member states is, of course, limited by the principle of subsidiarity introduced in the TEU (Article 5 ex 3b). This principle allows member states to enact measures to meet the legislative requirements of the EU in ways that reflect their institutional and cultural custom and practice. Effectively this amounts to an acceptance that, in the first instance, policies should be made at the national or sub-national level, with the EU only

Table 1: Projected demographic trends in the six member states

Country	Greece		Italy		Portugal		UK		Ireland		Sweden	
Dimension	1960	2030	1960	2030	1960	2030	1960	2030	1960	2030	1960	2030
Life expectancy at birth (years)												
Male	68	78	67	79	61	77	68	78	68	79	72	80
Female	71	84	72	84	67	83	74	83	72	84	76	85
Percentage of population												
aged 65 years and over	8	25	10	30	8	23	12	23	11	18	12	25
aged 80 years and over	1	7	1	8	1	6	2	6.5	2	5	2	8.5
	2000	**2030**	**2000**	**2030**	**2000**	**2030**	**2000**	**2030**	**2000**	**2030**	**2000**	**2030**
Lifetime years spent in work												
Male	37	33	33	27	39	33	38	34	38	34	37	33
Female	21	32	19	27	30	39	32	38	24	38	34	36
Old age dependency ratio[a]	2	1.5	2	1	3	2	3	2	3.5	2.5	2.5	1.5

Note:

[a] The 'old age dependency ratio' indicates the number of people aged 65 and over compared with people aged 16-64.

Source: Figures from OECD (2000). See pp 131-217 for more details of limitations of data

intervening when its objectives cannot (or are not) efficiently met by policies instigated by lower level political institutions. The implementation of social policy thus remains very much a national prerogative and overall the impact of EU policy in relation to welfare and old age remains limited (Geyer, 2000).

Different worlds of welfare: international retirement migration and the importance of location

In the past the welfare systems of the six member states under consideration in this book have been variously classified in relation to a number of criteria by theorists engaged in comparative analysis (for example, Esping-Andersen, 1990; Lewis, 1992; Giarchi, 1996). The construction of a detailed typology of welfare states in relation to social security and care in old age lies beyond the remit of this book. Nonetheless, a brief exploration is warranted on the grounds that continuing differences in the levels and types of provision at member state level have a particular importance in relation to international retirement migration (IRM) in the EU. Esping-Andersen's (1990) influential study was an attempt to construct a typology of welfare states based on the different ways in which they are organised in relation to market forces, social structures and political interests. He classified a number of states according to three basic 'ideal types' of welfare regime. 'Liberal/Anglo-Saxon' countries typically developed their welfare systems against an historic backdrop of strong class antagonism, which often resulted in residual social welfare schemes reserved for poor people, with private and occupational welfare available to the middle classes. In contrast, the 'conservative/corporatist' welfare states of continental Europe are typified by strong occupational, contribution based, social insurance welfare schemes for paid workers and lower rate social assistance benefits for those outside the PLM. The third group of 'social democratic/Scandinavian' states are distinguished from the others by welfare systems based very much on universalist services, full employment and equal opportunity, in which access to welfare is less dependent upon activity in the PLM.

A fourth category, variously described as a 'southern' (Ferrera, 1996), 'rudimentary/Latin rim' (Leibfried, 2000), has since been added to Esping-Andersen's original classification. The key elements that distinguish southern European welfare states have been laid out by Ferrera (1996), although debate continues as to the extent that southern welfare states are different to their conservative/corporatist continental cousins (see Katrougalos, 1966; Guillén and Matsaganis, 2000). In the context of this book two points are of particular relevance. First, what Ferrera (1996) calls the polarisation of social protection in retirement. Typically, southern welfare states have a "fragmented income maintenance system: generous retirement benefits for 'protected categories', but modest benefits for the rest, plus a low social pension for those with insufficient contributions" (Guillén and Matsaganis, 2000, p 123). Second, the role of informal, familial care, especially that given by women, is seen as crucial for plugging gaps in formal provision for senior citizens (Symeonidou, 1996).

In terms of the nations central to this study, Sweden is often seen as a very definite example of the social democratic/Scandinavian ideal. The UK, particularly in light of developments in the past 20 years, best fits the liberal/ Anglo-Saxon classification (Esping-Andersen, 1990). According to the schema outlined above, Greece, Italy and Portugal fit into Ferrera's (1996) southern welfare state model. Ireland has proved more difficult to classify (see Cousins, 1997; O'Donnell, 1999), but it has in the past been categorised as 'rudimentary' and similar in character to the welfare states of southern Europe (Leibfried, 2000). Indeed, discussions by Cousins (1997) and O'Donnell (1999) in relation to the Irish Republic serve to illustrate many of the problems inherent in comparative approaches that attempt to locate often diverse national systems within clusters of ideal types.

Guided to some extent by our previous research, our knowledge of the geography of post-retirement migration flows, and the range of literature on welfare regimes noted above, our selection of countries included key sending and receiving regions. The importance of a basic awareness of the diversity of welfare provision[8] across the EU becomes clearer when one understands the legal basis of citizenship entitlement under the free movement provisions and the implications of the non-discrimination principle. Put simply, location has a major influence on access to social welfare. Welfare status thus reflects the wider geography of mobility and the welfare mix of both sending and receiving countries. It is also life course sensitive because social welfare, in the narrow sense of access to services and so on, may figure little in the priorities shaping the initial migration decision of both economic migrants and retirement migrants. The decision of whether or when to return, on the other hand, suggests a much higher concern with access to welfare. This certainly proved to be the case in earlier work on gender and migration, which found little evidence of initial migration decisions motivated by concerns around access to formal welfare (see Ackers, 1998). Subsequent decisions about prospective return and the development of welfare needs on the part of themselves and their family, in the home and host state do, nonetheless, raise the determinative influence of welfare considerations (cf Dwyer, 2000a, 2001).

Outline of chapters

The structure of this book reflects our commitment, as scholars of citizenship, to overcome the kind of disciplinary myopia that has, in the past, restricted an holistic and comprehensive socio-legal understanding of the interplay of rights, responsibilities and experiences. As such it necessarily involves some attention to the detail of Community law on the one hand and comparative social policy on the other. However, we hope that our readership will draw from a spectrum of disciplinary backgrounds, encompassing European studies, geography, social gerontology, social policy and law. A number of readers may find some of the chapters in this book cover material that is less familiar to them. While we believe that the breadth and depth of coverage is essential to the endeavour as a coherent socio-legal project, we hope that readers from a variety of disciplines will find the material accessible.

In order to operationalise the concept of citizenship, we first have to define and explain our interpretation in the context of this study. This delivers the parameters of interest for our study. Consequently, Chapter Two opens with a discussion of the concept of citizenship and its relationship to equality and well-being.

Chapter Three considers citizenship of the Union in terms of formal legal rights. It outlines the legal framework underpinning the mobility rights of post-retirement migrants. Through an examination of the relevant legislation and its interpretation by the European Court of Justice, this chapter identifies a hierarchy of entitlement reflecting both location and forms of social contribution. It then demonstrates how the relative weight attached to different forms of contribution (via paid work and 'favoured' family relationships) shapes the social status of retired migrants. The chapter then moves on to consider the problem of fixed legal categories as the basis of citizenship entitlement in the context of the phenomenon of migration and the evolving unpredictability of life course in old age. These questions not only raise concerns around the awareness and ability of individuals to exercise legal rights, but also about equity in more general terms (and why certain forms of behaviour are privileged in retirement).

The fourth chapter of the book has two main elements. A brief discussion concerning the extent of IRM within Europe and the problems of arriving at reliable estimates of the numbers involved is presented in part one. The second part of the chapter combines an overview of the existing literature on IRM (much of which is written by geographers) with a more detailed consideration of data from our own fieldwork. In short, the chapter provides an overview of the motivational factors and issues that underpin the migratory movements of the respondents included in our sample.

In Chapter Five we consider the importance of formal health and care provisions and their influence on the migratory decisions of retired EU migrants. It begins by presenting a comparative outline of the formal health/care systems available to senior citizens in the six member states at the heart of this study. Recent reforms and debates related to general healthcare and the arrangement of institutional and community care services are outlined and discussed. Against this backdrop of diverse provision, the chapter moves on to examine the healthcare status and experiences of retired EU migrants. It explores the tactics and techniques that they employ in order to maximise access to the health and care services that they may require as and when their personal circumstances change. By using the example of healthcare, the chapter illustrates how the differential ability to move, through the manipulation of residency rules and/ or private resources, impacts upon an individual citizen's access to social rights.

The focus in Chapter Six falls on aspects of financial security in retirement and old age. Initially a brief consideration of some relevant issues in relation to social security provision for senior EU citizens is offered. This is followed by a comparative outline of the pension and social assistance of the six states included in the research. Reforms instigated in the last ten years and their effects are discussed. The chapter then addresses the impact of differing individual financial circumstances and wider institutional and economic arrangements across Europe on the migratory movements of our retired respondents.

Chapter Seven develops the more formal discussion of healthcare in Chapter Five to address wider issues of care and, in particular, the neglected relationship between care and mobility. The material presented in this chapter, based mainly on the interviews with returnees, raises a number of issues about the characterisation of older people as passive and dependent recipients of care. This reflects the contingent nature of the mobility rights of post-retirement migrants and the assumption that this population constitutes a potential drain on host social security systems (and are not 'economically active'). The evidence presented paints a rather different picture of retired people both as active care providers themselves and as active agents in their own care planning. The chapter finally questions the legitimacy of legal distinctions between paid and unpaid work and the narrow construction of the concept of economic contribution.

The conclusion (Chapter Eight) presents a synthesis of the respective components of the research presented in this book by drawing together the core theoretical ideas, the legal and policy analysis and the qualitative findings of our research. It concludes with a summary of the nature of status differentiation within the population of European citizens and, more specifically, the sub-population of retired migrants and the impact this has on individual well-being and autonomy.

Notes

[1] What this means in practice is that migrants are entitled to the same level of provision as nationals in that country. Community law, as such is not concerned with welfare diversity across member states. These issues are developed throughout the book.

[2] The European Commission has recently issued a number of draft Directives with the objective of regularising the status of legally resident third country nationals in the European Union, based on a minimum period of residency.

[3] Article 20 extends a right to diplomatic and consular protection from any Member State while in a third country and Article 21, the right to petition the European Parliament and apply to the Ombudsman.

[4] A list of Directives is provided at the front of the book under 'Relevant EU legislation'.

[5] These include a project on gender and migration funded by the European Commission (DG Employment and Social Affairs) (Ackers, 1998); a project on the impact of migration on children of migrant workers funded by the Nuffield Foundation and the European Commission (Ackers and Stalford, 2002); a project on the mobility of women researchers funded by the European Commission (DG Research) (Ackers, 2001).

[6] All four projects have evidenced the tendency for migration to 'run in families'. Family members are thus often geographically dispersed across at least two countries.

[7] The Community Charter of the Fundamental Social Rights of Workers, Luxembourg, states: "Every worker of the EC must, at the time of retirement, be able to enjoy resources affording him or her a decent standard of living. Any person who has reached retirement age but who is not entitled to a pension who does not have other means of subsistence, must be entitled to sufficient resources and to medical and social assistance specifically suited to his needs" (CEC, 1990, p 19; quoted in Geyer, 2000).

[8] It is important to reiterate here that our aim is not to construct a detailed typology of welfare regimes in relation to welfare services for senior citizens in Europe. This brief discussion is merely offered to illustrate that diversity in welfare provision matters in relation to post-retirement migration. We are aware that Esping-Andersen's original (1990) approach has been much criticised, contested and, indeed, subsequently developed, and that alternative approaches to the classification of welfare states exist (for example, Lewis, 1992; Giarchi, 1996; Ploug and Kvist, 1996; Bonoli, 1997; Gough, 2001). For an accessible introduction to debates and issues in relation to the comparative analysis of welfare states, see Alcock and Craig (2001) or O'Donnell (1999).

TWO

Citizenship, well-being and agency in the European Union

Introduction

Citizenship remains a highly contested and 'slippery' concept, with many authorities challenging its value as a vehicle for the promotion of well-being, equality and agency (for example, Ferge, 1979; Bottomore, 1992; Walby, 1994; Pringle, 1998). Indeed, in the context of the promotion of gender equality, Walby has raised the question as to whether:

> Citizenship is so imbued with gender specific assumptions related to the public sphere and the nexus of the market and state that it is necessarily only a partial rather than a universal project. (1994, p 379)

When considering comparative social policy, Esping-Andersen builds on the Marshallian approach to citizenship which he operationalises through his decommodification index. Decommodification occurs, according to this approach, "when a service is rendered as a matter of right, and when a person can maintain a livelihood without reliance on the market" (1990, p 22). Social citizenship or decommodification thus becomes the 'mark of a civilised society'. Esping-Andersen's work has attracted criticism by feminist analysts on the grounds that the methodology theoretically privileges social class, equating autonomy with independence from waged labour and thus fails to adequately account for the role of the family and the position of women in relation to social welfare (Bussemaker and van Kersbergen, 1994). Similar concerns have been expressed in the context of ageism and children's rights. Pringle thus refers to the:

> ... failure of Esping-Andersen's analysis to consider a range of social oppressions that are central to both the formation of social problems and the functioning of welfare systems. The issues which his analysis almost totally ignores include oppressive power relations associated with sexism, racism, heterosexism, disablism and ageism.... Esping-Andersen's approach ... focuses too exclusively on issues related to class and neglects other determinants of oppressive social relationships – one major form of social oppression is ageism. (1998, pp 13-14)

These criticisms focus on the primacy attached to the relationship between the citizen and the labour market in traditional approaches to citizenship. In that sense, existing use of the concept and its operationalisation may have limited potential in terms of capturing the experiences of those persons whose relationship with paid work is less determinative. Although Pringle (1998) is concerned primarily with children's rights, the reference to ageism suggests a more general concern about the relevance of these approaches to the experiences and well-being of older citizens who are no longer in paid work.

While Walby's analysis reveals some key concerns around the compatibility of citizenship with the "male-dominated family-household" model, she nevertheless concludes that the concept is "potentially suited to the conceptualisation, investigation and theorisation of the varying degrees of social integration and participation in contemporary society" (1994, p 393). Pringle also chooses to adopt Esping-Andersen's approach to citizenship as the basis of his evaluation of children's rights, notwithstanding its flaws, on the grounds that "so many of the debates about social policy in Europe have started from his analysis" (1998, p 10). A further relevant, if pragmatic justification for 'sticking with' the concept, despite its inherent limitations as a measure of well-being and social equality, lies in its importance as a foundational principle shaping European Union (EU) policy, particularly in the context of intra-Community mobility. To the extent that the research reported upon in this book represents an exercise in policy evaluation, 'Citizenship of the Union' constitutes a core policy objective and must, therefore, form a tool in the evaluation process in its own terms. Engagement in the policy discourse at EU level promotes the ability of research to actively inform policy making.

The purpose of this chapter is to outline the development of the concept of citizenship and its role as a fundamental principle moulding the evolution of EU law and policy[1]. Clarity of definition is important not only in a theoretical sense but also in operational terms in detailing the scope of the study and the research approach. The chapter looks first at the relationship between citizenship and concepts of equality both within the theoretical literature but also in EU social law and policy. It is important to establish in an evaluative study such as this, the objectives of policy. Citizenship has been used to describe a continuum of approaches ranging from the provision of basic 'safety net' services designed to reduce poverty and social exclusion, to more redistributive, egalitarian measures to promote inclusivity (Dwyer, 2000b, Chapter Three). The chapter thus considers different conceptions of equality in the context of EU policy and citizenship strategy.

Having charted the evolution of EU policy objectives from an initial concern with the improvement of living standards for workers to the more progressive commitment to redistributive equality (in the first section), the chapter turns to consider the material scope of citizenship. In order to evaluate the impact of European Union policy, it is necessary to define the notion of 'well-being' and to determine the parameters of analysis. Research on the redistributive impact of welfare by British social policy theorists (for example, Le Grand, 1987; Mann, 1992; Titmuss, 1958) has cautioned us against taking a narrow view of policy. In defining social citizenship in terms of the ability to access the range of resources and conditions promoting social well-being, the research encompasses a wide range of policy areas and resource frameworks and, importantly, the interaction between these.

The relationship between rights and responsibilities remains an issue of central importance to any notion of citizenship. At EU level reciprocity between rights and obligations is central to the Maastricht Treaty, which underpins the concept of European citizenship. Article 17 (2) thus states that "Citizens of the Union shall enjoy the rights conferred by this Treaty and shall be subject to the duties imposed thereby". The third theme explored in this chapter therefore considers issues of eligibility and the relationship between contribution (responsibility) and social entitlement (rights). The concern here is twofold. In the first instance, it seeks to identify the interpretation of the notion of 'contribution' in EU social law and policy and the extent to which this effectively privileges certain forms of behaviour, calling into question the inclusive nature of Community citizenship. In addition to questioning the moral judgements underpinning these distinctions we also raise concerns around the problems of operationalising such fine legal distinctions in the context of a population whose employment, family relations and migration status are constantly in flux.

Finally, the chapter considers the relationship between citizenship and agency. It is not only the material quantity of rights that impacts upon citizenship experience, but also their quality and the extent to which they enhance or inhibit autonomy and the exercise of agency. In the context of this book, key concerns are, first, the extent to which social rights facilitate or restrict mobility and, second, the relationship between the social division of welfare and the transportability of social rights and resources.

Citizenship, equality and European Union social policy

Marshall (1992 [1949]) describes the development of citizenship, and social citizenship in particular, as a 'civilising force' insulating members of a given society from the vagaries of the market. Marshall defines the 'social element' of citizenship as encompassing:

> ... the whole range [of benefits] from the right to a modicum of economic welfare and security to the right to share to the full in the social heritage and to live the life of a civilised being according to the standards prevailing in society. (1992, p 8)

In many ways this definition conflates two very different conceptions of equality. The reference to a 'modicum of social welfare' suggests, on the one hand, a residual 'safety net', formal equality approach. On the other hand, the reference to prevailing standards and sharing in the social heritage infers a more redistributive and egalitarian commitment to inclusivity, participation and substantive equality. In order to evaluate citizenship and its impact on well-being, it is necessary to distinguish these approaches and be clear about the objectives of policy.

The concerns around poverty and social exclusion in Marshall's definition echo the objectives of early EU social policy to the general raising of living standards. Indeed, competence in the early phase of European Community (EC) social policy was shaped by the reference in Article 117 (now 136) to the "promotion of employment, improved living and working conditions". This Article formed the legal base of EU social policy and suggested a commitment to 'levelling-up' rather than social redistribution[2]. Even this commitment to the improvement of living standards was arguably more motivated by concerns to promote a level economic playing field than inclusive citizenship as such. The only reference to equality as a policy objective in this early phase of EU social policy is contained in Article 119 (now 141), which refers specifically to the principle of equal pay for male and female workers. Szyszczak argues that even this limited commitment to gender equality in the labour market was "introduced for competitive reasons" (2000, p 78).

Notwithstanding the lack of clarity in Marshall's definition of citizenship and its egalitarian potential, his analysis of the development of social citizenship rights as the mark of the maturity of relationship between the state and its populace is perhaps interesting in the context of the development of 'social Europe' in recent years. Concerns around democratic deficit have led to increasing recognition of the importance of capturing the imagination and harnessing the support of the European populace as a means of conferring legitimacy. This underlying motive behind the extension of citizenship rights leads D'Oliveira to cynically postulate that:

> The populations of the Member States have not asked for citizenship; it has been graciously bestowed upon them as a cover-up for the still existing democratic deficit. (1995, p 83)

The importance of the emergence of a European identity as the basis for the development of the European Union itself is identified by Chalmers and Szyszczak who refer to the perceived need to "build up a common identity of Europe through processes of common cultural heritage and the creating of notions of citizenship rights" (1998, p 49). Laffan (1996) similarly argues that the EU has reached a 'critical' period in its development and needs to develop measures that go beyond the extension of purely economic rights to ensure the promotion of a sense of European identity.

Building on these arguments and the importance of cultivating, within the wider European populace, some form of collective identity, Chalmers and Szyszczak refer to the "conceptual isolation of economic rights and [the] divorce from political and social rights" (1998, p 52) as a key factor contributing to the perceived 'legitimacy' crisis in the EU. The first report from the Commission on Citizenship of the Union emphasises the constitutional significance of citizenship:

> The introduction of these new provisions underscores the fact that the Treaty of Rome is not concerned solely with economic matters.... For the first

time (since the Treaty on European Union) the Treaty has created a direct political link between citizens of the Member States and the European Union … with the aim of fostering a sense of identity with the Union. (COM (93) 702 final)

These concerns around democratic deficit and the relationship between citizenship, identity and integration have led to a policy commitment on the part of the European Commission to the promotion of Union citizenship and a 'Europe closer to its citizens'. They reflect a more holistic approach to citizenship as representing an interconnection of civil, political and social rights. All three rights elements must form "an indivisible triad for universal citizenship to be a reality" (Meehan, 1993, p 10). As Twine (1994) notes, any attempt to advance a vision of citizenship that ignores a substantive social element is of little use.

The role of citizenship policy in underwriting support for, and conferring legitimacy on, EU activity perhaps explains the difficulty of securing a precise and detailed characterisation of the concept in European law and policy as the basis for evaluation. Various authorities have talked of the 'dynamic' and evolutionary quality of Union citizenship. Referring to the commitment (expressed in Article 22 EC) that permits the Council to adopt provisions to "*strengthen or add to* the rights laid down in [Articles 17–21]" (emphasis added), Closa describes the character of Union citizenship as "determined by the progressive acquisition of rights stemming from the dynamic development of the Union" (1992, p 400). Subsequently, Closa (1995) has argued that this dynamic quality might allow the progressive incorporation of new rights, particularly social rights. Identifying the tension between the development of social citizenship rights on the one hand, with the implication of an active and even interventionist state, and the commitment to a free European market on the other, Closa suggests that:

> As the welfare state establishes principles of distributive justice that depart from free market principles, it has to be legitimised on the basis of solidarity that comes from free common membership of a human community … [citizenship implies] the consciousness of an obligation towards the common European good. (1995, p 508-9)

The European Commission has also endorsed this dynamic character and the commitment to a progressive evolution of citizenship and especially of social rights:

> [Union citizenship] reflects the aims of the Union, involving as it does an indivisible body of rights and obligations stemming from the gradual and coherent development of the Union's political, economic and social dimension. (Commission contribution to Inter-Government Conference, reported in Weatherill, 2000, p 401)

Weatherill concludes his discussion of the concept of Union citizenship by saying, "it has provided a solid basis for further enlargement of the catalogue of rights attached to citizenship" (p 410).

The previous chapter has demonstrated the close link between the development of European citizenship and mobility. Indeed, for those citizens who do not move within the European Union, citizenship remains a somewhat hollow concept. It is under the development of rights attached to mobility that the tension between economic and social rights is most evident and the incursion into areas of domestic social policy most apparent. The 1985 Adoninno Report, entitled 'A people's Europe', identified free movement as a fundamental right of Community citizens[3]. This was reiterated in the Commission's guidelines for a Community policy on migration, which stated that the free movement provisions should be driven not merely by labour market interests but by the desire to embrace the wider social aspects of European citizenship (Supplement 9/85, Bull EC, p 5). The evolution of this broader conceptualisation of citizenship is evident in recent cases on the free movement of workers (discussed in more detail in Chapter Three). An example of this can be seen in Advocate General Trabucchi's contention that the migrant worker is not regarded by Community law as "a mere source of labour but is viewed as a human being" (*F v Belgian State*, Case 7/75). This broader view, suggesting a commitment to a wider notion of citizenship and equality, was also expressed by Advocate General Jacobs in his opinion in *Konstantinidis*:

> Community law does not regard the migrant worker ... purely as an economic agent and a factor of production ... it regards him as a human being who is entitled to live in that State in 'freedom and dignity' ... and to be spared any difference in treatment that would render his life less comfortable, physically or psychologically, than the lives of the native population. (para 24)

The concept of citizenship has thus evolved from a fairly narrow concern with formal equality (at least in the context of discrimination in the labour market on grounds of nationality and gender) to embrace a broader concept of equality.

The relationship between citizenship and concepts of equality is specifically alluded to in Ruth Lister's definition of citizenship as a relationship encompassing membership of a community and "the rights and obligations that flow from that membership, and equality" (1997, p 14). The remainder of this chapter moves on to consider the constituent elements of citizenship (as a relational concept involving notions of rights/claims and responsibilities/contributions) in the context of a discussion about equality.

Citizenship and well-being

One approach to an evaluation of Union citizenship would be to simply chart or enumerate formal entitlement under Community law (an exercise undertaken in Chapter Three). Inquiries into citizenship, however, need to look beyond formal legal definition and argument. Citizenship is concerned with philosophical and political questions (Faulkes, 1998; Dwyer, 2000b) and also relative degrees of incorporation and empowerment (Harrison, 1995). Researching the impact of law and policy on life chances and well-being demands an imaginative and grounded approach encompassing the wider resource framework and the relative value or priority people attach to different rights, resources and opportunities over the life course.

Understanding the relationship between law and citizenship experience and the redistributive impact of law and policy (and the extent to which it promotes inclusivity, for example), requires an approach that moves beyond the listing and critiquing of formal entitlement to consider the interface of law with other dimensions of social life. In attempting to define the framework of resources and opportunities constitutive of the well-being of citizens in the European Union and the distributive impact of EU policy on citizenship outcomes, the following section examines three linked issues. We consider first the issue of territorial justice and the EU's response to persistent inequalities in the spatial distribution of social resources across member states. This is followed by a discussion of the nature of the mixed economy of welfare and the consequences of differential ability to tap into the various sources of welfare provision. The concern here is that policy attention to the role of the state as the provider of social goods and well-being may neglect the growth of other sources of welfare provision, which complement and interact with statutory resources with important implications in terms of redistribution and inclusivity. The key lies in the EU's ability to intervene and regulate this wider resources framework and to identify fundamental policy tensions that might, inadvertently, compound polarisation and inequality (through measures to privilege insurance-based and occupational schemes, for example). Finally, we examine the concept of 'social good' itself and the definition of well-being.

Citizenship, equality and territorial justice: the problems of uneven provision

The statement by the Advocate General in Konstantinidis, while broadening the concept of equality to encompass a more holistic view of the human condition, also alludes to the non-discrimination principle. The reference to the 'native population' in the final sentence echoes one of the fundamental limitations of the non-discrimination principle, at least in terms of its ability to deliver what Closa (1995) refers to previously as 'distributive justice'. Generally speaking, distributive justice in the context of free movement rights and citizenship infers a comparison of the formal legal status of Community nationals. This concern extends to both status differentiation between Community migrant workers and host nationals, and also to differentiation within the population of Community migrants itself. So, one might question the respective valuation of paid and unpaid work as an indication of exclusivity and injustice reflected in somewhat arbitrary distinctions in the social status of different groups of retired migrants (an issue picked up in detail in the next chapter). Equality, in that sense, refers to a demand for a broad equality of formal mobility and social rights.

More important in some respects than the allocation of formal, individual rights (which might have little more than symbolic potential), the notion of distributive justice in domestic social policy often denotes concerns around territorial injustice and regional or spatial inequality. This has been seen, for example, in the context of debates around 'postcode prescribing' and parental choice in relation to schooling[4]. A universal right to healthcare or education may thus mean something very different in different areas. A significant brake on the ability of the EU to 'deliver' equality in a meaningful sense lies in the interpretation of the subsidiarity principle[5] in the context of domestic social policy. The consequence of this 'hands-off' approach to domestic social policy is a veneer of Community-level protective legislation, underlain by a framework of social provision that remains largely untouched and continues to be characterised by diversity and regional inequality. The optimum entitlement realisable on the basis of Community citizenship reflects the status of host nationals; in practice this may involve a levelling down of their own status on migration. This is of particular concern to post-retirement migrants, most of whom are moving in the direction of southern European member states. As suggested in Chapter One ('the importance of location'), destination remains the key to welfare status. In that context, the language of rights may sound rather hollow when equality of status translates into equal access to stigmatised and residual welfare. Chapters Five and Six consider the implications of this situation in terms of retired migrants' access to healthcare and income support.

The justification for the subsidiarity principle lies in concerns around the allocation of powers and responsibilities in areas of shared competence and the notion that decisions should be taken as close as possible to the citizen. Linked to fears of loss of sovereignty, responsibility for policy in areas such as healthcare, housing and social assistance, for example, should rest with member states except in so far as there is a Community dimension at issue. Community-level intervention should only take place where action would be demonstrably more efficient and effective, either because there is a cross-border dimension or because we are dealing with policy externalities generated as a result of Community intervention itself. The validity of this interpretation of the subsidiarity principle has been examined primarily in the context of the apportionment of responsibility in the relationship between EU and domestic social policy and in terms of the consequences for member state nationals.

Where concerns have been voiced about unevenness in domestic social policy and the implications of this in terms of migration, this has been typically in the context of the consequences for the Single Market and competition policy. The arguments around 'social dumping' thus reflect concerns, albeit in the context of employment law, that companies might be encouraged to relocate to areas with less restrictive protective (and expensive) legislation. Elsewhere, the language of 'welfare tourism' or 'benefits shopping' echoes fears, with little basis in empirical evidence, that Community nationals might be motivated to migrate by considerations around the relative merits of respective social assistance systems.

Relatively little consideration has, however, been paid to the possibility that territorial injustice or welfare diversity might constitute a barrier to mobility, despite the fact that 'facilitating mobility' has become a key driver in the development of free movement rights (see Chapter Three). Seen through the lens of migration, the issues of cross-border effect and efficiency arguably tip the balance in favour of a more interventionist social policy in order to ensure that potential migrants are not deterred from moving nor indeed disadvantaged as a consequence of intra-Community mobility.

This persistence of profound inequalities in the provision of social resources across the European Union has a major impact on the citizenship status and experience of migrants. The precise consequences of this in terms of access to social resources depends on the geography of the move. The impact of domestic social policy on the incoming migrant might, however, be mitigated by the ability of the persons concerned to insulate themselves from dependency upon social assistance and state-provided services. The following section argues for a more comprehensive approach to the evaluation of social policy and draws into the frame the relative contribution of other sources of welfare provision.

The mixed economy of welfare across European social space

Clearly, access to the range of welfare services and benefits provided directly by the state (often taken as the yardstick of social citizenship) is only one dimension of an increasingly complex resource framework, the negotiation of which forms the basis of individual citizenship experience. Notwithstanding the importance of statutory provision to an analysis of welfare and social exclusion, an understanding of the role of the state at domestic and EU level in promoting citizenship and social equality demands a wider approach. The tentacles of the state extend beyond the parameters of direct state provision to impact on more diverse dimensions of provision controlling access to key social resources. In this regard it is perhaps worthwhile revisiting Richard Titmuss's work on the 'social division of welfare' and the emphasis it placed on occupational and fiscal welfare in shaping social redistribution. Titmuss (1958) describes three interlinked systems, which are functionally similar, but can be distinguished on the basis of "an organisational division of method which, in the main, is related to the division of labour" (p 42). The first of these he identifies as 'fiscal welfare', referring to the "remarkable development of social policy operating through the medium of the tax system" (p 42) as transfer payments. Fiscal policy, he suggests, may be indistinguishable from social policy. Szyszczak, in the context of EC labour law almost 50 years later and the increasingly blurred boundaries between macro-economic, fiscal and social policy, suggests that:

> ... the link between employment measures and fiscal policy, always in the shadows at EC level, has now been brought into the full glare of political decision-making and economic debate. (2000, p 1)

Moving to consider the other key sector so often missed in evaluations of social policy, Titmuss refers to occupational welfare and the extent to which occupational benefits have grown to:

> ... formidable and widespread proportions.... The goods themselves range from realisable or material goods to the 'most intangible forms of amenity' [and] are in effect if not in administrative method, 'social services' duplicating and overlapping social and fiscal welfare benefits. The rapidity of their growth in recent years has increasingly diminished the value and relevance of salary, wage and income statistics ... the benefits have increasingly favoured wealthier taxpayers.... In that sense they function as concealed multipliers of occupational success. (1958, pp 52-3)

He concludes that occupational and fiscal welfare "nourishes privilege and narrows the social conscience ... enlarging and consolidating the area of social inequality" (p 52). In later work Hilary Rose describes the subsequent neglect of this 'increasingly important' sector of employer-provided benefits particularly to the middle classes who, 'secure an impressive share' and the consequences of this neglect, "in terms of the paradigm's capacity to study the inequalities of class and gender" (1981, p 493). Adrian Sinfield (1978) also points to the continued relevance of Titmuss's analysis to contemporary work, suggesting that the limitations of the paradigm lay in its partial implementation and the relative neglect of the third category (of occupational welfare). Of course Titmuss was writing in a very different time and context (in the post-war British welfare state). Neither he, nor indeed Rose or Sinfield, could have predicted the impact of recent economic, political and demographic trends on social equality and the ability of domestic and supranational welfare systems to promote social redistribution.

The concern expressed in the 1950s that such schemes widened class and vocational divisions through the "provision of differential welfare benefits based on occupational achievement" (Titmuss, 1958, p 54) raises important questions about the EU's commitment to the principle of equality and social inclusion. Recent trends, observable across EU member states, would indicate the increasing significance of occupational benefits to welfare status and well-being. These include concerns around demographic change and the sustainability of pension and welfare systems, the residualisation of social welfare (partly in response to convergence criteria), the 'cultural' dominance of occupational-based schemes in European welfare systems, the globalisation of labour markets and the increased propensity for international mobility. Also, in recent years, social welfare in many European countries, particularly in relation to unemployment-related benefits, has become increasingly conditional, with issues of individual responsibility rather than rights dominating policy debates and initiatives (Lister, 1997; Dwyer, 1998, 2000b; Lødemel and Trickey, 2000).

In an interesting discussion of the logic promoting the increasing contribution of occupational welfare, Titmuss suggests that:

... many of these forms of occupational social services express the desire for good human relations in industry. Their provision is part of the model of the good employer. (1958, pp 52-3)

This concern about the 'drive' to 'buy good human relations in industry' would seem to be particularly apposite in the context of skills shortages in European labour markets and the increasing concern with retention. The requirement for labour mobility now also brings with it attempts by companies to lure staff into mobile careers and compensate them with generous relocation 'packages' that include housing, educational services for the children of mobile workers[6], travel and bonuses.

Taken together these changes have perhaps raised the significance of occupational welfare, not only in the sense of material contribution to well-being, but also in the differential ability of citizens to transport benefits and effect mobility. In that sense, reliance on social welfare not only translates typically into lower material benefits but also potentially restricts the mobility of recipients. The EU has had quite an important influence here with its measures to promote the aggregation and portability of contributory benefits. Arguably its confidence in some of these areas of occupationally-related social policy, arising from its greater legal competence in this field, may actually promote the kind of privilege and social polarisation Titmuss refers to in a domestic context and effectively confound the achievement or realisation of equality now embedded within EC labour law.

Before moving on to consider the concept of social good itself, it is important to remember that the mixed economy encompasses not only the three sectors referred to previously, but also the contribution of voluntary, informal/family (cf Rose, 1981) and private sources of support. While the latter three sectors were not considered so relevant in the Titmuss era, increasing emphasis has been placed upon them in more recent years. In a migration context, analysis of the impact of international moves on citizenship experience demands some understanding of the relative balance of provision within this wider mixed economy of welfare. Retirement migration raises particular concerns in this regard because of its highly focused nature and the fact that older people are, in the main, moving away from more highly developed statutory support and into those regions which place great emphasis on family and informal care and, as such, have less well-developed systems of institutional and community care. Of course, the majority of retired migrants do not have access to family care in the host state and eventually may be entering a phase in their lives associated with progressively increasing dependency (see Chapter Seven).

The importance of family care to well-being should not be underestimated. Access to family care reflects factors such as family size and proximity, gender roles (and women's labour market participation) and the ability of potential family members to provide care in the widest sense. Some of these issues fall well beyond the scope of EU or indeed domestic competency. Many of them are, however, influenced by social policy at member state and EU level. In a more general context, EU measures to promote gender equality, childcare and the reconciliation of work and family life may be expected to encourage care giving and promote fertility. More specifically, in the context of the current project, the restricted definition of family in Community law, coupled with the failure to recognise unpaid family care as work (discussed later), doubtless restricts the ability of retired migrants to both access and provide informal care.

In the context of the discussion around occupational benefits (considered previously), we identified the advantages of the ability to tap into this sector for would-be migrants, as reflecting both their greater material value but also their greater transportability. Of course, the most 'footloose' of resources are those provided by the private sector, reflecting differential access to personal income and wealth. The opportunities this creates for the exercise and management of citizenship is an issue returned to later. Citizenship experience and social redistribution thus reflect not only the ability to tap into infrastructures of statutory services and income support, but also to access occupational and fiscal welfare, informal care, the voluntary sector, private resources and the 'mixed economy of welfare' in its broadest guise.

Well-being and the concept of 'social goods'

The previous section has considered the contribution of the mixed economy of welfare to well-being and the distributional implications of differential access to the various sources of provision. It has sought to demonstrate how any individual need for, say, housing or healthcare may be met through a combination of different providers (see Chapter Five for a discussion of healthcare). The ability to spread dependency across these sources of provision may both increase access to material resources and promote mobility.

The following section looks at the concept of a social good or resource itself. The importance of income or housing to well-being is well-established, but our research suggests that other forms of good and the contribution of these to well-being may have been neglected. We have thus attempted to take a more grounded and broader view of the contribution of different kinds of resources and their relative value or priority at different points over the life course. It may be that housing is a priority at one point in time and exercises considerable influence on migration decisions at that point, whereas access to informal care may emerge as a more influential factor several years later, tipping the balance in favour of another move.

Resources such as income or housing are 'material' in the sense that they can be 'measured' to some extent and introduced into some form of cost-benefit analysis. On the other hand, an important concern of many senior citizens that is less amenable to quantification, but has a significant impact on decision-making, is the value of social contact and concerns about loneliness. Health status is similarly a function of a wide range of 'inputs', some of which are measurable (such as hospital or domiciliary services, for example), but other components are not (social support, for example). These kinds of 'resources' are, nevertheless, a fundamental part of the citizenship experience and differential access to them constitutes a dimension of inequality.

While Titmuss (1958) encouraged us to consider the relationship between social welfare (as that provided by the state) and private, occupational and fiscal sources in shaping citizenship experience, he was perhaps unable to foresee the importance of adding to that menu the issue of climate as a welfare resource. Cahill (1994) certainly draws attention to the importance of leisure ('playing') and travel as social policy, but climate is more than simply leisure. Some respondents mention climate as a determinant of their location decision not just as a 'quality of life' factor (although this is referred to) but, on occasion, as a health resource, particularly in cases of chronic arthritic, cardiac or respiratory conditions. Quite simply, but of great significance, retired migrants (and particularly those from Sweden and the UK) often talk about the extent to which they can get out and about and do things in the host state which they were unable to do back home due to climate. Temperate climate thus promotes social interaction, physical mobility, social participation and well-being in a very direct sense (for more discussion see Chapter Four). Environment is also an increasingly important resource, which figures quite highly in some migration decision-making processes[7].

Cahill presents what he calls a 'social life analysis of social policy', arguing that the disruption of traditional patterns of life and work have transformed everyday existence. Stressing the importance of defining resources such as communicating, viewing, travelling, shopping, working and playing as dimensions of social policy, he suggests that, "inequalities and divisions are manifest in these areas and ... new ones are being created" (1994, p 5).

A comprehensive understanding of the relationship between mobility and citizenship and of citizenship as a redistributive mechanism thus demands an imaginative analysis encompassing the 'mixed economy' of provision in the widest sense. We need to broaden our understanding of well-being to encompass resources such as climate and leisure, travel or social contact not simply as free-standing social goods, but also as factors interacting with more formal resource frameworks to shape well-being. Evaluation of the inclusionary and egalitarian potential of EU social policy demands a definition of social citizenship that encompasses the operation of redistributive mechanisms across all welfare sectors in as comprehensive a fashion as possible, the full range of resources and the priority accorded to them by citizens.

Citizenship, equality and contribution

The previous section has considered the material scope of citizenship and the range of social goods constitutive of well-being. It is in this context, of an evaluation of material entitlement, that the relationship between citizenship and equality is typically examined. Social citizenship is generally understood as a status reflecting the articulation of both obligations and rights or duties and claims. Marshall thus described citizenship as:

> ... a status bestowed on those who are full members of a community. All who possess the status are equal with respect to the rights and duties with which the status is endowed. (1992, p 18)

In a European context, the focus has been very much on the enumeration and evaluation of the rights end of the equation. The relational dimension of citizenship is thus often lost. So, while Kleinman (2002) refers to the explicit recognition in the Maastricht Treaty of citizenship as involving "reciprocal rights and duties" (p 197), the subsequent discussion focuses entirely on an evaluation of the rights dimension. Where he subsequently refers to issues of status differentiation based on economic activity and the ways in which the EU is effectively promoting new forms of stratification (p 199), he does not contextualise this within a discussion around contribution and duties. Closa goes a step further suggesting that while "Citizenship implies rights and duties ... characteristically, the citizenship of the Union regulates only rights" (1995, p 509). The failure to locate some of the key concerns around the status of work and family, for example, within a wider debate around contribution and, impliedly, merit or 'dessert', represents a significant weakness of existing analyses of European citizenship.

In the context of our work on intra-Community mobility, we start from a different perspective. Rather than arguing that the social dimension of EU citizenship is merely symbolic and rhetorical (as Kleinman contends), we would suggest that the 'basket of goods' on offer to certain sections of the European populace, albeit depending on where they move to, has a fundamental impact on well-being. They underwrite meaningful and material welfare claims to healthcare, education and employment – indeed all dimensions of social welfare – for the persons concerned and members of their family. Citizenship of the Union, in that context, is worth having and delivers immediate benefits. The key concern, in relation to status differentiation, lies in an evaluation of the personal scope of the provisions and the processes by which the entitlement of certain European citizens is more heavily circumscribed.

The following section thus moves from a concern about the relationship between rights or claims and equality to a consideration of equality in the context of contribution. The inference, in Marshall's definition, of rights deriving from a universal ability to contribute or at least contribute in a legally significant way is problematic in a number of ways. The first concern lies in the definition of employment and the valuation of different forms of contribution and, in particular, the legal significance of different forms of work. More specifically, what benefits accrue to the citizen-carer or citizen-volunteer? This question also raises the issue of family relationships, gender and caring roles and the legal significance of these. The second concern lies in the assumption that all forms of contribution via paid work are equally meritorious (and give rise to a broad equivalence of legal status, if not financial return) and also that access to employment and the costs of undertaking paid work are evenly distributed.

An important focus of our research has been on the subject of contribution and the legal regulation, at EU level, of the personal scope of entitlement. In other words the basis on which migrants can make claims in the host state. A key dimension of the personal scope of entitlement, at least in EC law, lies in the ability to demonstrate contribution – via labour market participation – as the basis of the status of 'privileged alien'. Pringle explains the more limited citizenship status of children as a reflection of the priority ascribed to paid work:

> ... the European Union concentrates on workers' rather than citizens' rights as far as social protection is concerned ... children are not workers and are therefore not a primary focus for European Union attention. (1998, p 134)

The concept of work and worker in Community law is discussed in much more detail in Chapter Three. The point here is to raise it as a fundamental issue affecting the status of retired migrants, both in terms of their employment histories and the rights that accrue from these and their current status in the host state. An issue of real concern here, particularly to retired women, concerns their involvement over the life course in unpaid caring work.

Citizen-carers and the valuation of unpaid work

McKie et al identify the failure to address care work as a fundamental weakness in citizenship theory, arguing that:

> ... contemporary debates around concepts of citizenship emphasise the obligation to paid employment but fail to tackle the gendered division of caring activities and organisation of care. (2001, p 233)

In a similar vein, Leira (1992) suggests that even the more progressive Scandinavian welfare states privilege citizen-workers over citizen-carers and concludes that what is lacking is a concept of citizenship which recognises the importance of care to society. The problem of the legal valuation of unpaid work and, in particular, caring work is present throughout Community law and indeed the domestic law of most member states[8]. It has been raised in the context of discussions about gender equality and the valuation of unpaid work undertaken by women mainly in the home. The failure to recognise these forms of social contribution as capable of giving rise to rights has led feminists to question the relevance and value of the citizenship concept to feminist analysis and strategy. Expressing frustration at the continuing tendency for "dominant conceptualisations of citizenship [to] marginalise private caring", McKie et al conclude that:

> Citizenship as a concept and a focus for debates does not appear to have moved issues on: in fact it may well have produced a smokescreen to gender inequalities. (2001, p 254)

This issue was discussed at some length in Ackers' work on gender and migration, which identified the impact of migration (1998, pp 183-223), partnering and family on the labour market participation of mobile women. The current study, with its focus on retired migrants, underlines the importance of these relationships and their cumulative effect, over the life course, on the citizenship status and autonomy of mobile women in retirement. The relevance of this becomes particularly clear when we examine the relative advantages of occupational and private benefits to the financial status of retired migrants (see Chapter Six). While interruptions in women's careers have long-term knock-on effects in terms of access to independent income in retirement, the interviews also raised a number of issues around the legal recognition of the work of older carers, many of whom were men (see Chapter Seven).

The concept of family and parasitic rights

It would be incorrect to say that unpaid, caring work as a form of social contribution remains completely unvalued in law. Indeed, presumptions about gender and family roles permeate Community law and policy. Certain forms of care work undertaken within legally sanctioned contexts (notably the Community law concept of family) are explicitly recognised and give rise to derived forms of benefit. The failure to recognise the contribution of carers as capable of giving rise to independent social entitlement, however, leaves informal carers in a vulnerable situation. Access to social citizenship for this group of citizens depends on the extent to which their family relationships are recognised. If they are members of legally defined families, then they should have access to derived social rights on the basis of their relationship to the worker-citizen. This raises important questions about the definition of the concept of family, of spouse, child, 'ascendant relative' and, more generally, of dependency in Community law and the qualitative value of what have been referred to as parasitic or adjectival rights. These issues and the ways in which the law operates to privilege certain forms of social behaviour and personal relationships are discussed in more detail in Chapter Three.

Differential access to and experience of work

The lack of formal recognition of the status of citizen-carer is not only problematic in the sense that this form of work fails to give rise to independent social entitlement, it also restricts the ability of the persons concerned, mainly women, to fulfil their citizenship obligation through paid work (to participate in the labour market). In that sense, carers have a more limited opportunity to perform legally recognised forms of work. The ability to assume the duties of citizenship are unevenly distributed and not only reflect the sexual division of labour in the domestic sphere, but also other forms of discrimination (based on age, sex, race, disability, and so on) prevalent in the PLM and wider society. Indeed, much of the literature that has emerged from the disabled people's movement since the 1960s has emphasised that disabled people have been systematically denied enjoyment of the equal rights and responsibilities that are central to any substantive notion of citizenship (refer to Hunt, 1966; UPIAS, 1976; Fincklestein, 1980; Oliver and Barnes, 1991; Barton, 1993; Oliver, 1996).

In addition to issues around the equality of access to labour markets, the costs of contribution through paid work may also be distinguished. Some forms of work are intrinsically more rewarding (through higher salaries and occupational entitlements) and more easily combined with caring responsibilities and flexible working. In that sense, the relative benefits of more progressive employers (typically in the public sector) may mitigate the problems associated with motherhood and caring, enabling women to fulfil their caring roles without withdrawing from paid work.

The nature of some forms of work may, however, have an even more immediate impact on well-being. We have already referred to the contribution of occupational welfare to well-being in terms of employment-related perks. These may include, in addition to the kinds of housing, travel, health and educational benefits mentioned above, access to healthier working environments, working hours and conditions. The converse of this can be seen in those forms of work that generate their own externalities or dis-welfares, the severity of which may pose a threat to the continued ability to work itself. Evidence of this can be seen in the interviews with our sample of returning southern European workers, many of whom reported some degree of work-related illness or disability as a consequence of time spent in hazardous working environments[9] (see Chapter Four). The relationship between different forms of work and the ability to contribute is neither equally distributed nor experienced and may contribute to inequalities in health and general well-being.

Contribution over time and space

The work of both Marshall (1992 [1949]) and Titmuss (1958), in common with many other citizenship theorists, presumes a process of contribution (via paid work) over a person's working life, followed by a period of receipt during retirement. As such, the reciprocity relationship is based on an assumption of a linear and chronological evolution of work and family relationships (the predictability of retirement and the stability of marriage, for example) and fails to take account of the kinds of fluctuations and fluidity so common in careers and family circumstances today. The 'model' also distinguishes relatively fixed and mutually exclusive populations of 'providers' and 'dependants'. As such it fails to capture the reality of reciprocity and exchange and the fluidity of relationships that characterise the lives of many people. In particular, in the context of our current project, the presumption of dependency in old age fails to acknowledge the contribution that many retired people make as family carers, consumers and volunteers. Neither does it deal with the fact that so many retired persons are both caring for and being cared for simultaneously; they are both providers and recipients of care.

The development of citizenship in theoretical and policy terms has generally taken place within the confines of domestic welfare systems. Based on actuarial principles it has implicitly assumed a more or less boundaried and fixed populace. Contribution via paid work in one location was thereby rewarded in times of sickness or retirement by access to social benefits in that same location. People were assumed to have grown up, been educated, worked, had children, experienced periods of ill health or retired in a common location. Migration has brought with it more dislocated patterns of contribution and receipt over time and space that test the ability of social institutions in an increasingly European and global context. The 'age of migration' according to Lister strengthens the case for the development of "stronger institutions of global citizenship" (1997, p 61)[10].

Citizenship and agency

We have already referred to the notion that rights may have both an immediate material impact, conferring tangible and quantifiable benefits, and a qualitative dimension. The example we have given so far concerns the issue of transportability and the extent to which it promotes or restricts mobility. Mobility is thus a right in itself and also a very concrete manifestation of agency shaping the well-being of those people concerned. The relationship between citizenship, equality and agency (or autonomy) is emphasised in Ruth Lister's work. Indeed, Lister argues that autonomy is the key, "linking the theorisation of social citizenship with that of human need ... citizenship as rights enables people to act as agents" (1997, pp 17 and 36). Echoing the concerns expressed by Meehan (1993), in the absence of the positive rights to welfare associated with social citizenship, political rights may exist in a vacuum and amount to little more than symbolism. Citing Marquand (1991), Lister goes on to suggest that the:

> ... typical justification [of social rights] is agency ... social rights (at least in theory) enable citizens to exercise their political and civil rights on equal terms and create the conditions for full social and political participation. (1997, p 34)

Understanding the relationship between citizenship and equality thus demands consideration of the mechanisms by which EU law and policy delivers social rights and translates into the differential ability to exercise agency.

In the previous sections, we have identified the importance of placing any evaluation of the redistributive implications of citizenship within the context of the mixed economy of welfare and also of taking a broad and grounded view of the concept of social resources. Citizenship experience, therefore, reflects access to these diverse resource frameworks in the widest possible sense. Of course the ability to respond to these concerns to maximise individual health, fiscal and housing status is not evenly distributed. They are not choices that everyone can make with equal ease, but rather reflect differential ability to access and transport pensions, benefits and personal wealth. The social division of welfare, in that sense, reflects the social and sexual division of labour, pre-retirement employment trajectories and family circumstances. In particular, it reflects the ability to spread dependencies across the welfare sectors promoting autonomy and freedom of choice in decision-making.

While the respective benefit of these sources of support are generally enumerated in terms of levels of benefit (or amounts of income), it is also important to consider the quality of the benefit and the flexibility it offers the recipient. Generally speaking, contributory and private goods and benefits are more transportable and, as such, facilitate mobility, whereas the rules governing access to non-contributory forms of social assistance include residence requirements, and are generally not transportable and thus impede mobility. The ability to access personal wealth and private sources of finance and support is perhaps the most advantageous in terms of promoting 'footloose' decision-making and maximising autonomy. Income and wealth is important not only in its own terms (as the means of promoting freedom of choice), it also provides a trigger to social benefits. The relationship between entitlements in the different sectors was particularly evident in the differential ability of some of our respondents to manipulate residency and thereby make welfare claims. Retention of property in the home state thus retains important health and welfare rights for the persons concerned. In this context, Lasch's (1995) reference to the "cosmopolitanism of an international elite ... divorced from the principles and practices of citizenship" (cited in Lister, 1997, p 57) raises a number of questions. It is perhaps not so much that this 'elite' subsection of the retired migrant population is divorced from citizenship but rather that their superior wealth and property actually enables them to negotiate preferential status across supranational and domestic welfare systems.

Dependency on forms of social assistance or social welfare on the other hand, effectively ties the recipient wishing to move in retirement, to residency in that state and restricts their ability to move and (potentially) take advantage of the lower property values and better climates of southern Europe. A move abroad for this group of retired people, dependent on the benefits derived from national citizenship, would consequently impact severely on their command of resources and social well-being. Recipients of private and/or occupational benefits are thus not only often better off in material terms, but are also more footloose and able to exercise greater autonomy in terms of deciding where to live in retirement. The ability to move and exercise choice in terms of post-retirement location is clearly one component of citizenship in itself, but also in terms of the access mobility provides to other dimensions of well-being (such as climate or cheap housing, for example).

Certainly, for retired migrants, the resource framework within which they are negotiating their individual citizenship 'portfolio' spans international geopolitical space, as occupational and private benefits are increasingly transportable and the relative benefits of domestic fiscal and welfare systems (both in terms of statutory and voluntary sector provision) more transparent. In a global context, fiscal welfare and the ability to manipulate domestic taxation regimes adds further potential for the exercise of 'agency'. Skilful management of citizenship, both in terms of the location of contribution and receipt, enables some retirees to extract maximum benefit from the respective welfare systems. In practice, retired migrants are often making informed choices between the benefits of registering residency (a legal obligation which many avoid without penalty) in the host state and incurring forms of national and local taxation.

In an interesting twist, the articulation of private benefits with statutory services in the context of international space creates a situation in which access to resources may bear an inverse relation to need. Those pensioners with sufficient resources to retain a second property 'back home' thereby preserve their access to welfare in the 'home state', while those pensioners who have to sell up completely in order to finance their move relinquish these rights. Referring to the need to take a wide view of well-being and the resource frameworks it encompasses Cahill concludes:

> It is quickly clear from any study of the major forms of social life that the prosperous and the powerful can utilise their position to maximise their welfare. The social changes described and the emerging political consensus on markets and the state have put the self-maximising individual at the centre stage. But this can mean that the weak ... and others will see their position and interests deteriorate in this new world. (1994, p 7)

These examples illustrate the importance of taking a broad and comprehensive view of citizenship in order to identify the redistributive impact of national and international social law and policy. While on the one hand, legal analysis may identify a group of citizens with inferior formal rights, in practice, this denial of rights may not translate into an inferior ability to access to resources promoting well-being. As Ruth Lister suggests:

> People can be, at the same time, both the subordinate objects of hierarchical power relations and subjects who are agents in their own lives, capable of exercising power in the 'generative' sense of self-actualisation. (1996, p 41)

Conclusions

The starting point in our analysis of the citizenship status of retired migrants involves detailing the framework of legal rights that form the basis of 'Citizenship of the Union'. Citizenship, however, implies something more than simply documenting formal rights and comparing access to material resources. It also demands consideration of the quality of entitlements and the rules governing their use and the effect of accessing them on the recipient's ability to exercise autonomy and make choices in relation to their well-being. The interviews reported in this book reflect an appreciation, on the part of the respondents, of citizenship and social well-being as a synthetic and evolutionary status comprising social resources from across the welfare sectors and geographical space. Accessing cheaper housing is one reason cited for migration, as people are keen to realise optimum amenity value for their money. In that sense, people are negotiating private property markets to their advantage and realising the benefits of domestic house price inflation through purchase in weaker regions. The ability to make fiscal gains is another reason given for choice of location, enabling the people concerned to 'manage' fiscal regimes (the contributory dimension of citizenship) and safeguard their income. While concerns to minimise taxation may shape location decisions in early retirement, these may be reversed in subsequent years as the need to access social infrastructures increases with growing frailty and dependency (see Chapter Six). The negotiation of citizenship is an evolutionary and, at times, unpredictable process.

Concerns about health also figure highly in the decision-making process of retired migrants. Some cite the beneficial impact of Mediterranean climates on health as a factor shaping migration decision-making and improving their social well-being. Once again, however, health figures highly in reasons cited for subsequent return moves, as often the same, typically chronic, condition (arthritis, respiratory or heart problems, for example) which derived benefit from the initial move, intensifies and requires treatment and access to formal healthcare (see Chapter Five). In that sense retired people are involved in a series of ongoing decisions and 'trade-offs' in an attempt to maximise their social well-being at any point in time.

The legal framework providing the right to free movement and residence constitutes an important dimension of citizenship. The extent to which it is determinative depends on its engagement with the other conditions and resource frameworks we have alluded to. The following chapter outlines the scope of free movement rights in Community law as the basis for the subsequent analysis of retirement migration decision-making.

Notes

[1] In this sense the chapter is examining the concept and operationalisation of citizenship, rather than developing or critiquing welfare regime theories.

[2] Although some commentators have referred to the alternative means of achieving compliance with equality objectives via a 'race to the bottom'. See, for example, Szyszczak (2000, p 9).

[3] Second Report of the Ad Hoc Committee on a People's Europe to the European Council, Supplement 7/85, Bull EC, p 18.

[4] Postcode prescribing refers to recent policy concerns in the UK in relation to healthcare provision and the differential ability to claim certain medicines and services depending on local area of residence. Residence within a particular locality is also an increasingly important factor in the allocation of school places.

[5] The principle was formally introduced as Article 3b in the Treaty on European Union. For more discussion see, O'Keeffe and Twomey (1995).

---

[6] The rights attached to the employment contracts of many mobile workers include payment of private school fees, boarding school, and so on, and family travel costs, as well as accommodation allowances and assistance in locating and financing housing. In some cases the value of these 'fringe' benefits may be greater than the salary itself (see Ackers and Stalford, 2002).

[7] See Ackers and Stalford (2002) for a discussion of 'ecological migration' in Portugal, for example. Some respondents in the current project also referred to the draw of what they perceived to be a cleaner environment as a factor precipitating their move. This was particularly evident in relation to the Irish sample.

[8] For more details see Ackers, 1998, 2001; Hervey and Shaw, 1998; Szyszczak and Moebius, 1998; McKie et al, 2001.

[9] One form of work commonly associated with ill health and disability is, of course, caring work both in the paid and unpaid sectors.

[10] This discussion is developed in Chapter Eight.

THREE

Shades of citizenship: the legal status of retirement migrants[1]

Introduction

We have already referred, in the context of our discussion about Community citizenship, to the existence of status differentiation. This chapter outlines the evolution of social and residency rights under the free movement of persons' provisions to detail the hierarchy of entitlement that exists under Community law and the importance of contribution to the citizenship status of retired migrants. It begins with a study of the provisions and the personal and material entitlement of different groups of post-retirement migrants.

'Citizenship of the Union', as Article 17 suggests, does not replace national citizenship but rather 'complements it'. In that context, formal citizenship status reflects not only Community law but also the specific benefits deriving from national citizenship (which vary considerably between member states, not only in a substantive sense but also, importantly, in terms of their transportability). The contribution of national citizenship as a fundamental source of social entitlement is of particular importance given the diversity in domestic welfare systems and the fact that non-discrimination remains the basis of welfare claims in the host state[2].

As a piece of socio-legal research this level of analysis takes us only a part of the way, however. Having outlined the forms of status differentiation institutionalised in Community law, the discussion turns to consider the articulation of formal legal status with other forms of social status and social processes to shape citizenship outcomes. As such, it recognises both the tension between the static and fixed nature of legal categories and the sheer complexity and fluidity of social life and human relationships, as well as the role of agency in shaping the effect of the law. As the empirical findings suggest, individuals do not respond in a passive or predictable and uniform way to legal scenarios, but rather engage with them at different levels. Individuals may effectively 'manage' or negotiate citizenship portfolios specific to their own and their family's needs. The determinative effect of the law and the ability to execute this form of 'rights management' thus reflects differential awareness and access to cultural, social and economic resources. The second part of the chapter accordingly examines the role of agency in shaping citizenship experience and the potential for differential outcomes (and social divisions) based on the articulation of Community rights with national rights and other forms of status.

The right to freedom of movement in community law: the provisions

Title III of the Treaty establishing the European Community provides for the 'free movement of persons, services and capital' throughout the Community. Individuals who wish to enter, work and reside in another member state can do so on the basis of Article 39 EC (formerly Article 48), which provides that:

> Freedom of movement of workers shall be secured within the Community. Such freedom of movement shall entail the abolition of any discrimination based on nationality between workers of the Member States as regards employment, remuneration and other conditions of work and employment....

Article 43 details the freedom of establishment of nationals to include, the right to "take up and pursue activities as self employed persons" and Article 49 contains a prohibition on restrictions on the freedom to provide services within the Community[3]. The constitutional right to free movement has been substantiated by secondary legislation that adds 'flesh to the bones' (Craig and de Búrca, 1998, p 697; Steiner, 1994, p 201; O'Leary, S., 1999, p 68) of the Treaty and enables the migrant worker to overcome certain financial and social obstacles, which arise as a result of exercising free movement. This has been achieved through the development of two principal mechanisms. Regulation 1612/68[4] implements Articles 39-43 EC (formerly 48-52) and is the main source of secondary legislation governing the free movement rights of workers. Most significantly, Article 7 (2) of Regulation 1612/68 entitles Community migrant workers to the "same social and tax advantages" as nationals in the host state. Regulation 1408/71[5], on the other hand, seeks to coordinate rather than harmonise domestic social security systems.

Social entitlement in the host state and the geography of retirement migration

Access to social resources in the host state reflects the ability to both transport benefits attached to national citizenship and to access domestic welfare systems. For the purposes of this research, we are primarily interested in the developing framework of Community rights and not so much in the extension of national citizenship (in the form of transportable rights), although we return to consider the relationship between the two of these later in this chapter[6]. Access to social citizenship entitlements under the free movement provisions is based on the principle of non-discrimination (Article 12 EC). A key recital to Regulation 1612/68 outlines the rationale for this extension of Community competence into the social sphere:

> Whereas the right of freedom of movement, in order that it may be exercised by objective standards, in freedom and dignity, requires that equality of

treatment shall be ensured in fact and in law in respect of all matters relating to the actual pursuit of activities as employed persons and to eligibility for housing, and also that obstacles to the mobility of workers shall be eliminated, in particular as regards the worker's right to be joined by his family and the conditions for the integration of that family into the host country.

While Robin Allen refers to freedom and dignity as, "the essential ingredient of substantive equal treatment" (Allen, 1999, p 32)[7], economic objectives have proved the momentum fuelling the evolution of the law. In *Ministere Public v Even & ONPTS*, the Court interpreted the scope of Article 7 (2) of the Regulation to include:

> ... all those [advantages] which, whether or not linked to the contract of employment, are generally granted to national workers primarily because of their objective status as workers or by virtue of their residence on national territory and the extension of which to workers who are nationals of other Member States therefore *seems suitable to facilitate their mobility within the Community*.

Following the impact of this, and many other cases (cf O'Keeffe, 1985; Hervey, 1995; Ackers, 1998), Meehan (1993, p 93) describes the Court's approach as having, "blurred customary distinctions between security and assistance so much that discrimination in almost any welfare benefit might be regarded as contravening Community law".

Community law cannot guarantee a standardised platform of social entitlement, but it does provide for a very broad application of the non-discrimination principle, giving favoured EU citizens full and equal access to welfare benefits in the host member state, including forms of social assistance. Robin Allen QC has recently described the evolution of social entitlement under the social advantages concept as "covering situations extending from before the cradle and up to the grave ... 'social advantage' can cover most of the serious rights [sic] of passage" (1999, p 35).

Although the provisions may create pressure for harmonisation (perhaps to reduce the opportunities for benefits tourism), in practice material entitlement depends on the welfare system of the receiving state. The specific geography of retirement migration is thus pivotal in determining access to resource frameworks. While movements into Nordic social systems, based on social democratic principles and social redistribution may thus enhance citizenship status, movements into southern European 'mother-daughter' economies – or 'rudimentary' welfare systems – based firmly on principles of family care and support may imply a reduction in social status, particularly for migrants who lack access to such informal resource networks. Retirement migration thus raises some interesting questions in terms of material entitlement.

1 The population is generally moving at a time in their lives associated with progressively increasing dependency (in other words when access to care becomes increasingly important).

2 Retirement migration flows are characterised by a move away from relatively generous welfare systems (where care for senior citizens is socialised to a greater extent) to locations in southern European sunbelt countries and coastal and rural regions. The geography of these moves is highly specific and clustered and the favoured locations typically lack a comprehensive infrastructure of community care and support services.

3 With the exception of some returnees, the majority of retired migrants are also moving away from potential sources of informal care (their families).

Notwithstanding the diversity of national welfare systems, Community law clearly provides an important basis for welfare claims in the host state. For the citizen-worker 'Citizenship of the Union' conveys some valuable and tangible material benefit. However, the exercise of the right to move and reside in another member state following retirement does not confer universal status on Europe's 'senior citizens'. Analysis of the legal consequences of post-retirement mobility reveals a hierarchy of entitlement that bears little, if any, relationship with social need, but rather echoes the spatial and temporal character of pre-retirement forms of social contribution and the complex interplay between life course, economic trajectories and mobility. In practice, the law privileges paid work and marriage as the basis of Community entitlement. The following section documents the legal consequences of different forms of post-retirement mobility.

Issues of eligibility and the 'personal scope' of entitlement under the free movement of persons' provisions

The rights of retired Community migrant workers

As we have seen, the 'basket' of social goods available to 'favoured' intra-Community migrants extends beyond contributory and employment-related benefits to encompass all aspects of welfare available to nationals in the host state. In that sense it is legitimate and meaningful to use the language of citizenship to refer to this collection of social rights. The ability to access these goods, however, depends on the ECJ's interpretation of the personal scope of the provisions (defining eligibility). The rationale for the development of social rights attached to the freedom of movement derives from concerns to promote labour mobility in a Single Market (Ackers, 1998; Craig and de Búrca, 1998). Achievement of the status of Community migrant worker thus provides the trigger to full, independent citizenship in the host state. This is of particular significance to the legal status of retirement migrants for two reasons. Firstly, the rights of the Community migrant worker encompass a right to remain in the host state following retirement[8]. Secondly, it determines the social status of those retired migrants who resume work, following retirement migration, in the host state[9]. Evaluating the scope and consequence of these rights demands some discussion of the concept of work and worker in Community law.

The concept of work in Community law

Given the focus on retirement in this book, it is not the intention in this section to provide a comprehensive and detailed discussion of the concept of work in Community law but rather to identify those dimensions which may play a determinative role in shaping the social entitlement of retired migrants (for further discussion see Ackers, 1998; Craig and de Búrca, 1998). Employment status is of importance here in two contexts: firstly, in terms of employment history and the life course implications or long-term consequences of acquiring the status of Community migrant worker. In that sense, the pre-retirement occupational histories of the respondents and especially retired women have a determinative effect on the citizenship status of retired migrants. Secondly, the increasing emphasis (explicitly promoted by EU policy) for flexibility in retirement and for more fluid relationships with labour markets has encouraged an increased prevalence of forms of return to paid work in the post-retirement period. Resumption of work in the host state may thus have a significant impact on citizenship.

Article 39 EC and Regulation 1612/68 refer specifically to the "freedom of movement for workers". The European Court of Justice has interpreted the concept of worker broadly to encompass part-time work and irregular hours (see Ackers, 1998, Chapter Four for a discussion of the concept of worker in Community law). There is no earnings threshold as such, nor a requirement to demonstrate financial autonomy. Indeed, the Court's insistence on an 'objective' definition can be seen in its ruling in *Levin v Staatssecretaris van Justitie*, a case involving the claims of a woman whose wages fell below the national minimum wage, in which it was successfully argued that a person's status as a Community worker depended not so much on their financial self-sufficiency, but on their economic contribution. The Court held that the enjoyment of the rights for workers could not be made subject to national legislation on minimum wage levels, "so that the field of application ratione personae of the Community rules might vary from one Member State to another". Referring to Article 117 EC (now Article 136) and the Treaty commitment to an "improved standard of living for workers", the Court argued that part-time work was an important and effective means of achieving that objective. In an interesting judgement the Court showed itself prepared to take account of changing socio-economic and cultural conditions, arguing that restricting eligibility to full-time employees would jeopardise Treaty objectives by, "excluding very large, and probably increasing numbers of persons [including] women, the elderly and disabled [sic]" (para 17).

In this case, the Court also considered the issue of motive, responding to the suggestion that Levin should be disqualified on the grounds of instrumentalism (she only sought work as a means to securing residency). Preferring an 'objective' definition, the Court found that motive or purpose was irrelevant, provided that the person was engaged in the pursuit of effective and genuine activities. This line of reasoning was taken still further in a case involving a person who sought to supplement his earnings with a claim for social security in the host state (cf *Kempf v Staatssecretaris van Justitie*). The Court found that reliance on social assistance did not automatically undermine his status as a worker. Such forms of work qualify, provided they are not 'purely marginal and ancillary', by virtue of their economic nature, even when they are to the economic detriment of the receiving state.

The definition was extended further in *Raulin v Minister van Onderwijs en Wetenschappen* to include employment in irregular, 'on-call' contracts, which:

> ... provide no guarantee as to the number of hours to be worked, with the result that the person concerned works only a limited number of days per week or hours per day ... in so far as the activities pursued are effective and genuine activities to the exclusion of activities on such a small scale as to be regarded as marginal and ancillary.

Under pressure from member states to provide more concrete guidance, the Court, in *Lawrie-Blum v Land Baden-Württemberg*, found that a trainee teacher qualified as a 'worker' on the grounds that:

> The essential feature of an employment relationship, however, is that for a certain period of time a person performs services for and under the direction of another person in return for which he receives remuneration.

The concept of remuneration was returned to in *Steymann v Staatssecretaris van Justitie* in the context of a claim by a person who undertook voluntary work for a religious community in return for 'pocket money'. The Court held that, under the Lawrie-Blum formula, Steymann provided services of value to the religious community which would otherwise have had to be performed by someone else (and presumably paid for) and, on that basis, he qualified as a worker. His contribution to the community via some plumbing work, general housework and participation in the outside economic activities of the organisation (a disco and laundry service), while unremunerated, nevertheless did:

> ... constitute economic activities in so far as the services which the community provides to its members may be regarded as the *indirect quid pro quo for genuine and effective work*.

The ruling in Steymann is clearly good news for those workers engaged in more marginal forms of 'work', the majority of whom are, and will be, women. Furthermore, if the concept of remuneration under the Lawrie-Blum formula can be strained so substantially to include pocket money and the notion of indirect economic 'savings' as opposed to income, then resumption of only limited part-time employment in the host state may have significant impact on the formal entitlement of post-retirement migrants.

The valuation of unpaid 'voluntary' work and informal care

The Court applied a more restrictive approach, however, in a case involving a person who was undertaking therapeutic 'work' as part of a Dutch social employment scheme (aimed at reintegrating people into the workforce). Work in sheltered employment schemes does not constitute genuine and effective economic activity. Concern over the implications of this interpretation of work and the implications for voluntary workers was expressed by the Commission in its submission to the case:

> The claim that the activity pursued ... is not an economic activity but has a purely social purpose amounts to refusing to regard as workers within the meaning of Community law those who are employed in foundations, associations or other non-profit organisations. (*Bettray v Staatssecretaris van Justitie*)

It would appear that forms of voluntary activity in the host state either prior to or following retirement would not elevate the status of the persons concerned to the more favoured status attached to Community migrant workers[10]. Evidence from the interviews indicating a fairly high level of voluntary activity among the expatriate retired community would suggest that this ruling impacts quite significantly, restricting the legal status of this population and the welfare claims they can make.

The opportunity to discuss the status of unpaid caring work in Community law was presented in *Martinez Sala v Freistaat Bayern*. Sala, a Spanish national and single parent, claimed a child-raising allowance from the Bavarian government. She was not entitled to a residence permit, which formed the grounds for refusing her the benefit, as she had left work in order to look after her children. Szyszczak and Moebius argue that the fact that the referring Court:

> ... did not ask whether Sala could be seen as a 'worker' on the basis that she was caring for two children, but rather whether she could still be considered to be a 'worker' as a result of her former employment (on the grounds that the status of worker 'may produce certain effects after the relationship has ended') meant that the Court 'implicitly rejected the idea that care for children per se could be considered 'work'. (1998, p 129)

In so doing:

> ... the Court and the Advocate General failed to address the fundamental problem of how, in future, women who choose (or are forced) to give up, or

interrupt, paid work, or who never take up paid work in order to care for children and other family members, should be dealt with in Community law.

The problem of the legal valuation of unpaid work and, in particular, caring work is present throughout Community law and indeed the domestic law of most member states (Ackers, 1998, 2001; Hervey and Shaw, 1998; Szyszczak and Moebius, 1998; McKie et al, 2001). It has been raised, in the main, in the context of discussions about gender equality and the valuation of work done by women mainly in the home. The failure to recognise these forms of social contribution as capable of giving rise to rights has led feminists to question the relevance and value of the citizenship concept to feminist analysis and strategy. Expressing frustration at the continuing tendency for "dominant conceptualisations of citizenship [to] marginalise private caring", McKie et al conclude that, "Citizenship as a concept and a focus for debates does not appear to have moved issues on: in fact it may well have produced a smokescreen to gender inequalities" (2001, p 254).

Szyszczak and Moebius (1998) similarly challenge the validity of the distinction between paid and unpaid work, reflecting on the relative advantages, in terms of citizenship status, of 'raising pigs and children'[11]. Arguing in favour of an extension of the concept of worker to include persons who perform unwaged care work for children, sick and older people, the authors suggest that the current formulation, which excludes informal care from the notion of work, "undermines women's experience of citizenship in the European Union" (p 125).

The long-term consequences for women of taking time out of the formal labour market in order to support families, in terms of forgone earnings, lost pension entitlements, and so on, is well documented (see Szyszczak and Moebius, 1998, p 153 for a discussion of the economic value of women's unpaid care work). Recent research suggests that, in a mobility context this trend is particularly marked, as the dislocation of informal sources of support, the primacy attached to male careers and the often repeated nature of mobility results in an increased withdrawal of women from paid work (Ackers, 1998, 2001). In failing to recognise or acknowledge the genuine and significant economic contribution made by informal carers in terms of savings to welfare systems and also the economic burden to the carers themselves in forgoing paid work, the insistence on the exercise of paid work as the trigger to citizenship entitlement disadvantages carers. This disadvantage extends beyond their working lives, denying them access to the trappings of paid work (in terms of social protection and other forms of 'occupational welfare') but also, in the context of this research, in terms of their ability to exercise mobility in later life[12].

In that sense the failure to recognise unpaid care work as work has a multiplier effect: for those persons (predominantly women) engagement in unpaid work during an earlier phase of their life course reduces their own recourse to care services and benefits in the future. As Hervey and Shaw point out in their analysis of EC Sex Equality law, providing care (re)produces dependency:

> Care-giving work can be the result of a dependency situation (of children or
> frail elderly [sic] relatives on women), and itself give rise to a situation of
> dependency upon the state because that care-giving work is not (economically)
> valued. (1998, p 44)

The interpretation of the concept of worker and work under the free movement
provisions, however, further restricts access to even this 'safety net' of statutory
support in the host state (as a consequence of the resources requirement).
Thus, as participation in unpaid care reduces labour market participation (and
command of economic resources in a wider sense), so reduced labour market
participation restricts an individual's ability to access statutory support. Szyszczak
and Moebius suggest that this 'double bind' situation may act as a barrier to
mobility:

> The woman's chances of migration are undermined by the fact that her status
> as a mother or carer is not seen as a sufficient basis for the exercise of her right
> to free movement within the Union. (1998, p 148)

In many cases, as our previous work has shown, people move with little
knowledge of their rights. Family formation, family breakdown and bereavement
often catapult women into a stark realisation of their highly circumscribed
status (Ackers, 1998, note 37). These concerns around the status attached to
unpaid caring work, the costs of undertaking such work and withdrawing
from paid employment fall, in the main, on women. However, it is not only
women who care. The focus in much of the literature and research to date has
been on the issue of childcare and the period of women's lives associated with
this form of care. Increasing attention is being paid, however, in the context of
demographic change to the 'problems' of caring for a population of increasingly
frail, older people. The gender and intergenerational issues raised here are
somewhat different, with a significant incidence of spousal care. It is perhaps
in this context that the role of men in caring for old and disabled partners is
most apparent, as Fisher suggests:

> We are so used to arguing for equity in community care policy in the name
> of women, that we are surprised to find the need to integrate older men into
> this argument. The legitimate concern to identify the major task of caring as
> falling on daughters has had the unintended effect of blurring the picture of
> the care given by older people, and thus by husbands to wives. (1998, p 136)

So, while many male carers will have undertaken paid employment during
their working lives (and as such will have greater access to contributory-based
benefits and occupational welfare), the population of retired migrants will include
a significant population of old male carers who will, as a result of their status as
unpaid carers, share the experience of discrimination in terms of welfare claims
against the host state (cf Chapter Seven).

The derived rights of family members (joiners) and the concept of family in Community law

In addition to their personal entitlement, Community migrant workers (including those who retire in the host state) are entitled to be joined or accompanied by members of their families (who as a consequence of their relationship with the community migrant workers derive social rights) (cf Ackers, 1998; Craig and de Búrca, 1998; Ackers and Stalford, 2002). The extension of citizenship rights to the family members of Community workers was deemed necessary in order to *facilitate the mobility* of workers (*Ministere Public v Even & ONPTS*). An understanding of the impact of these provisions, and their potential in terms of promoting a more inclusive form of citizenship, demands an analysis of the concept of family in Community law. Article 10 of Regulation 1612/68 begins to set out a Community definition of family:

> The following shall, irrespective of their nationality, have the right to install themselves with a worker who is a national of one Member State and who is employed in the territory of another Member State:
>
> (a) his spouse and their descendants who are under the age of 21 years or are dependants;
>
> (b) dependant relatives in the ascending line of the worker and his spouse.

While dependency remains an important consideration when assessing entitlement there are no clear guidelines as to what exactly constitutes dependency. The case law of the ECJ infers that dependency must be of a financial nature to trigger entitlement to social protection in other member states. The anomaly lies in the fact that once a claim for social protection is made on the very basis of this financial dependency a family member becomes financially independent (since they can obtain support from the state rather than the worker). Dependency, therefore, is a matter of initial fact. It does not matter why the family member is dependent on the worker or whether they could support themselves by paid employment. The fact that a dependent family member may be eligible for a social security benefit, and claims it, should not result in the loss of that person's status as a dependent member of the family (CPAG, 1997).

This, coupled with the fact that there is no requirement that the family member live under the same roof as the worker (see *Diatta v Land Berlin*), implies that dependency is merely an initial qualifying criterion. However, what it fails to consider are other relationships of dependency, which are perhaps of greater consequence to the family member but which, because they are not of an economic nature, potentially fail to qualify as 'dependency'. In relation to older people, for instance, the family member may be financially autonomous but heavily reliant on family members for informal care and emotional support.

Article 10 refers to a Community worker's right to be accompanied by 'his spouse'. The concept of spouse is not specified in the legislation and it has been left to the Court of Justice to define. The interpretation of this concept is, however, of crucial importance to the citizenship status of the population of non-working partners moving throughout the Community. If they qualify under the provisions as family members they derive a significantly greater benefit than those persons who do not.

The concept of 'spouse' in Community law

Regulation 1612/68 simply refers to 'his spouse'. This definition leaves scope for some ambiguity, with important implications for the rights of the partners of Community migrants. In particular, concern has arisen over the definition of 'spouse' in Community law, the entitlement of cohabitants (including those in same-sex partnerships) and the implications of separation and divorce on spousal rights.

In *Netherlands v Reed* the Court of Justice was asked whether the term 'spouse' included a cohabitant. Advocate General Herr Carl Otto Lenz emphasised the importance of a Community-wide definition:

> The term 'spouse' has a specific meaning in Community law – [therefore] divergence in the application of the law on an issue important for freedom of movement, would be just as unacceptable as divergence with regard to the term 'worker'.

Ms Reed argued that in the light of legal and social developments, in applying Article 10 of Regulation 1612/68, and in particular the word 'spouse', to circumstances such as those of this case, unmarried partners must, in so far as possible, be treated as spouses. The Court rejected Ms Reed's argument and found that:

> When, in support of a dynamic interpretation reference is made to developments in social and legal conceptions, those developments must be visible in the whole of the Community; such an argument cannot be based on social and legal developments in only one or two Member States. (para 10)

The term 'spouse' in Article 10 thus "applies to marriage partners only and does not include cohabitation"[13]. Kathleen Kiernan's recent analysis of the rise in cohabitation and childbearing outside marriage in western Europe contends that "few developments in family life have been quite as dramatic as the recent rises in unmarried cohabitation" (2001, p 1). One would therefore expect cohabitation to become increasingly prevalent among the retired population in the next couple of decades. Our previous research, together with the findings of this study, suggest that many men and women spend at least a part of their lives cohabiting.

The implications of separation and divorce

There is, as yet, very little case law concerning the effect of divorce and separation on a spouse with Community nationality. The cases discussed later all involve non-Community spouses. Some uncertainty exists over whether a spouse with Community nationality would be dealt with similarly. The cases raise broader issues, however, concerning the relationship between marital status and social entitlement under Article 7 (2) Regulation 1612/68. The English High Court considered the impact of separation on the rights of a non-Community spouse of a migrant worker in *R v Secretary of State for the Home Department* (*ex parte Sandhu*). The judge in the case (Comyn, J.) described the issues as follows:

> Can an EEC national admitted to this country as such together with her non-EEC husband deprive him of EEC protection by, for example, deserting him, separating from him, by going to live elsewhere in this country, by going back to her native State or by going somewhere else abroad? If she can automatically and over any interval of time do that, it would ... add a new terror to marriage. (para 12-13)

The Court held that Mr Sandhu should be allowed to stay indefinitely and permanently; separation and divorce did not automatically extinguish spousal rights. The Court of Appeal, however, took a different view on the grounds that the worker's right to be joined by his family did not imply:

> ... put the other way around, the family's right to join the worker. There is a right given to a spouse as a member of the family, it is a right not to come here independently of the other spouse, but a right to install themselves with a worker who ... and note it is in the present tense ... is employed in the territory of another member state ... in the present case the husband can only make a claim to a right for permission to stay in this country as long as the wife herself is exercising it.

The ECJ considered the impact of separation in another case involving the Senegalese wife of a French Community worker living in Germany, who had separated with the intention of seeking a divorce (*Diatta v Land Berlin*). The question of whether the spouse is required to live with the migrant worker in order to retain her rights was referred to the Court of Justice. Ms Diatta claimed that the provisions of Regulation 1612/68 (Article 10) do not impose an express obligation to cohabit. The Commission proposed a broader interpretation, arguing that:

> The severance of the family relationship – in this instance the marital relationship – should not have the effect of automatically withdrawing 'the protection of Community law' from the members of the family who benefit from it. (para 7)

The Court interpreted EC law to the effect that the marriage subsisted until divorce and there was no requirement to live under the same roof, and consequently Ms Diatta was still a member of her husband's family. The Court was, however, insistent that any right of residence for a spouse derived from their relationship with the Community worker and was not an independent right.

In a subsequent case involving a couple who were part way through divorce proceedings, the Court held that Community law protected a spouse up until the point at which the marriage was finally dissolved. Once again it failed to clarify the impact of divorce itself on spousal rights, reflecting its reluctance to deal with the issue (*R v IAT and Surinder Singh ex parte Secretary of State for the Home Department*). The problem in relation to spouse's rights is clearly most acute where the spouse is not a national of a member state, as in the previous cases. A spouse who is a 'Citizen of the Union' may derive an independent right of residence under Directive 90/364 (or now, arguably Article 18). However, while protecting such a spouse from the risk of expulsion, this new Directive does not provide for access to the panoply of social rights available to migrant workers and their spouses.

The parasitic nature of family rights

We have seen in the previous discussion how the benefits accruing to workers under the free movement provisions (including access to social advantages) extend to those persons who fall within Community definitions of 'family'. Such "specifically included family members" (Craig and de Búrca, 1998, p 704) have broadly similar substantive rights to those of the worker. The status of family members and workers differs, however, in a fundamental sense, in that the former only have derived entitlement. Families thus gain their social entitlement indirectly through the economic contribution of the worker. The problems of financial dependency within marriage are summarised by Lister:

> When married or cohabiting women do not have a wage or other source of personal income in their own right, their male partners have enormous power (potential or realised) over the resources at these women's disposal. (1990, p 450)

Where marriage determines not only the allocation of resources within the family (the breadwinner's wage), but also access to key social goods, then this problem is clearly compounded. The availability of social advantages to members of migrant worker's families depends on the existence and subsistence of marriage or, in the case of an ascendant relative, proof of dependency. This has significant implications for the autonomy of family members reinforcing relationships of dependency within families. Where, for example, a worker loses his or her employment and where this is construed as being 'voluntary' resulting in a loss of vital social entitlement, the family's derivative rights are also at risk. This 'subjective' interpretation of worker's motivation has dramatic implications for any family members. The Court made it clear in *Lebon* that once a child of a migrant worker reached the age of 21 and was no longer dependent on the worker, benefits to that child could not be construed as an advantage to the worker:

> … members of a worker's family, within the meaning of Article 10 of Regulation 1612/68 qualify only indirectly for the equal treatment accorded to the worker himself by Article 7 of Regulation 1612/68. Social benefits … operate in favour of members of the worker's family only if such benefits may be regarded as a social advantage, within the meaning of Article 7 (2) of Regulation No 1612/68, for the worker himself.

Blake QC describes family rights as 'adjectival' on the grounds that:

> The rights subsist while the principal is exercising Treaty rights in the Member State and the person remains a member of the family. They are not free-standing rights of entry given to people who happen to be family members; the family rights are adjectival on the exercise of Treaty rights by the principal. (Blake, 1999, p 8)

Commenting on the exclusion of unmarried and de facto relationships, in spite of their inclusion within the expression of family in the ECHR, Blake concludes that:

> … families do break up and separate. Marriages end in divorce … it is harsh and inappropriate that past residence as a family member is disregarded or of little weight. (1999, p 16)

As it stands the definition of family in Community law currently leaves many migrants in a highly dependant and vulnerable position. The female partners of retirement migrants, many of whom will not themselves have undertaken paid work prior to retirement, are at particular risk following divorce or should their partners leave the member state. The personal status of family members thus meshes with pre-existing divisions, based upon economic contribution, to create a matrix of distinctive legal scenarios which, in reality, neither derive from Community nationality or 'membership' in an inclusive sense, nor bear any relation to objective measures of need[14].

The rights of ascendant relatives

The concept of family in Article 10 of Regulation 1612/68 encompasses not only the rights of the spouses and children of Community migrant workers, however, but also those "*Dependent* relatives in the ascending line of the worker and his spouse" (para 1). A Community migrant worker thus also has a right to be joined by his or her older and dependent parents or parents-in-law and to make welfare claims on the basis of equal treatment under Article 7 (2)

Regulation 1612/68. In *Castelli v ONPTS* the Court found that an Italian widow who moved to live with her migrant worker son in Belgium was entitled to a minimum income allowance paid to all older persons under Belgian law. Since she had a right under Article 10 Regulation 1612/68 to install herself with her son, she was also entitled to the same social and tax advantages as Belgian workers and ex-workers. Applying the *Even* formula, the Court held that Castelli was entitled to the old age benefit by virtue of her 'settled residence'[15].

Evidence of the exercise of this right to join family members in the host state and some of the problems of translating such formal legal rights into caring practices is developed in Chapter Seven (see also Ackers, 1998, Chapter Eight).

The rights of such 'joiners' who are senior citizens are derived rights and exist to benefit the Community migrant worker and to promote labour mobility. They are based on an assumption of simple provider-recipient relationships, as the wording of the Regulation suggests, and both require and reinforce relations of dependency. As such they raise important questions of the parasitic nature of such family rights and the implications of a subsequent move on the part of the qualifying Community worker on older dependants' rights and autonomy. In principle, the rights of the family member in the host state are strictly coterminous with those of the qualifying CMW; a decision on the part of the CMW to move again would therefore presumably extinguish the claims a family member can make in the host state. This may in practice also impede the mobility of the Community workers themselves.

The impact of the death of the worker-citizen on family rights

While the derived rights of family members give cause for concern in circumstances of family breakdown and the subsequent mobility of the worker-citizen, the situation facing family members of deceased workers is rather more clear-cut[16]. Regulation 1251/70 extends the right to remain to family members, provided the qualifying worker acquired the right to remain before his death (Article 3). Furthermore, if the worker died before having acquired that right, members of his family nevertheless have a right to remain in the host state, providing that:

> ... the worker had resided continuously in the territory of that member state for at least 2 years; or his death resulted from an accident at work or an occupational disease; or the surviving spouse is a national of the State of residence or lost the nationality of that state by marriage to the worker. (Article 3, para 2)

The social status of surviving family members was discussed by the ECJ in *Cristini v Société nationale des chemins de fer français*. The Court held that family members could make applications under Article 7 (2) of Regulation 1612/68 following the death of the migrant worker. Indeed, the existence of family members' right to remain in the host state following the death of the migrant worker under Article 3 (1) Regulation 1251/70 would be superficial if it were not accompanied by a continued right to claim the social advantages previously available to them. This ruling provides an important legal basis for the social entitlement of non-working and retired spouses of Community migrant workers and members of their family (as defined in Community law).

The social entitlement of the groups of retirement migrants referred to so far (those who wished to retire in situ following a period as a Community worker themselves and those who moved to join their Community worker children) derives from Regulations 1408/71 and 1612/68. In other words, notwithstanding the limitations of derived entitlement for family members, these persons have full access to domestic welfare systems. The following section moves to examine the very different legal status of another group of retired migrants.

The legal status of post-retirement migrants (PRM)

Directive 90/365 further extends residency rights to those Community nationals who have ceased their occupational activity in the 'home state' and who wish to move to another member state on retirement. An important distinction exists, however, in terms of the social entitlement that this form of residency gives rise to, for in order to exercise this right the persons concerned must demonstrate that:

> ... they themselves and the members of their families are covered by sickness insurance in respect of all risks in the host Member States and have sufficient financial resources to ensure that *they will not become a burden on the public purse* and social security system of the host Member State during their period of residence.

To that extent, what has become known as the 'resources requirement' severely restricts the formal welfare claims that this group of retired people can make against the host state. In theory, at least, they have no formal social citizenship status.

Implications

Reference was made earlier in the chapter to the presumption of static relationships underpinning legal categories. In defining the research questions during the very early stages of the research and setting out the sampling strategy, the project team underestimated the difficulties of defining and identifying a sample of retired migrants. In reality, basing the sampling strategy on our awareness of Community law distinctions and the hard and fast legal categories contained therein, proved immediately problematic in the field. Respondents rarely 'fitted' comfortably within these categories and if they did, it may only be for a certain period of time. In many cases the issue reflected the assumption that retirement (almost by definition) marked the end of paid work or economic activity. Of course this 'problem' of the need to define, in operational terms, populations for research purposes is not unique to this project and may be expected to present ever-increasing challenges as traditional parameters breakdown. Phillipson similarly identifies social trends, suggesting:

> ... a blurring of boundaries between different stages of the life-course; the growth of different work categories and statuses in between full-time work and complete retirement. (1996, p 219)

In practice, many of our respondents moved in order to retire (it was their plan not to work), but recommenced some form of work in the host state; others did plan to work for a short while prior to retirement, perhaps not so much for the economic gains and legal status attached to that but rather to facilitate their social integration. For this group of persons or, to be more correct, for this period of residence, the persons concerned and their families can, presumably, claim the more favoured entitlement attached to the status of Community migrant worker (on the basis of the rulings on part-time work discussed previously)[17]. While the case law referred to earlier suggests that someone who resumes paid work, perhaps selling ice-creams or conducting tours, automatically climbs a tier in the citizenship hierarchy, the requirement of remuneration would appear to rule out other forms of contribution (such as caring or voluntary work) irrespective of their economic consequences and social importance.

The legal status of returnees

The social status of returnees (those people who either return home after finishing work in another member state or return after spending a period of retirement abroad) is to a large extent a function of national law and policy (and once again the infrastructure and quality of support in the home state). It also reflects the ability to aggregate and transport occupational and statutory benefits. In recent years, however, the European Court has had to consider the legality of certain national laws potentially restricting the social status of returnees (on the grounds that their economic contribution has taken place in another state). A case in point is the UK's habitual residence test. This test, first introduced in 1994, requires that an EU citizen moving to the UK should satisfy certain criteria in determining their access to a range of social security benefits[18]. These criteria relate to the number of years the individual has lived outside the UK. As such, the habitual residence test operates to withhold benefits to EU citizens and returning nationals until residence is considered to have been (re)established.

Defining 'habitually resident'

There is no formal legal definition of 'habitually resident'. It is therefore "open to highly subjective, restrictive and inconsistent decision-making by adjudication offices and social security appeal tribunals. Particular groups tend to be targeted, including EU nationals and people (especially from ethnic minority Communities) who spend lengthy periods overseas" (CPAG, 1998, p 72). Following a series of Social Security Commissioner decisions, a number of principles were established in defining the meaning of 'habitually resident'[19]. Firstly, it was emphasised that there are no definitive factors by which to determine a person's habitual residence, each case being considered individually according to its own specific circumstances. Secondly, the claimant must demonstrate a 'settled intention' to reside in a country, either temporarily or permanently. This intention is established according to activities and arrangements made by the individual subsequent to their arrival in the UK. Thirdly, the claimant must have resided in the UK for an 'appreciable period of time'. Again, an 'appreciable period' is judged according to the facts of the case.

Certain issues will be taken into account in considering whether an individual is 'habitually resident', such as whether they have a permanent job in the UK, the nature of their work, future intentions, reasons for coming to the UK and the continuity of their residence in the UK and elsewhere. Furthermore, an individual who migrates to another country for a temporary period of time may retain their habitual residence in the UK so that they will become habitually resident from the first day of their return home (CPAG, 1998, note 74, p 73). There are also cases in which an individual can qualify as habitually resident in more than one country concurrently.

The habitual residence test is applied to all claimants, including British citizens, but not partners or dependants. If the claimant is unsuccessful in satisfying the test, however, their partner may then make a similar claim in their own right. EU or EEA nationals are exempt from the test if they are a migrant worker within the remit of Regulation 1612/68, either in the UK or another member state and making a claim for means-tested benefits under Regulation 1408/71, or if they are exercising their right to remain under Regulation 1251/70 as retired EU migrants (*Di Paolo v Office National de L'Emploi*; see also *R v IAT and Surinder Singh ex parte Secretary of State for the Home Department*).

The test has significant implications for retired EU migrants in that it jeopardises a right to claim social protection for both British returnees and retired migrants who are nationals of other member states. The existence of the test certainly presents a real as opposed to a merely perceived or theoretical problem. According to a Eurolink Age report: "In 1995/6, 6,089 British citizens failed this test on return from overseas, as did 6,326 people from the EEA and 7,308 others, many of whom were older people" (Eurolink Age, 1996a, p 4). More recent figures (April 1998 – March 1999) indicate that 113,000 claims to Income Support and Jobseeker's Allowance were subject to the habitual residence test. Of these approximately 18,500 claims did not pass the test, of which some 10,500 claims were from UK nationals (DSS, 1999). The habitual residence test potentially impedes mobility and particularly return migration. Furthermore, following the death of a spouse, for example, retired widows who wish to return to their country of origin may find themselves in a situation where they are unable to support themselves since they are prevented from claiming essential financial assistance. In this respect, they are faced with a Hobson's choice of remaining in the host country, perhaps without important emotional and familial support, or returning to their country of origin, the UK, where they will have insufficient financial resources.

In recognition of these issues, both Eurolink Age and the DSS have recommended reforms to the test, which afford greater social protection to older people returning to the UK after a period abroad. Among the main reforms proposed is that UK and other nationals returning to the UK from any country overseas who are re-establishing their ties are to be accepted as habitually resident immediately upon their return. These proposals follow an ECJ decision relating to the case of Robin *Swaddling* (*v Adjudication Officer*), a UK citizen who lived and worked in France for a number of years. On subsequently returning to the UK (he was unemployed at this time and unable to find work in France), his claim for Income Support was rejected on the grounds that he had yet to complete a qualifying period of residence. The ECJ, ruling in favour of the claimant, rejected the UK requirement stating that the imposition of such a test was in contravention of the free movement of persons' provisions:

> Article 10(a) of Council Regulation 1408/71 ... precludes the Member State of origin – in the case of a person who has exercised his right to freedom of movement in order to establish himself in another Member State, in which he has worked and set up his habitual residence, and who has returned to his Member State of origin, where his family lives, in order to seek work – from making entitlement to one of the benefits referred to in Article 10(a) Regulation 1408/71 conditional upon habitual residence in that State, which presupposes not only an intention to reside there, but also completion of an appreciable period of residence there.

Although in this case the person concerned was seeking work, one would hope that the same reasoning would be extended to retired migrants.

Temporary residence and the legal status of 'tourists' and 'seasonal' migrants

For many retired people the decision to move to another country is taken incrementally over a period of time, often with the person deciding to initially spend extended vacations in an area they enjoyed visiting as tourists during their working lives. The concept of 'snowbirds' is thus popularly associated with Nordic countries and evident in the literature on international retirement migration[20]. A common pattern would be a period of tourism shading into seasonal and finally more permanent settlement, often culminating in an eventual return 'home'.

Although the Treaty itself does not refer to service recipients, Article 1 of Directive 64/221 (implementing the right to provide services under Articles 49-55) protects the position of service recipients who travel to another member state for that purpose. Article 1(b) of Directive 73/148 also requires the abolition of restrictions on the movement and residence of "nationals wishing to go to another member state as recipients of services". In *Luisi and Carbone v Ministero del Tesoro*, the Court confirmed that the Treaty articles extended to cover the situation of recipients. This furnishes tourists with important rights under Community law to move in order to receive services and to equality of treatment in that respect. The services must, however, be economic in nature and must be provided for 'remuneration', although this definition has been held to extend to recreational or sporting services. It would not, presumably, extend a right to move in order to receive informal care. In practice, as our findings suggest, many retired migrants, keen to preserve their welfare entitlement back home through the retention of residency in that country (and to avoid local taxation, and so on) live for the majority of the year as 'tourists' in the host state. However, this status does not give rise to the beneficial social entitlement referred to previously.

The impact of Article 18 on social entitlement

The second report from the European Commission on Citizenship of the Union (CEC, 1997a) described the right to free movement as a fundamental and personal right conferred on every citizen of the Union, which may be exercised outside the context of an economic activity. The impact of Article 18 EC on the citizenship status of retirement migrants (and in particular the extent to which Article 18 effectively replaces the residency directives and the inherent distinction they imply) remains a matter of contention. Eurolink Age[21] submitted its views to the Commission that "those (older persons) who have ceased their occupational activity should not be excluded from the right to move freely and reside anywhere within the European Union, as set out in Article 18" (Eurolink Age, 1996a, p 1). The Commission recognised, however, that Article 18 EC does not constitute a comprehensive legal base from which all free movement rights derive. Article 18 cannot take the place of existing legal bases dealing with the distinctions and limitations of the various categories of persons granted free movement rights under Community law (cf Chalmers and Szyszczak, 1998, p 66). The Commission proposed the upgrading of Article 18, "to a specific legal basis apt to revise the complex body of secondary legislation. This would certainly increase the transparency of Community law, ease implementation measures and increase the citizen's understanding of the rights effectively conferred" (CEC, 1997a, p 4).

The constitutional status of Article 18 has been discussed in a series of Court of Justice cases. In *Skanavi and Chryssanthakopoulos* the Court of Justice held that while Article 18 sets out generally the right of every citizen of the Union to move and reside freely within the territory of the member states, it finds specific expression in Article 43 EC (that is, the Right of Establishment). The question was raised again in *Stober and Pereira v Bundesanstalt für Arbeit*. The cases concerned German legislation requiring the children of self-employed people to reside in Germany in order to qualify for a children's allowance.

Advocate General La Pergola urged the Court to address the relationship between Article 18 and the free movement provisions, arguing that the German rule was in conflict with Article 18. The Court chose not to address this issue but rather dealt with the matter on the grounds of Article 18 itself.

A similar expansive approach to Article 18 was presented, however, by Advocate General Ruiz-Jarabo Colomer in *Shingara*:

> The creation of citizenship of the Union, with the corollary described above of freedom of movement for citizens throughout the territory of the Member States, represents a considerable step forward in that, as the Commission rightly points out, it separates that freedom from its functional or instrumental elements (the link with an economic activity or attainment of the internal market) and raises it to the level of a genuinely independent right inherent in the political status of the citizens of the Union.

The potential of European citizenship as an instrument for producing substantive social rights, was further explored in the important case of *Martinez Sala v Freistaat Bayern*. The facts of the case have already been outlined in the context of the valuation of unpaid work, however, the case also raised wider issues concerning the legal impact of the post-Maastricht citizenship provisions. The claimant argued that the refusal to grant her a child-raising allowance was in direct contravention of Article 6 EC (now Article 12), which provides a general prohibition of discrimination on the grounds of nationality. The crux of the decision, however, lay in whether Sala, as an unemployed non-national with no 'family' connection to rely on, fell within the *personal* scope of the free movement provisions. The Court approached the issue on the novel basis of Article 8a EC (now Article 18), which endows all EU citizens with a general right of residence in all member states. Sala's status as a de facto European citizen was deemed sufficient for her to exercise the general right of residence[22]. Furthermore, this automatically entitled her to rely on the non-discrimination principle enshrined in Article 12, a right attached to the status of Union citizenship (for a critique of this decision see Fries and Shaw, 1998). The decision adds considerable substance to the symbolic notion of Union citizenship and calls into question the continued significance of the 'layered entitlement' previously granted according to individuals' economic value. It also overcomes the complexities involved in applying different dependency-related criteria. Indeed, Fries and Shaw (1998) argue that it may indicate a general right to 'all manner' of social welfare benefits for all EU migrants, whether or not they are (have been) engaged with the PLM.

> ... it would appear that something close to a universal non-discrimination right including access to all manner of welfare benefits for all those who are Union citizens and who are lawfully resident in a Member State has now taken root in EC law. (p 536)

Weatherill (2000, p 403) concludes:

> Martinez Sala may prove to be the key ruling that breaks the ground between
> the orthodoxy of economic rights for economic migrants and new horizons
> lit up by comprehensive rights to equal treatment for Union citizens.

The ruling also has potentially far-reaching consequences (and indeed benefits)
if applied to retired individuals, and particularly the surviving family members
of former workers. Firstly, it extends the opportunities for benefits claims by
economically inactive family members who remain in the host state
independently of the former worker. In this respect, they would be entitled to
claim state benefits as a means of supporting themselves without falling foul of
the dependency test[23]. Secondly, it implies that all citizens of the EU who are
lawfully resident in the territory of the host state can rely on Article 12 of the
EC Treaty in all situations which fall within the scope of Community law
(including therefore claims based on Regulations 1408/71 and 1612/68). This
includes situations in which member states refuse or delay awards of benefits
on the grounds that the claimant does not satisfy a length of residence test.

From legal rights to citizenship experience: the problem of fixed categories

The difficulty with the complex matrix-like structuring of legal rights described
previously, lies not only in the impact on legal certainty and administration of
Community law, but also in the assumption of binary and fixed relationships.
In particular the law assumes that it is possible to identify, within families,
dependants and providers, reinforcing the association of retirement with the
condition of dependency (cf Ackers and Stalford, 1999) and of senior citizens
as the consumers of care. McKie et al make a similar point:

> It has been common to consider citizenship in terms of a series of binary
> oppositions, that is, public and private, active and passive, and rights and duties.
> Feminists and ecological theorists have moved debates away from such binaries
> to configure citizenship as dynamic, as interweaving these oppositions. (2001,
> p 247)

In practice family relationships are not characterised by this degree of certainty
and unilateral flows of support. The interviews with retired migrants demonstrate
the importance of understanding the fluid nature of caring relationships, of
reciprocity and interdependency over the life course. Indeed, perhaps the most
surprising finding in this respect was the extent to which respondents' migration
decisions were shaped by their desire or need to *provide* care rather than receive
it (for more discussion see Chapter Seven). As we shall see, the tendency to
categorise retired persons as 'dependants' and as the recipients of care thus flies
in the face of empirical reality.

Linked to the assumptions about dependency are equally problematic assumptions about personal relationships (marital status) and employment status. Previous research on the experiences of migrant women evidenced the constant shifts in marital status within the research population, with some women reporting five or six changes during their period of residency (perhaps moving initially as single women, then marrying, divorcing, re-partnering and subsequently becoming widowed) (Ackers, 1998).

The concept of retirement and the cessation of economic activity is equally problematic when, in practice, many retired migrants resume some form of work, either on a voluntary, part-time or self-employed basis in the host state, perhaps moving into and out of paid work. These shifts in both work and marital status raise legally significant questions around the concept of worker and spouse in Community law and the effect of these in determining which 'rung' the person occupies on the Community citizenship ladder.

In addition to assumptions about the fixed nature of dependency relationships, are the equally stereotypical, normative assumptions about migration behaviour, which both determine the identification of barriers to mobility (as the basis of policy development) and impose a legal straitjacket on relationships, with important consequences for welfare claims[24]. The mobility of older people is thus caricatured as a movement of passive, non-contributing dependants whose caring needs may create undue demands on receiving welfare systems. The findings of research with older migrants reinforce the importance of understanding the fluid nature of this kind of migration, described by Karen O'Reilly (2000b, p 483) as a 'peripatetic process'. We have already described the incremental approach taken by many older migrants who move, in the first instance, as tourists or on a seasonal basis. In practice, respondents often made a series of moves, with each move triggered by a different balance of events and considerations as they and their families' lives unfolded and new situations arose and were responded to in the endeavour to 'manage kinship' transnationally. Hard and fast legal categories are thus insufficiently flexible to deal with the kind of transitions and complex negotiations of interdependency that form a feature of people's lives.

The articulation of legal status with other forms of social status

The discussion in the first section of this chapter has identified the link between different forms of retirement migration and social entitlement. The retired Community worker stands at the apex of the citizenship hierarchy, at least in terms of their access to independent legal rights under the free movement provisions. In practice material status is more than simply a reflection of formal legal rights. The formal status of a migrant, in Community law, articulates with other forms of legal and social status shaping their ability to spread dependency across the resource frameworks available to them. In the main those persons exercising their right to return home following a period spent working in another member state represented a group of 'labour migrants' in the traditional sense of the term. They typically moved under pressure from depressed home labour markets and the draw of advantageous wage levels and work opportunities abroad often in the period prior to accession. This group is characterised by a movement of blue collar, manual workers who primarily return to weaker southern European welfare systems[25].

To the extent that the mobility of this group of workers enabled them to access the more favourable statutory and occupational benefits systems of northern and western European countries, return migration places these people in a position of relative economic advantage on return (in the sense that they can transport these benefits with them and continue to make claims against the welfare systems of their previous country of residence). However, as the interviews indicate (see Chapter Five), a number of this group returned home with serious health problems and industrial diseases resulting from periods of work in hazardous industries. Furthermore, their ability to tap into informal networks of support, so important to welfare status in southern Europe, has often proved more limited due to the dislocating effect of migration on family resources. Many of them had children who moved with them or to join them and have not returned 'home'. Indeed the research uncovered reports of the exodus of entire populations of younger, male workers resulting in significant demographic distortion in the home region. In that sense, the returning Community workers have, as a result of migration, more limited access to informal care and family support on their return than their non-migrant peers.

The mobility rights of that group of retired persons who wish to move following the cessation of economic activity do not, as we have seen above, extend to full citizenship entitlement in the host state but remain conditional (on their ability to demonstrate financial autonomy under the 'resources requirement'). The impact of this highly circumscribed status on the individuals concerned reflects their pre-retirement economic status and, in particular, their ability to aggregate and transport certain statutory and occupational benefits and pensions. A clear division is evident here between those persons who have contributed to occupational and private schemes during their working lives and those reliant upon means-tested state benefits and forms of social assistance. In general the former have access to both more generous and more portable forms of benefit. They are thus more footloose and can effectively move their entitlement with them.

In addition to insulating them from reliance upon welfare systems, in some circumstances post-retirement movers are able to use their wealth as a means of maintaining a right to claim against the welfare systems of their home state and in some cases a number of domestic welfare systems. This is achieved through careful articulation of fiscal and residency status[26]. This ability to manage citizenship through residency and location decisions is not specific to retirement migration, but has been identified in a whole range of areas. In this context, however, it takes on a specific transnational flavour. Effectively circumnavigating the formal nexus of national and Community legal rights, and often moving in the shadows of the law in order to maximise their social citizenship entitlement, the mobility of this second group is lubricated by their superior ability to access and transport private and insurance-based systems of support. In practice many are able to negotiate their own personalised citizenship 'package'. An important factor here concerns the ability to maintain residency status in the home state (through property ownership there) and by not claiming residency in the host state. Post-retirement migrants may thus make a conscious decision not to move themselves out of a status as tourist or seasonal visitor. In that sense the impact of the resources requirement (under Directive 90/365) is minimal as the persons concerned are forgoing entitlement in the less generous host state by maintaining formal residence 'back home'.

In general these people are moving away from those countries associated with more 'generous' and importantly, culturally acceptable (less contested) infrastructures of elder care in the direction of the mother–daughter, welfare societies of southern Europe. In contrast to the returnee group, their mobility is often highly focused, resulting in high levels of residential segregation and the effective colonisation of previously depopulated coastal regions.

The geography of this form of mobility has other consequences in terms of access to welfare and the ability to make welfare claims. On the one hand, the concentration of specific expatriate communities supports the development of strong voluntary and self-help initiatives (through churches and other voluntary organisations). These groups provide a wide range of services to the retired population, including not only social support but also elements of community care (cf Chapter Five). On the other hand, the residential concentration of this population at local level, may force a situation in which resources are provided irrespective of formal entitlement. This situation reflects the relative political and economic clout of these populations and their ability to make political demands, supported by the Citizenship provisions themselves (and the right to vote in municipal elections under Article 19). Their power as consumers within local economies thus further enables them to command social resources over and above their formal legal entitlement (cf Betty and Cahill, 1999). In that sense, although the returnee sample may achieve the highest level of Community protection, as privileged aliens, this does not necessarily translate into optimum ability to access social resources. It may be that post-retirement migrants are best able to maximise their access to social resources (through their ability to manage their residency status and to underwrite the costs of repeated moves between the home and host state). The point here really is to emphasise the articulation of formal legal status with other forms of status in the shaping of resource frameworks: formal legal rights do not translate in any straightforward and simplistic fashion into citizenship experience. This underlines the importance of understanding the distinction between formal legal rights and the exercise of the law.

The limitation of the categorisation outlined so far lies in the implied determinism. The qualitative work reported on in the subsequent chapters evidences the danger of assuming a precise relationship between resources and life experience. Life course events such as ill health, bereavement and relationship breakdown can rapidly catapult people from relative security into poverty and need. The experiences of the respondents in this research evidence not only the ease with which wealth can be exhausted but also the limited value of economic wealth in the face of certain forms of human condition, in particular isolation, loneliness and illness. While insurance and wealth doubtless enables some citizens to cope more easily with the vagaries and unpredictability of life courses, some situations are difficult or impossible to plan for and insulate oneself from.

Conclusions

In its second report on citizenship, the Commission stated that citizenship of the Union is to be regarded as a "fundamental and personal right within the EC which may be exercised outside the context of economic activity" (CEC, 1997a, para 4.1). The extent to which this represents a move towards a more inclusive 'Citizens' Europe' encompassing the social needs of those whose contribution falls outside the currently defined 'economic nexus' (such as retired migrants) has provided perhaps the most significant challenge to the European Community in the last decade (Closa, 1992; O'Leary, 1992; O'Keeffe, 1994). This chapter first described, and to some degree critiqued, the hierarchy of citizenship status attached to different groups of retired migrants on the basis of their social contribution (via paid work) and family status. It then moved on to outline the limitations of hard and fast legal categories in responding to real life situations, which are, typically, complex and fluid. Finally, in recognition that the law remains only one dimension of social status (the determinative effect of which varies depending on access to wider social, economic and political resources) the chapter has considered the interface of legal rights with other forms of status. In so doing it has also raised the question of agency and the differential ability of citizens to negotiate and manage formal rights to their advantage.

A central objective of this socio-legal project has been to juxtapose the empirical reality of the lives of older migrants with the normatively based legal constructs that underpin Community law. With this in mind, many of the issues raised here are revisited in subsequent chapters which flesh out some of the concerns in more specific contexts (on health, pensions and care, for example) before reflecting once again upon the extent to which Community law shapes the citizenship experience of retired migrants in the concluding chapter.

Notes

[1] This chapter is based on a paper presented to the Socio-Legal Studies Association Conference in Belfast in April 2000, jointly written by Professor Ackers and Dr Stalford.

[2] Community law, in this context, is not concerned to promote harmonisation in the social policy field but rather recognises diversity.

[3] Although the focus here is on the concept of worker, it is important to bear in mind these other provisions, particularly as many retired persons may become involved in small business enterprises and the provision of services in the host state, at least in the

early stages of their residency. The rights attached to service providers extend to service recipients.

[4] OJ Sp Ed 1968 No L257/2, p 475.

[5] Adopted pursuant to Article 42 EC (formerly 51), OJ 1971 I 149/2 supplemented by Regulation 574/72, OJ Sp Ed 1971 II, p 416, which provides detailed rules for implementation in individual member states.

[6] Warnes (2002) presents a more sceptical view of the potential of European citizenship to deliver social welfare and concludes his analysis by suggesting that "bilateral agreements ... will be the best way to advance the goal of raising the welfare of expatriates" (2002, p 150).

[7] The point about freedom and dignity as the basis for the extension of social rights is discussed in more detail in the Conclusion.

[8] Article 2 (1) of Regulation 1251/70 EC extends a permanent *right to remain* to "a worker, who, at the time of termination of his activity, has reached the age laid down by the law of that Member State for entitlement to an old age pension and who has been employed in that State for at least the last twelve months and has resided there continuously for more than three years". Articles 1-9 of Council Directive 75/34, OJ 1975, No L14/10 applies similar conditions to previously self-employed individuals who wish to remain in the host country following their retirement.

[9] This is discussed in more detail later.

[10] In a recent ruling, the Court has confined *Bettray* to its specific facts, ruling that a post organised and funded by public authorities may nevertheless constitute legal employment; *Mehment Birden v Stadgemeinde Bremen*, judgement of 26 November 1998.

[11] The title used in this piece is based on a German publication dated 1921, which when translated reads: "Those who raise pigs are productive while those who raise children are unproductive members of this society".

[12] In addition to this and of particular relevance to this form of mobility, given its highly focused geography, is the failure to take into account the economic contribution made to the often weak regional economies via consumption. The relationship between consumption and citizenship is raised in the Conclusion.

[13] However, a member state that grants such an advantage to its own nationals cannot refuse it to workers who are nationals of other member states without being guilty of discrimination on grounds of nationality.

[14] The status of these groups is currently under a raft of Commission proposals for amendments to extend protection to cohabiting couples, same-sex relationships and divorcees.

[15] This 'facilitating mobility' approach has been further supported in *de Vos v Bielefeld* and in *Schmidt v Belgian State*.

[16] Indeed this has been used as the basis of an argument to bring the rights of divorcees in line with those of widows/widowers.

[17] Of course, in many cases, the persons concerned were not formally registered as working and were effectively in the shadows of the law – working 'casually' in the 'black economy'.

[18] Including Housing Benefit, Income Support, income-based Jobseeker's Allowance and Council Tax Benefit.

[19] CIS/1067/1995; CIS/2326/1995; paras 20747-48 AOG.

[20] These issues are dealt with in more detail in Chapter Four.

[21] A European non-governmental organisation representing the rights of older people (now known as 'AGE').

[22] Article 18 (2) provides the basis for this decision in that it empowers the Council to adopt provisions with a view to facilitating the exercise of Union citizenship.

[23] The extent to which this interpretation of Union citizenship will provide tangible benefits for economically inactive individuals remains to be seen, although any imminent departure from the current, stringent application of the law relating to dependency and facilitating mobility seems unlikely.

[24] The gendered assumptions underlying migration theories are discussed in Ackers (1998) and Ackers and Stalford (2002).

[25] One would expect this situation to change in the future, as intra-Community mobility is increasingly characterised by forms of skilled and professional mobility (we may see echoes of this situation in the aftermath of enlargement).

[26] Thus avoiding problems in proving 'habitual residence'.

FOUR

Movements to some purpose?

Introduction

This chapter explores the dynamics of international retirement migration (IRM) in relation to EU nationals within Europe and is divided into two main parts. Initially, the extent of IRM within the EU is briefly considered. The chapter then moves on to provide a more detailed exploration of the motivational factors and triggers that are influential in retired EU migrants' decisions to relocate. This section combines an overview of relevant literature on IRM with qualitative data drawn from our fieldwork[1] to consider some important factors that precipitate movement.

The extent of senior citizens' retirement migration in the EU

It has been argued (for example, Laslett, 1989; Warnes, 1993) that a number of significant changes have occurred in western European society that modify the ways in which many of us experience old age and retirement. Improvements in incomes, increased educational opportunities and attainment, and changes in occupational structure (for example, increasing numbers of professional and technical, rather than manual jobs), have combined to impact upon the aspirations and choices available to people in later life. It is not suggested that such a positive experience is universal; old age for some is still characterised by poverty, lack of opportunities and debilitating illness. The argument is, however, that in contemporary Europe we are now able to differentiate between a 'third age' of "well resourced and healthy retirement" (Warnes, 1993, p 451) and a 'fourth age' of later life starting in the late seventies in which the onset of old age-related illness and need for care become important considerations (cf Laslett, 1989). Longer holidays, experience of overseas travel and the possibility of a period of early retirement have increasingly become a feature of many people's lives in recent decades. Indeed, a number of comparatively wealthy retirees, often in possession of significant occupational and private pensions, are able to consider relocating internationally on retirement.

When discussing IRM much of the established literature (for example, Williams et al, 1997; King et al, 2000; O'Reilly, 2000a, 2000b) has focused on the migratory movements of UK pensioners who relocate towards the warmer regions of southern Europe in retirement. This study has attempted to broaden the focus of such work by also considering the migratory movements of some other groups of retired EU migrants, that is those who have moved around Europe during their lives as paid workers and, subsequently, retired either to their country of origin or another host EU state. All the respondents that took part in this research can loosely be labelled as 'retired EU migrants', that is EU nationals who have moved across national borders *within* the Union at some time and who are now regarded as retired in the sense that on reaching a certain age they have chosen or been required to give up paid work. They are generally reliant on various types of pension and/or personal savings to meet their financial needs. Within this widely defined category it is, however, important to make a further initial distinction. First, 'post-retirement migrants' are those people who migrate to a second EU host country following retirement. A second group 'returnees' are nationals of one EU member state who having previously migrated to another EU state(s) then return to their country of origin. The group labelled 'returnees' can itself be further differentiated into two groups with 'returning workers' being those migrants who have returned to their country of origin after a period of work in another host member state. A more accurate label for those whose initial movement was motivated by the desire for work would be 'returning workers and their partners/spouses'. Many women included in this group did engage in paid labour while resident in a host state, indeed in a lot of cases it was imperative that they earned a wage. This group, however, also includes a number of women who were engaged in unpaid domestic/childcare work throughout their period of residence abroad. 'Returning retirees' on the other hand can be defined as individuals returning to their country of origin following a period of retirement in another EU member state. Differentiation within a generic category of 'retired EU migrants' is important given that the various groups outlined above effectively have different rights as EU citizens in respect of residence and access to social provisions (see Chapter Three for details).

The lack of coherent and reliable statistical data on IRM has been widely commented on (Williams et al, 1997; O'Reilly, 2000a, 2000b; Warnes, 2002). Estimates vary but it appears that IRM is becoming an increasingly important aspect of migratory movement within the EU. It is also suggested that official population figures do not evidence the true extent of EU nationals' migratory movement in retirement. Table 2 illustrates some of the problems in trying to gain an accurate picture. A number of countries fail to differentiate by age at all, and, while the figures give an indication of the number of older EU nationals officially resident in another member state, there is no way of assessing how many of them moved following retirement. Nor do the figures record those who are resident in host countries but who fail to inform the official authorities. O'Reilly's comment (made in relation to British retirees relocating to Spain) that, "existing statistics are both difficult to obtain and to trust because of the fluidity, undocumented and unofficial nature of this form of migration" (2000b, p 481) holds true when considering IRM across the whole of Europe. For example, King et al (2000) note that there are 82,156 recipients of British pensions living in the Irish Republic, yet Table 2 records a mere 5,900 UK nationals aged 65 plus as resident. While some of the recipients may well be Irish nationals who have returned home to retire, the huge discrepancy between

Table 2: Numbers of EU nationals resident in another member state, by age[a]

Country	Age			
	50-54	55-59	60-64	65+
Austria	3,900	2,900	1,900	6,600
Belgium	11,441	33,373	29,563	71,809
Denmark	4,078	2,974	1,709	2,582
Finland	656	513	434	1,586
France	99,729	88,973	73,642	58,622[c]
Germany		1,850,032[b]		
Greece	3,344	2,301	1,391	2,573
Italy		133,512[b]		
Ireland	Not available	Not available	Not available	5,900[d]
Luxembourg		131,410[b]		
Netherlands	14,066	10,971	6,542	11,077
Spain		219,790[b]		
Sweden	18,163	12,893	8,875	13,782
UK	65,000	66,100	56,400	137,900

Notes:

[a] Data for Portugal unavailable.

[b] Total for all age groups 0-100 years. Indicates that numbers differentiated by age are not available.

[c] This figure relates to those aged 65-69 only.

[d] This figure is for UK nationals only. No other figures available.

Source: Figures adapted from Eurostat data provided by ESRC/R.cade service in 1999

the two figures serves to illustrate the current problem of trying to assemble accurate quantitative data on IRM.

The problems referred to in the introduction, in terms of defining and categorising the population of retirement migrants is reflected not only in terms of legal categories but also in terms of identifying a population from which to sample. The availability of secondary data generally reflects methods of legal classification and the political or policy priorities of the parent or funding body. The focus within EU policy making on paid work and the population in employment (favoured citizens) is thus reflected in current Eurostat data sources (cf Ruxton, 1996; Ackers, 1998; Singleton, 2000; Ackers and Stalford, 2002). The peripatetic nature of many post-retirement moves, coupled with the desire on the part of some migrants to negotiate residency status in order to maximise personal financial gain and welfare status renders a significant proportion of the potential target population effectively 'hidden'. In many ways the heavily circumscribed welfare entitlement of post-retirement migrants is itself a factor prohibiting formal registration of residency in the host state. This all translates into a general lack of coherent and reliable statistical data on international retirement migration and effectively rules out the possibility of recruiting a representative sample in the strict sense (cf Williams et al, 1997).

Figure 1: Extract from grid analysis on motivations and triggers to movement

Respondent's number	Stated motivation/triggers
R005	Holidays Lower house cost Better living standards on pension/lower living costs R Nuisance neighbours R Health R Health and climate R Funeral culture clash

Note: R indicates a motivational factor in a return movement to country of origin following a period resident in a EU host country.

IRM triggers and motivations to movement: an overview

Discussing internal retirement migration within Britain, Warnes (1993) notes that migration decisions in old age are often the culmination of a careful consideration of a number of factors. The importance of a cumulative combination of issues and circumstances as a precursor to international retirement migration decisions has similarly been noted elsewhere (King and Patterson, 1998) and was very much evident in our study. A typical example is presented in the grid analysis extract in Figure 1.

A consideration of the qualitative data that this grid refers to indicates that respondent R005 (a female British returnee) spoke of prior holidays in Spain and lower housing/living costs as all being important elements in the initial post-retirement migration decision. The decision to return to England some years later was influenced primarily by concerns over her husband's failing health, combined with a desire to escape particularly noisy neighbours and what had come to be viewed as an oppressively hot climate. A culture clash in relation to burial rituals acted to confirm the decision to return. Subsequent chapters of this book argue that specific issues (especially concerns related to health, finance and care) can and do play a large part in migratory movement in retirement; indeed, they feature in the particular case offered here. However, in the majority of cases respondents outlined several factors as influential in decisions to relocate.

R005 an example of multiple triggers to movement

The original decision to move on retirement: Holidays/Region appeal/Lower cost of living:

> "Well, I'd been to Spain in the 1950s, when Benidorm was a village, which shows how long ago that was, I fell in love with the place and talked to some people who were retired, and they said how far their pensions went and I

thought, 'Ah, that's for me!' and you know, forgot it. Retirement was a long way off then, and didn't think anything much more about it, you know it was just one of these pipe dreams."

Lower house prices:

"Well, we chatted about it, you know, he wanted to go back to E. Sussex which is where his parents had lived, but the property was a dreadful price and we just couldn't afford that, because we would have to have bought outright, we couldn't have got a mortgage at our age, not then you couldn't, and the rental was not available much."

"Oh yes, we got it [the flat in Spain] for seventeen thousand. It was very small, but it was very compact and just right for two people."

On the decision to return to England: Health/Climate/Nuisance neighbours:

"My husband had a heart condition, and he had a heart attack while we were out there, and we had a private doctor and he nursed him and got him well, when he would do what he was told, and then before that I hadn't been very well, and I'd been to see the quack and he said the rhythm of my heart wasn't right, and gave me some pills which put it right, but these wretched pills meant that if I went into the sun I came up in prickly heat, so I spent half the day in the shade on my patio – which wasn't really the reason why we went to a warm climate to live. And every summer it seemed to get more and more humid – the last summer we were there it was like being in a Turkish bath! Then there was this little locale underneath us, which was bought by a fisherman who had won the lottery and turned it into a Spanish bar. Well the room was small, but the Spaniards start drinking at eleven o'clock at night, so we thought 'to hell with this, we're not having this!', so we decided that we would move, and we started to look, we put the place up to sale."

Burial at home:

"Then one of our friends died, and we went to his funeral, and it was really ... [pause] I can't describe how it was – our funerals are so reverent aren't they – there's a little bit of decorum about it, and poor Graham, he was kind of trundled onto a push-cart, all down these aisles, and he was a very big man, he'd been a colonel in the army, a very big man, and well they were going to put him into the wall right at the top, and the man that was doing it had a red pullover on and they pushed the coffin up and they shoved him into the wall and then before you could say 'knife' somebody came along with some cement and started sealing him in and I said 'Well, I don't care what happens, I am not going to die in this country', and that was that!"

The data from R005 also illustrate the extent to which IRM can be an ongoing process. Different factors may emerge as the life course unfolds which precipitate subsequent moves.

Routes to retirement

Recent work (Williams et al, 1997; King et al, 1998; Rodriguez et al, 1998) outlines some reasons why an increasing number of nationals from northern European states relocate to southern Europe on retirement. Williams et al (1997) offer three main explanations as to why southern Europe is attractive. First, cheaper house prices and lower costs of living and heating mean that it makes economic sense to relocate south. Furthermore, certain southern regions may be more beneficial in terms of fiscal and tax policies. In these ways northern migrants, who, it is argued are mostly "either retired or 'active young elderly' [sic] persons with above average wealth and incomes" (Williams et al, 1997, p 116), are able to simultaneously export and build on their already advantaged economic position. Second, the chance to live in a warmer climate has an obvious appeal to many who wish to escape (permanently or temporarily) from the colder northern regions of Europe. Third, it is argued that certain retirement movements are characterised by a search for landscapes, cultures and lifestyles that fit a kind of idealised middle class myth. Other factors such as prior holiday visits and certain previous occupations have also been noted as influential in decisions to migrate internationally post-retirement (King et al, 1998).

Taking the above issues into account, Williams et al (1997) note discrete groups within a more general category of post-retirement migrants. Seasonal migrants (snowbirds) who spend variable periods in their host country are differentiated from those who permanently reside abroad following a total displacement from their country of origin. Others are classified as 'second homeowners' or 'third age long-stay international tourists'. A further significant group, labelled 'lifetime expats', consists of those who were previously employed by the military, international agencies/companies or as high ranking civil servants who have experienced prolonged and continued movement and relocation throughout most of their adult working life. An argument can be made here that among post-retirement retirees there is a significant number of 'multiple movers' who have developed what can crudely be termed a migration mentality and for whom post-retirement migration appears to be almost a mundane decision (Ackers, 1998). In addition, Williams et al (1997) argue that many such lifetime expats are essentially 'tax dodgers' who on retirement choose southern European locations in order to store their accumulated wealth in offshore havens, thus avoiding the higher tax regimes in their northern European countries of origin. The above discussions have a relevance to our present research project as each category of migrant outlined is represented in our sample. To give two examples; seven from a total of 20 Swedish returnee respondents fall into the 'lifetime expats' category and 20 respondents among the 125 post-retirement migrants interviewed identified themselves as seasonal migrants at the time of interview.

The category of migrant that can be loosely labelled 'returning worker' also merits further consideration. The Swedish 'lifetime expat' returnees noted previously are returning EU workers who, to a large extent, previously made positive choices to move internationally *with* work in order to further their careers. However, when discussing IRM in the EU, consideration must also be given to a group which has tended to be overlooked; that is those migrant workers and their families who initially were to a large extent compelled to move *for* work (often at great personal sacrifice) in order to escape poverty and unemployment. All bar one of the Greek, Portuguese and Italian returnees (65 respondents) interviewed fell into this category. In a direct contrast to the great majority of northern European nationals, their return movement back to a southern homeland, often in retirement, was always preceded by an initial move to northern Europe seeking employment. Perhaps not surprisingly the Irish returnees shared similar migratory patterns only in this instance – most had moved east to the UK for work and returned west to Ireland on retirement. The motives and triggers that precipitate the movements in retirement of these 'returning workers' are often (though not always) different from the northern European post-retirement migrants looking to move south that are the focus of much current debate. Nonetheless, this group of essentially returnee labour migrants need to be considered in any full discussion of IRM within the EU.

Discussions so far have indicated the extent to which IRM within the EU is a complex phenomenon in terms of migration patterns and the motives behind movements. A more detailed exploration of the qualitative data generated in our present study illustrates that a wide variety of factors is important to an informed understanding of respondents' migratory decisions. As analysis progressed, however, it became clear that motivations and triggers for movement could be assembled into five loose clusters:

- *Economic issues:* for work, with work, lower living costs.
- *Family issues:* domestic care, proximity to family, marriage effect, that is remaining following an intended short visit to marry a local, loss of partner (divorce, separation, bereavement), for children.
- *Welfare state issues:* health/care services as a factor in initial and, especially, return movements.
- *Life course issues:* the wish to be buried 'at home', enforced unemployment, retirement plan.
- *Regional issues:* region appeal, holidays, climate, a desire to return to one's roots/homeland.

It is important to remember that these five clusters are not mutually exclusive of each other. The category 'retirement plan' fits well within the life course issues cluster, but how and when an individual retires is linked to a number of factors including economic and welfare state issues. As previously stated factors working in combination with one another are often influential in migration

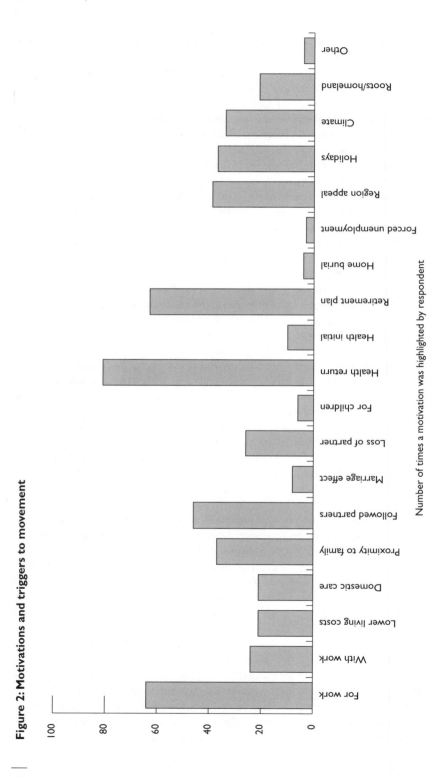

Figure 2: Motivations and triggers to movement

decisions, however, as Figure 2 illustrates certain single issues are of significance to a large number of respondents (see also Dwyer, 2000a). Figure 2 should not be seen as a crude attempt at quantitative analysis, but should be viewed as a tool that allowed the qualitative analysis to proceed. When faced with a large number of texts each giving complex and often differing accounts of personal experiences, a chart that records a simple count of the number of times an issue was raised helps to clarify important issues.

Economic issues

When looking at economic issues it is clear that prior to retirement, movements both *for* and *with* work are important, particularly the former. Poverty and a search for prosperity were initially the obvious spurs to many:

> "Everyday I had to go on foot and with the donkey loaded with vegetables from #### to #### trying to sell them from house to house. I prayed to God to help me sell them all. I went through unbelievable misery and unhappiness till I was 32. My husband was working in construction he didn't have a steady job. I had to leave our young children alone all day long; those were difficult years...."

> "I couldn't stand it anymore, people were leaving the villages ... they used to go to Australia, Germany.... The teacher at #### suggested to me that if we wanted to start a new life, we should send the children to a boarding house in #####.... I told my husband and also the children, they didn't say anything...."

> "My husband and I left together, my husband left through a contract, I left as a tourist. We got exhausted ... to make money in Germany was not as easy as it is said nowadays, it was cold and lonely, we didn't know the language, we would come back home and not talk to each other.... I was patient, I didn't cry because my husband had warned me that if I got sad because of the children he would take me and we would come back to Greece."

> "My daughters came to Germany when they finished primary school. I missed them, they had stayed at the boarding school till they were 12 years old.... This is my story." (R402 Greek woman who worked in Germany for 22 years)

> "I would never have left if it wasn't for the money. When I left [Portugal] I made PTE 10,000 per hour. There [France] I earned PTE 100,000 per hour." (R304)

> "There was poverty ... we had just sold our tobacco crop and yet we were still in debt. We could not make ends meet our children were small, we had to

take care of them. My husband left first and then I followed … as did everyone else." (R409)

For those respondents who had the opportunity to move *with* work the experience of economic migration prior to retirement tends to be much more positive. This Dutch naval engineer had worked around the globe and stayed on in Portugal post-retirement:

"There were two main reasons that made me come to Portugal. First, it was a big professional challenge…. The second, was the climate; climate in Holland is terrible and here it's great!" (209)

Interestingly, moving to access lower living costs or lower rate tax regimes were cited as significant on comparatively few occasions. There were certainly some respondents who were honest about the financial motivations behind their move. The most candid was a wealthy Swedish woman who maintained three properties; two in Sweden, another in France. A seasonal migrant who returned home regularly, she was registered as a French resident for tax reasons.

"I didn't want to get registered in France, but the taxation authorities forced me to. We have to spend at least six months a year in France. I was kind of forced to get registered in France." (R218)

It may be the case that a considerable number of people were reluctant to cite essentially selfish financial reasons as important considerations in any post-retirement migration discussion. Certainly, the possibility of some kind of financial advantage as a spin-off from migration regularly appears elsewhere in the data as something that many respondents had previously considered. This Italian wife who followed her husband post-retirement was clearly unhappy that financial considerations had overridden her own wish to stay in Italy and care for her mother:

"He recalled Portugal as being a country in which it was cheaper to live in, in which one could lead a good life. Our daughter was here, and now we have two grandchildren, besides he enjoys playing golf. I would rather go back to Italy, because my mother is old and she needs company." (324)

Similarly:

"Yes, it's cheaper to live in Greece than it is in England. Quite a lot cheaper." (418)

The importance of financial matters in migratory decisions is explored more fully in Chapter Six and it would appear that the possibility of moving to secure some kind of financial advantage was often an important consideration for a number of northern Europeans who moved south.

Family issues

The relative importance of family matters is illustrated in Figure 2 and a fuller consideration of the impact of family and informal care is offered in Chapter Seven (cf Ackers, 1998, 2001), nonetheless, two points are worth noting here. First, it appears that to a large extent women yield to their male partners' decisions concerning migration in general and retirement migration in particular. Approximately three times as many women, as opposed to men, spoke of following their partner's wishes when moving.

> "It was something my husband had always wanted to do, and which I had been dubious about [pause], and then, after my husband retired from the navy he had constant ill health, various things happening to him, he had the most horrific medical history, you know, he had an aortic aneurysm, he had carcinoma of the larynx, and so on, and I knew at that point that he would have possibly five years, and this is something he dearly wanted to do, so against my better judgement we did it. So that's how it was rather a precipitous thing, and we had a family crisis at the same time and he just said 'Up sticks! We're going' and that was it." (R007)

> "Oh yes, he'd always wanted to live abroad, and we always said it was a pity he didn't do it earlier, because he'd been retired about fifteen years by then and we could have done it then, mind you I wouldn't have done it on my own because I'm not the adventurous type, I'm the stay at home type." (R015)

Second, while concerns about proximity to family to a certain extent illustrate the importance of familial care networks, the count showing domestic care as a trigger to movement is not as straightforward as it may first appear. When respondents spoke directly of domestic care they were often referring to migratory movements that occurred in order to *provide* care for other members (both children and older parents) of their families, rather than moving to access informal care from relatives to meet their own needs.

> "I first came over, we both came over to help settle our grandson into school because my daughter had the business, which left nobody to look after him, so we decided to come out for 6 months. And we haven't gone back." (419; British woman, a post-retirement retiree who resides in Greece)

> "Because of my father's death. My mother remained by herself, she was quite old, you see. We wanted her to join us in Munich, but she refused, so I had to come back and it was me who came back because I'm single, you see ... my sister has a family to look after." (R112 Italian man; returnee worker)

Such evidence tends to refute dominant, negative stereotypes that construct retired/aged people as an undifferentiated group of costly dependants with little to offer once employment in the paid labour market has ceased (see Chapter Seven for a fuller discussion of this issue).

Welfare state issues

Chapters Five and Seven discuss at length the importance of formal and informal health/care issues in relation to IRM and are not considered in detail here. Two allied points related to ill health are, however, worth mentioning. First, the extent to which a warm climate can be seen as a valuable health resource that promotes individual health or well-being and consequently plays a part in some IRMs should be noted. On a number of occasions the therapeutic powers of a move to the warmer regions of southern Europe were commented on by northern Europeans who had moved to southern Europe.

> "Well it really all started because I had a problem with my chest – lung trouble – and the doctor said a warmer climate would help. And Barry's mother, who lives with us had a stroke. A warmer climate would help her health also." (R012; British woman who migrated to Spain)

> "We lived in Germany for about two years but then we had to come back down here because she [his Italian wife] kept having health problems connected to the weather. We went to see a consultant and he clearly stated that the German weather was not good for her and we had to go back to Italy." (103; German man)

> "We moved because of my husband's health [he suffers from rheumatoid arthritis] and no other reason." (R204; Swedish woman)

Second, a large percentage of the southern European respondents (particularly men) who moved to look for work were engaged in heavy and at times hazardous industrial labour. This work ultimately had a detrimental effect on the health of the migrant workers.

> "When I left Italy there were 40 young people on that bus to Belgium ... only 3 of us came back. It was the dust that killed us. Every vein we extracted we got covered in a thin layer of silica dust, we breathed it all, and in time we all got silicosis ... had we known at the time we could have worn masks but nobody warned us. We could have refused to do certain things but we were young and strong and we were lured by the money." (R118; Italian man who worked in Belgian mines for ten years)

> "[Following an industrial accident] ... the doctor told me I'll give you your invalidity certificate now. You should take care of your health and return to your country." (R314A; Portuguese man who worked in France)

Life course issues

At risk of stating the obvious, when considering life course issues, a significant number of respondents talked about putting into practice some form of retirement plan. What is worth noting, however, is the limited impact of enforced redundancy from the paid labour market (classified as UB40 in Figure 2) in early retirement decisions. Very few respondents talked of being forced from the workplace against their own wishes; a planned withdrawal from paid employment, often at a relatively early age[2], was much more the norm, while enforced redundancy and the wish to be buried at home overall were of little numerical significance within the sample. Their importance to the individuals who discussed them should not, however, be overlooked. For example, the previously noted sentiments expressed by respondent R005 in relation to her wish to be laid to rest in England are strongly expressed and of obvious importance to her individual decision to return home.

Regional issues

An examination of regional issues again springs few surprises with many respondents discussing the appeal of a particular region for any one of a number of general reasons (natural beauty, local lifestyle, people, culture, and so on) or because it met a personal recreational requirement, such as sailing or fishing. Likewise, past holiday experiences and/or a preference for a sunnier climate were mentioned as precursors to a more permanent relocation on retirement (cf Williams et al, 1997; King et al, 1998; Williams and Patterson, 1998). The pull of a homeland was (obviously) an influence cited overwhelmingly by returnees, with the wish to return to one's roots particularly evident among returnee Irish and Swedish respondents. The following Swedish man, for example, moved to work as a marine attaché at the Swedish embassy in London prior to establishing his own shipping business. Eventually, he returned home in retirement to Sweden because of his wife's wish to go home.

> "My wife told me 'I want to get back to my roots'. I thought that as she had been very nice following me all these years it was only fair to pay her back."
> (R208)

Conclusions

This chapter illustrates that the motivations and triggers involved in IRM decisions within the EU are many and varied. A combination of different issues and events related to geographical location, age, and economic and familial relationships are significant in influencing the movements and preferred locations of retired EU migrants. Beyond these factors the importance of issues related to the provision of welfare benefits and services and the differences in availability and scope in various EU member states should not be overlooked. Many retired EU migrants are actively seeking to maximise the enjoyment of their later years by relocating in retirement. The next three chapters illustrate the extent to which assembling a package of welfare services that meet what individuals consider to be their personal requirements and needs is an important element in initial migratory decisions and subsequent movements after retirement. The ability to access certain types of health and care provision are issues of importance, particularly with regard to return migration decisions linked to serious illness or increased frailty in old age. A consideration of the importance of formal health/care systems and issues related to how respondents access such systems are explored in the next chapter.

Notes

[1] Where material from the interviews is cited in the book an interview number is provided in the text. The prefix to this number reflects the category of respondent. All of those with a prefix 'R' are returnees; 'L' refers to interviews with key informants some of whom were retirees themselves. Those without a prefix are post-retirement migrants resident in a host country at the time of interview. The location in which an interview took place is indicated by the first digit of the respondent's number as cited in the text. Zero (0) indicates UK; 1 denotes Italy; 2, Sweden; 3, Portugal; 4, Greece; and 5, Ireland.

[2] The fact that 38% of the respondents were aged 65 or less at the time of interview indicates that early retirement was a significant feature of many retirement plans. See age profile of respondents in the Appendix for details.

FIVE

Health/care, well-being and citizenship

Introduction

This chapter focuses on the provision of formal health/care services and considers their importance in relation to retirement migration. Health status is central to well-being and considerations around access to constituent resources (such as health and social services and climate) form a key concern both in migration decision-making (on the timing and location of moves, for example) and citizenship experience in the host state. Health status is not only a primary concern in retirement in its own right, it is also central to the exercise of agency. Mobility, not simply in terms of international moves but also in the sense of 'getting about' is so important to participation and autonomy in a more general sense.

From the outset it is useful to clarify a number of points, not least how the notion of 'formal health/care services' is used in subsequent discussions. The term 'formal' is used to differentiate the health/care services provided by the state, private and voluntary sectors from the often extensive informal welfare support provided to senior citizens by family members. It should be remembered, however, that in reality the types and extent of formal services available are very much underpinned by (often female) informal provision and assumptions about the role of familial welfare in meeting needs. So while this book, for the sake of clarity, considers formal health/care services in this chapter and informal care in Chapter Seven, a symbiotic relationship exists between the two. When considering the care of senior citizens distinctions between health and social care are also problematic. The boundary between health services and social services is blurred when both may often be crucial to the overall well-being of an older person. Deliberate use is therefore made of the term 'health/care' on a number of occasions.

The chapter is divided into two main parts. The first part provides a comparative outline of the formal health/care provisions available to senior citizens in the six participant countries. Recent developments are discussed and similarities and differences in approach noted. We have already referred in Chapter One to the importance of location in terms of access to resources. Citizenship entitlement of Community migrants in the host state is based on the principle of non-discrimination and not harmonisation. Understanding the relationship between Community law and comparative social policy (and domestic policy context in the sending and receiving country) is thus fundamental to an understanding of the exercise and experience of citizenship. The purpose of this first section is to illustrate the importance of welfare diversity to migration decisions and citizenship status in the six countries covered in the study. As such it seeks to give a flavour of the differences between resource frameworks and the implications of moving between them. This is of particular relevance given the geography of retirement migration and the general trend away from northern and western member states and in the direction of southern Europe. It does not, however, purport to present a comprehensive and detailed evaluation of comparative healthcare.

The chapter then moves from a discussion of comparative social policy to an examination of the healthcare status and experiences of retired EU migrants. This section explores the ways in which migrants seek to meet their healthcare needs in the light of their personal circumstances and existing institutional arrangements and legislation. It serves to highlight two important points. First, the extent to which concerns about accessing formal health/care services are an important factor in precipitating migratory movements in retirement. Second, the tensions and confusions upon which the emergent notion of European social citizenship is being built. The chapter concludes with some reflections on the challenges of welfare diversity in the context of the EU's increasing commitment to equality and non-discrimination.

Health/care services for senior citizens in Greece, Italy, Portugal, the UK, Ireland and Sweden

This section offers a comparative overview of formal health/care arrangements for senior citizens in the six member states under consideration. Separate sections explore three important areas of provision for each member state. First, the general principles and institutional framework of healthcare are considered under the heading healthcare. Issues such as the terms of access to a general practitioner and hospital services are discussed. Second, institutional care, that is, care provided for older people in residential institutions away from the family home is discussed. Finally, a section on community care services in each national location is offered. As Dalley (2000, p 2) notes, community care includes a varied range of social and medical services that seek to keep individuals in their own home "supported by community based services and especially their families ... meals on wheels, home care (including both personal care and help with domestic activities), district nurses and so on"[1]. While there is some evidence of convergence in policy in relation to state-provided institutional care (with a general retrenchment) and also in relation to the increasing reliance on family care across member states, the extent to which this general trend is backed up by the development of Community-based services perhaps remains one of the key distinguishing features of European welfare systems. Southern Europe has, on the whole, been much slower to recognise the importance of such services to the sustenance of informal care and in promoting independent living.

Greece

Healthcare

In principle, Law 1397 (passed in 1983) established the national health service to ensure equal access to free medical care for all citizens on the basis of need. Under this legislation the Greek state formally accepted responsibility for the nation's health, put a stop on subsidies to private sector medicine, set about recruiting doctors on increased salaries and embarked upon an ambitious programme for the construction of NHS hospitals and health centres (Katrougalos, 1996; Symeonidou, 1996; Papadopoulos, 1997). While theoretically healthcare is organised according to the previously noted universal principle, certain well placed professional classes retain access to better hospital accommodation through use of their occupational social insurance funds as the current system has not completely replaced previous arrangements (Papadopoulos, 1997; Guillén and Matsaganis, 2000).

Substantial regional inequalities in healthcare also persist (Symeonidou, 1996; Papadopoulos, 1997) with rural districts generally suffering from a lack of trained healthcare personnel and an inadequate support infrastructure when compared to urban locations (Katrougalos, 1996). The large private sector continues to thrive alongside the state run system, which has itself been subject to cost controls and privatisation pressures throughout the 1990s (Symeonidou, 1996). Arguably, the need to meet convergence criteria as a prerequisite to European Monetary Union has added additional pressures in this context. In addition, a particular feature of the Greek system is the existence of a strong 'black market'. Although in principle the patient pays no fee for using NHS general practitioners or hospital services (CEC, 2000), the use of bribery and other improper practices to secure quick treatment or better service is not unknown. This can add substantially to the 'cost' of public healthcare and may be a factor in the recording of low levels of patient satisfaction (Symeonidou, 1996; Guillén, and Matsaganis, 2000).

Institutional care

Although 47% of aged Greeks suffer from some type of chronic condition related to ageing, the family expected to assume the main role in caring for its senior citizens. Institutional care is rare in Greece with only 0.8% of those aged 65 and over in geriatric nursing or care homes as opposed to the EU average of 8-11%. The vast majority of senior citizens live, and expect to remain living with, either their spouse and/or with their children. Generally, a family that places one of its older members in a care home is widely regarded as having failed in its duty (Symeonidou, 1996). In the absence of the formal provision of long-term residential care (LTRC) many families cope by hiring a low cost 'live in' immigrant worker to care for highly dependent older relatives (Blackman, 2000a).

Community care

The family is expected to play a major role in meeting the day-to-day needs of senior citizens. However, a limited system of personal social services (PSS) under the control of local authorities (LAs) was established in 1984 (Katrougalos, 1996). The most important institutions for senior citizens are the 'open care day centres' (KAPI), which provide health and social care services for those aged over 65. The idea behind these centres is to encourage activity and independence among older people while also providing the services of relevant healthcare professionals to ensure that people can remain in their own home (Giarchi, 1996). They are not designed to cater for those individuals who have serious health problems and who are unable to generally care for themselves. It has been argued (Symeonidou, 1996) that there is an urgent need for the state to provide better medical and psycho-social support if the needs of all OAPs are to be adequately met. Research also suggests that gender has an important impact on how KAPIs are utilised. Women use them mainly for preventative health checks as they are generally too busy with familial care work to make use of recreational facilities. Older men on the other hand see KAPI largely as leisure centres where they can interact with their friends (see Veniopoulou, 1988, referred to in Symeonidou, 1996).

Italy

Healthcare

Theoretically, since the establishment in the late 1970s of the national health service *Sistema Sanitario Nazionale* (SSN), all senior citizens have been guaranteed access to public health provisions as part of a wider commitment to universal free healthcare. Under present rules various charges are made for certain treatments and examinations. For those aged 65 plus visits to a general practitioner are free from cost, but patient contributions for hospital tests or visits to a specialist are subject to a means test. Those in receipt of a social assistance pension are exempt from any personal costs (CEC, 2000). In common with the other southern welfare states and exacerbated by the problems of internal migration and rural depopulation, the universality of the Italian system has been limited by the existence of regional inequalities, in this case between urban centres in northern Italy and the more rural areas of the south (Granaglia, 1996; Niero, 1996; King et al, 2000).

Since 1992, responsibility for the delivery of healthcare services has been transferred from LAs to independent local enterprises that must endeavour to balance the books. Alongside this development there has been an increasing role in public provision for the thriving private healthcare sector. For example, legislation states that public hospitals must allow adequate opportunity for doctors to do private work and that between 6% and 12% of hospital beds must be reserved for paying clients (Saraceno and Negri, 1994). This more expansive role for the private sector in the 1990s (which now provides the majority of specialist services) has coincided with a fall in spending as a percentage of gross domestic product (GDP) allocated to the SSN (Granaglia, 1996).

Institutional care

Long-term residential care in institutions plays a relatively minor role and families continue to provide the majority of residential care for older relatives by accommodating older generations within the family home (King et al, 2000). There are two main types of residential institution, but regional variations in the level and kinds of institutional care continue to exist. *Residenze Sanitarie Assistenziali* (nursing homes) provide both medical/nursing and social care for those with the greatest needs. *Presidi Socio Assistenziali* (residential homes) provide social care for those who do not need medical attention. The social elements of care in both types of institution are subject to means testing with wealthier users or their families forced to pay a substantial part of care costs to the municipal authorities. Recent research suggests that only 2.7% of senior citizens (aged 65 plus) are in receipt of long-term residential care (see discussions in Gori, 1999).

Community care

An integrated system of home nursing, physiotherapy and social care, the *Assistenza Donmiciliare Integrata* (ADI), is available for senior citizens who live in their own homes. The healthcare element of ADI is provided free of charge by the local health authority; charges are levied (subject to a means test) against a user or their relatives for social care (home help) services. The 102 municipalities are responsible for ensuring the delivery of such services, however, more than half of current provision has been contracted out to private providers. Since 1980 a national care allowance (*indennita di accompagnamento*) has been available for people with severe impairments (subject to assessment by the local health authority) to purchase commercial services or to give to relatives who provide care; approximately 70% of recipients are aged 65 plus. In the past decade a new local care allowance has been introduced by several regional and municipal authorities and this practice looks set to become more widespread in the future. Rather than providing residential or community care services the authorities provide an allowance payable to the dependent senior citizen or a family carer. Means tested and targeted at frail, low-income older people, this approach can be seen as an attempt to reduce the future financial costs to the state while at the same time bolstering the existing extensive role of informal family provision. Much of the money paid goes to daughters who would otherwise be expected to provide familial care services out of a sense of duty. Alternatively, the money is often used to purchase low cost 'care assistants' in the informal economy (see Gori, 1999).

Portugal

Healthcare

The Portuguese constitution of 1976 established a universal right for all citizens to access free public healthcare (Hampson, 1997a; King et al, 2000). In operation since 1979, *Servico Nacional de Saude* (SNS) is financed from general taxation and caters for the healthcare needs of approximately 75% of the population. The remaining 25% of citizens continue to make use of a parallel system of social insurance (*segura social*) provision, which predates the setting up of the SNS. This group consists largely of public sector employees, members of the armed forces and bank workers who retain cover for themselves and their dependants (Hampson, 1997a, 1997b). A position of relative advantage for certain well placed occupational groups continues to exist in the healthcare system, a situation similar to that previously noted in relation to Greece.

In general terms the health of the Portuguese population has improved greatly in the last two decades, however, Santana (2000) notes that a number of factors combine to limit the ability of many senior citizens to access public provision. Although the number of senior citizens as a proportion of the Portuguese population is increasing, due to a combination of longer life expectancy and declining fertility rates, the lack of financial and technical resources has a negative impact upon the level and quality of healthcare services available to meet the needs of older people. This situation is further exacerbated by the fact that generally "Ageing in rural areas is higher, begins earlier and is more rapid than in urban areas" (Santana, 2000, p 1029). Furthermore, many rural areas are poorly served in that hospital beds and specialist consultants are concentrated in the major conurbations and older people living in rural settings are less likely to consult their general practitioner. Beyond this simple urban/rural divide, the migration of young people in search of work in the past (1950-90) have left certain specific rural areas, most notably Alentjo and the central region, with high concentrations of older people living alone. While these areas do not form key locations for retired migrants to Portugal[2], the majority of retired migrants are locating outside of the main urban areas in rural coastal resorts in the Algarve and thus to some extent fall victim to the high levels of territorial injustice characteristic of the Portuguese health system.

In recommending the training of more specialists in gerontology and geriatric care, the setting up of local home care packages and the development of rehabilitative healthcare services for older people in the future, the government in its 'Health strategy for 2002' clearly recognises that there are problems to be addressed. However, as Santana (2000) argues there remains a necessity for increased investment in healthcare services for older people that takes into account variations in need and the level and quality of services if present regional inequalities are to be reduced in the future.

Institutional care/community care

The last 20 years have seen a reduction in the level of community-based personal social services available to Portuguese senior citizens. Similarly there has been a decrease in the number of residential beds (both long- and short-term) available to older people within the SNS. In relation to community care services (CCS) and institutional care (IC), because of higher numbers of older people living alone and limited local access to a range of services, again rural populations can be seen as being doubly disadvantaged. Rather than adapting to meet the needs of an increasingly aged population there has been a gradual transfer of state health/care responsibilities to private institutions and/or the family in provincial areas. "A considerable expansion of community services would be required to return to the level of services of the early 1980s" (Santana, 2000, p 1028).

In common with other southern European welfare states, access to formally provided care services for senior citizens is limited and the social expectation is that informal care provided by family members should meet the needs of senior citizens. In spite of the fact that Portuguese women have some of the highest levels of full-time employment in the paid labour market in Europe, much of this unpaid care work falls to female family members (Perista, 1999). In certain localities limited home help services are available from public or private providers. Where such provisions are unavailable, a small care allowance may be available on a local basis to enable individuals to directly purchase some support from their neighbours (Weekers and Pijl, 1998; Pacolet et al, 2000).

The United Kingdom

Healthcare

Established in 1948, the National Health Service (NHS) has long been held in high regard by the public and political parties of all persuasions (Taylor-Gooby, 1996). Funded in the most part from general taxation, healthcare in the UK is provided free on declaration of need at point of service and there are no charges for hospital or GP visits. All people aged 60 plus are exempt from prescription charges. Pensioners receiving Income Support as a Minimum Income Guarantee (MIG) are exempt from charges from dental treatment and spectacles; other senior citizens with low income may also be eligible for some help in meeting costs (CEC, 2000).

In recent years the NHS has been subject to fundamental reform. The 1990 NHS and Community Care Act, introduced by a Conservative government keen to enforce a managerialist ethic on public healthcare in an attempt to increase efficiency, promote consumer choice and drive down costs, saw the introduction of an internal/quasi-market system among providers of public healthcare services. Under this legislation a separation between purchasers and providers of healthcare was instituted, with hospitals being given NHS Trust status, and responsibility for providing services, while District Health Authorities are obligated to purchase 'best value' services from such providers on behalf of their populations. New Labour's overall strategy appears to be one of accepting and building upon the approach of their predecessors. Despite past declarations to the contrary the internal market introduced by the Conservatives in the 1990 NHS and Community Care Act remains, albeit with somewhat altered terminology with the words 'commissioning' and 'service management' replacing purchaser and provider respectively (Paton, 1999).

Contemporary public health services in the UK remain under considerable strain with many patients subject to a long waiting period to access non-emergency treatment. This, coupled with certain regional variations (so-called postcode rationing) in both the extent and quality of services provided, has prompted a dramatic and unprecedented rise in the numbers making use of the private sector. Browne (2000) reports that in 1999 some 160,000 people borrowed money or used personal savings to fund one-off surgery in the private sector, with companies reporting a rise in business of between 15% and 20% in comparison to the previous two years.

Institutional care

The past three decades has been characterised by a significant policy shift away from the provision of long-term residential care (either in nursing homes or hospitals) in favour of community care services which support older people in their own homes (Brown, 1996; Dalley, 2000). A number of major changes occurred in the 1980s: most notably a significant reduction in the state's role, accompanied by a massive increase in the number of long-term care beds supplied by the private sector. Between the period 1970 and 1994 there was a fourfold increase (to 358,000) in the numbers of places provided in private residential or nursing homes; simultaneously, the state provision of long-term residential care facilities for senior citizens fell from 69% of total supply in the 1970s to 24% in 1994 (Wistow, 1997).

In addition the 1990 NHS and Community Care Act marked a shift in long-term care away from free, universally available NHS services to more residual, means tested and discretionary ones under the control of LAs. While the acute/surgical needs of older people continued to be met by the NHS other aspects of care for the aged were classified as involving 'social' as opposed to 'health' care, leaving the individual or their family rather than the state to bear the cost (Baldock, 1997; Wistow, 1997; Glendinning, 1998; Dalley, 2000). The negative impact of these changes should not be overlooked. As Dalley states:

> Long-term care for older people in Britain is now located in the private sector because NHS hospital care is no longer available. And who gets what and who goes where is carefully controlled by local government – the local state. Because of its financial interest in the matter, financial considerations are sometimes beginning to outweigh clinical considerations. (2000, p 4)

It has been argued that these changes amount to a reduction in the social right to publicly provided care in old age (Glendinning, 1998).

The move towards individuals rather than the state footing the bill for long-term care has led to a wider debate about the future funding of residential care. Parker and Clarke (1997) argue that there is very limited support for the idea that people should pay for themselves. The majority of respondents in their survey believed that an older person in need of LTRC should not be forced to sell their home to finance care but should instead be allowed to pass on such assets to relatives in the event of death. The most popular idea (48%) was that the state should guarantee a minimum level of universal care and that individuals should be able to supplement this by taking out private insurance if they wished. Interestingly only 15% of those asked believed that such insurance should be compulsory. It would appear that most people want the state to take a lead role in the provision of care but few are prepared to fund such services by increased taxation or the sale of family assets.

The recent Royal Commission on Long-Term Care (Sutherland, 1999) recommended that both the health and personal care needs of senior citizens should be met from the public purse. To date, the New Labour government has agreed to meet only the health related costs of long-term care in old age, believing that the present system of means testing social care is adequate. This is not a view shared by the Scottish Executive which has recently opted to fund all long-term care in relation to senior citizens, including personal care, from the public coffers; thus highlighting a tangible difference in rights to care within the nations of the UK (Steele, 2001).

Community care

Underpinned by an overt ideological hostility to state welfare, the 1990 NHS and Community Care Act was seen by its Conservative instigators as an opportunity to create a mixed economy of welfare in the delivery of care services. In order to stimulate the private sector into providing services in the community care (CC) sector, a stipulation was built into the legislation that 85% of the local authority CC budgets had to be spent on the purchase of non-LA services. The result of this move is that private companies and voluntary organisations now have an increased role in providing care to the older population, with LAs managing and overseeing provision (Glendinning, 1998).

Evidence suggests that this fundamental reordering of CC fails to provide adequate services. Baldock (1997) notes that a number of individuals who need CC services are not getting them and that those that do receive on average only between four and five hours a week. Glendinning (1998) recognises that there are good reasons for closing large long-stay NHS institutions, however, she believes that the main objective behind such closures was a reduction in expenditure rather than an improvement in care. Both authors argue that it was unrealistic to set up a mixed economy of care and then sit back and expect the goods to be distributed equitably according to needs. Supporters of the changes outlined in the 1990 NHS and Community Care Act believed that the reforms would enable service providers to tailor flexible patterns of care to meet each persons specific needs. The outcome has been somewhat different. Local variations in both care and the charges levied for services are now widespread. Publicly funded services are only available to the poorest of older people and problems in coordinating the differing agencies delivering services has, in some cases, resulted in fragmented poor quality provision. The rhetoric of the 'empowered consumer' used to justify change has failed to materialise and most senior citizens face a distinct lack of choice. Overall, the 1990 reform of CC marks a diminution of the citizenship rights of older people (Glendinning, 1998). In the UK the state has always fulfilled a limited role in the provision of care for older people with the majority of support being provided informally by family members (Wistow, 1997; Taylor-Gooby, 1999) and the reforms of the 1990s increase the possibility that relatives will continue to carry such burdens in the future (Baldock, 1997; Dalley, 2000). Recent changes to the 1996 Community Care (Direct Payments) Act now allow disabled people aged 65 plus to receive direct cash payments so that they can directly purchase community care services from a variety of agencies rather than relying on LA provision. Unfortunately the Act only allows the use of direct payments for the employment of a close relative as a care assistant in exceptional circumstances (Leece, 2001). This could be seen as a counterproductive measure given the key role of family members in providing care to older relatives.

Ireland

Healthcare

The Department of Health oversees policy with eight regional health boards responsible for the provision of publicly provided hospital services and community care. Two basic principles underpin public health services in Ireland. First, services are to be available on the basis of need rather than the ability to pay, and second, those with greater means will be expected to make proportionally greater contributions towards funding services (O'Sullivan, 2000). Approximately 90% of funding for healthcare is raised from general taxation (Weekers and Pijl, 1998). Hospital care is free and financed by the state, with patients (subject to a means test) generally required to make some contribution towards the cost of visits to general practitioners and outpatient services (Fanning, 1999). Ireland provides a good example of a mixed economy approach to the provision of healthcare with the state involved in direct provision and funding and the regulation of other service providers. The voluntary sector (including a number of Catholic organisations) have long been involved in complementing state services[3].

Public healthcare provisions are available to all who are defined as 'ordinary resident'. The levels of co-payment required from a patient are determined according to different categories (Giarchi, 1996; Weekers and Pijl, 1998). Free care is available, but only to those on a limited income subject to a means test.

Individuals who qualify for 'full eligibility' status have the right to a medical card issued by the various health boards. It should be noted, however, that although national standardised income guidelines are issued by the government, regional variations exist in the way that capital and savings are assessed by different boards when issuing medical cards; eligibility in one area does not automatically confer a right to a card in another (Comhairle, 2001a, 2001b). Those who rely solely on non-contributory state pensions or widows/widowers pensions automatically qualify for a card[4]. A medical card entitles the holder to receive all GP services and prescriptions free of charge and also guarantees access to public health nursing and home help schemes (CEC, 2000). EU nationals resident in Ireland who are not in paid work and receiving a social security pension from another member state are able to get a card without having to be subject to a means test. The medical card brings with it access to other benefits, such as exemption from the 2% health levy which is collected as part of the PRSI system (Comhairle, 2001b, 2001c).

Those with middle range incomes who qualify for category two 'limited eligibility' status (including many retired persons) have more restricted rights to free medical services and are required to pay charges for GP visits and prescriptions up to a specified maximum. Beyond these two categories Irish citizens can either make use of the private sector services available and/or join the Voluntary Health Insurance scheme (VHI) if they want further assistance with charges for visits to GPs or outpatient departments. The amount of financial support given under the VHI relates directly to the level of premium paid. Around 37% of the population currently contribute to the VHI (Giarchi, 1996; Weekers and Pijl, 1998).

Institutional care

There are some 18,000 non-psychiatric residential care beds available in the public system in Ireland. In recent years the state's role in providing long-term institutional care has diminished with much demand now being met by private sector nursing homes (O'Shea and Hughes, 1998; cf Yeates, 1997). Ironically, those most likely to have need for residential care (older pensioners, usually women aged 80 plus), have benefited least from the recent more general improvement in the living standard of pensioners, and this has left many reliant on their children to meet the financial costs of residential care. These costs, and indeed the availability of an option between public and private provision, vary greatly according to geographic location. For example, while private long-term care in Dublin may be available to a greater degree than elsewhere it is likely to be especially expensive (O'Shea and Hughes, 1998).

The level of financial assistance offered by the state to support an individual in need of residential care varies according to whether or not a senior citizen is reliant on the public or private sector. Those with very limited assets effectively have to rely on public provision with the costs of their care met from general taxation. People entering private nursing homes are assessed in relation to predetermined levels of dependency (as decided by a health professional), and are also subject to a means test of assets and income, with state subsidy varying according to the individual circumstances (see Comhairle, 2001c). Regardless of the outcome of the formal assessment process, the state will only meet a maximum of two thirds of the costs of private provision, leaving the individual concerned (or their relatives) to pay the substantial shortfall (Yeates, 1997).

O'Shea and Hughes (1998) argue that present policy is promoting the emergence of a two tier system of residential care with the distinct possibility that in the future publicly provided care will become a second best service reserved for the poor. They believe that the introduction of a designated, public, long-term care social insurance fund that grants access to residential care on clear and strictly defined criteria of need, combined with a private insurance component, would provide a better way forward. Contributions to the state run social insurance fund would guarantee a right to state funded residential care for a stipulated length of time, with any longer period met by the individual through a private insurance package. In cases of hardship the state would step in and provide care free of charge, subject to a posthumous payment based on the deceased person's assets. With falling numbers of public beds available for LTRC, and the preferred solution of meeting an individual's care needs in their own home, the above system (due to the time limit on residential care) would help to free up public money which could then be redirected at improving community care services. O'Shea and Hughes (1998) believe that this is the best way to ensure the adequate and equitable provision of long-term institutional care in the future.

Community care

The Irish government is keen to emphasise community care services in preference to placing senior citizens in residential institutions. The provision of community care services is ultimately the responsibility of the Department of Health and Children, with the health boards given the task of regional delivery. In reality, however, access to public health nurses, meals on wheels, home help services and so on, is limited. Informal care provided by families remains the most important mode of provision[5] (Convery, 1998; O'Shea and Hughes, 1998; Fanning, 1999), with the voluntary sector (including a number of religious organisations) often playing a dominant role in the provision of more formal personal social services (Fanning, 1999). Due to the fact that services are provided by the health boards, regional variations exist in both the extent of provision and the levels of co-payment required (Larragy, 1993; Convery, 1998; O'Shea and Hughes, 1998). Expansion has occurred in the last three decades, but only 3.5% of older people receive home help services (Boyle, 1997). It has been argued that an ideology which sees a very limited role for formal provision continues to dominate and that the health boards see the provision of formal community care as appropriate only when, and if, informal familial care breaks down (Larragy, 1993; Fitzgerald, 2000).

Due to the recent relatively healthy state of the Irish economy, considerable new funding has been made available for financing care in old age, however, much of it has been used to finance expensive health provisions. It appears that social aspects of care in old age are somewhat marginalised due to the prevailing institutional arrangements. Convery (1998) argues that the role of community social workers in providing support for vulnerable older people is limited to the North Western Health Board and the area around Wexford, and that social work is seen as having limited relevance by a dominant medical profession, which is reluctant to look beyond strictly medical services in relation to the older population. Furthermore, legislation only empowers, rather than requires, health boards to provide home help services. As Fitzgerald (2000) notes, this may be because no legal right to social care in old age exists:

> Where people have a right to a service, the budget must expand to meet demand. But where access to service is discretionary as in the case of home support services for senior citizens, the level of service on offer is restricted by the size of its budget line. (2000, p 83)

Ireland looks set to continue with a selectivist approach to the community care of senior citizens; an increasing role for the private and voluntary sectors alongside extensive familial provision seems the most likely case in the near future (Yeates, 1997). For as long as community care services remain discretionary they are particularly vulnerable to cutbacks or elimination (Boyle, 1997). Although some recent progress has been made (see Brown, 1996), Fitzgerald (2000) argues that community care services must be given parity with institutional health and care services. He maintains that the 'fundamental human right' for senior citizens to stay in their own home will not become a reality in the Irish Republic until individuals attain legally enforceable social rights to community care services.

Sweden

Healthcare

Central government guarantees all residents equal rights to access healthcare and sets the general rules governing public healthcare services, which are provided by county councils (Gould, 1996; CEC, 2000). Financed by taxation and the social insurance system, money is allocated to the county councils, which in turn allocate devolved budgets to hospitals and other primary health centres (Weekers and Pijl, 1998). The last decade has seen a number of important reforms with an internal market type system introduced and an expansion in the role of the private sector instigated in an attempt to reduce costs to the public purse. Patients have to pay a range of charges when they visit a doctor or stay in hospital. In addition most pharmaceutical products involve a prescription charge up to a specified maximum amount. All the above charges have been subject to considerable price increases between 1989-93 (Gould, 1996).

Caring for senior citizens has long been one of the main functions of Swedish social policy. Since the early 1950s the Swedish state has emphasised an approach to support older citizens via a range of services that enable people to remain in their own homes if at all possible, while at the same time providing long-term residential care when needed. Korpi (1995) outlines five complementary elements to this approach. First, through the provision of a range of district nurses and doctors the state has attempted to improve the health of older people so that they are able to cope with everyday activities in later life. Second, by adapting individual's homes, providing meals on wheels, safety alarms and telephone calls to people alone, and so on, endeavours to improve the physical and social environment of senior citizens have been part of official policy. Third, the important role of informal, familial carers has been recognised with some family carers[6] supported by a basic salary provided by the municipality (see Weekers and Pijl, 1998, pp 277-81), and the provision of day care and respite/relief units. Fourth, the provision of an extensive range of home help (that is, non-medical services) for older people who remain in their own home. Finally, as noted above there has been a commitment to provide various types of institutional care; for example, homes for the aged, nursing homes long-term/geriatric hospitals, serviced accommodation, and so on (Korpi, 1995).

Although central government assumes some responsibilities in relation to the care of older people, the majority of formal provision is delivered by local government institutions, which operate within the legislative framework established by the state. Traditionally the (26) county councils delivered medical services and the (290) municipal authorities were obliged to provide various social services. However, following reforms in 1992 many medical services have been transferred to the municipalities, which now have responsibility for post-medical geriatric care, nursing services and long-term residential care alongside social services (Korpi, 1995; Gould, 1996; Blomberg et al, 2000).

Institutional care

Both levels of local government enjoy some degree of flexibility in how they react to central government directives/legislation and, therefore, there is a limited amount of regional variation in services. Since 1970 (in line with official policy) the number of places in long-term care institutions has fallen dramatically. Following the closure of large residential institutions in the 1980s by Social Democratic administrations that wanted to emphasise community care (Gould, 1996), the Conservative-centre government of the early 1990s encouraged the municipalities to allow the private sector a bigger role in the provision of long-term care. Recent increases in the proportion of the population aged over 80 do not appear to have been matched by a commitment from central government to meet any new LTRC needs that may arise. Approximately 33% of those aged over 80 continue to live in an institutional setting of one type or another (Korpi, 1995) and this leads some commentators to suggest that problems could arise in the future. For example, Gould (1996) has noted that although the municipalities were given additional responsibilities for the care of older people, they were denied permission to raise local taxes to meet their new duties.

Similarly, Blomberg et al (2000) argue that since 1994-95, when the municipalities assumed obligations to care for people with functional and mental impairments, the increase in local financial burdens and competition for beds in care institutions has been to the detriment of wider services for older people.

Community care

One distinct feature of the Swedish welfare state in the past has been the provision of an extensive range of personal social services for older people. Traditionally 'home help' type services have been used by all classes, but in the past decade it is argued that the scale, scope and content of home help services have been systematically reduced (Sundström and Malmberg, 1996). Recent developments, including stricter means-tested eligibility criteria, increased regional variations in provision, stricter needs assessment and higher fees for services from the municipalities, have combined to reduce what was once a universal service to a highly selective one (Korpi, 1995; Sundström and Malmberg, 1996; Blomberg et al, 2000). In the past decade home help services appear to have been concentrated increasingly on those aged 80 plus, those with severe problems and/or people who are living alone. Although there has been an overall increase in the number of hours of help provided, this has been accompanied by a relative decline in the numbers of senior citizens receiving home help (Korpi, 1995). Furthermore, research suggests that as home help is being restructured in Sweden, a more restrictive, medicalised perspective is beginning to dominate. Increasingly services that help people to perform the routine social tasks of daily life and homemaking are becoming marginalised or unavailable. Importantly, a cultural shift in relation to what Swedish citizens expect from the state may also have occurred. Evidence indicates that the growing number of applications for CC rejected by the municipalities discourage new applications. This has the knock-on effect of augmenting a reliance on familial or privately purchased alternatives (Sundström and Malmberg, 1996).

In drawing this discussion of formal care services for senior citizens to a close, it is worth remembering that even in the Swedish 'social democratic' welfare state informal care by relatives within a family setting remains the most significant provision. Indeed, cutbacks in both institutional and home help services make an increased reliance on family and/or private welfare in old age more probable in the immediate future (Korpi, 1995; Gould, 1996; Blomberg et al, 2000). Whether or not the financial pressures of the early 1990s and the moves to contain costs and increase efficiency in the public provision of senior citizens' care are part of a more general long-term trend in 'downsizing welfare' (Ahn and Olsson Hort, 1999) is debatable. It is reasonable to argue, however, that older people now have greater trouble establishing themselves as legitimate clients of the public CC system and that "cutbacks relative to demographic needs and probably also to actual needs have occurred nationally and locally" (Sundström and Malmberg, 1996, p 69; cf Herlitz, 1997).

Caring for senior citizens: a north/south divide?

All EU member states are currently trying to resolve questions about how to provide and finance long-term care for the increasing minority[7] of older Europeans who require additional support in old age (Pacolet et al, 2000). The importance of informal (usually female) care in meeting the day-to-day needs of senior citizens should not be underestimated; indeed, the overwhelming majority of care for senior citizens is provided by kin with formal provisions often playing a relatively minor role (Korpi, 1995; Hantrais, 2000). The trend towards higher levels of female labour market participation across Europe presents an additional problem, in that future generations of women may have less time to provide informal care for older relatives. The increasing emphasis on the 'expectation of mobility' in many careers (Ackers, 2001) with implications for women as employees and partners (as 'tied movers' or 'trailing spouses'), further exacerbates the potential spatial dislocation of family networks and the challenges posed by transnational kinship.

When considering the formal provision of older people's care in the six countries in question, a number of basic distinctions can be made. In the northern European states of Sweden, the UK and (more recently) to a certain extent in Ireland, there is an assumption that the state should be formally engaged in providing and/or financing care services for older people. A shift may have occurred in the last couple of decades in the relative importance of institutional and community care in meeting need, nonetheless, a view exists that the care of older people is a public as well as a private issue. In contrast, in many southern Mediterranean countries, including Greece, Portugal and Italy, the care of older people is seen very much as a private, familial responsibility. Two different cultures of care can be seen to exist on the basis of a north/south divide with the effect that the provision of formal care services within southern Europe is generally at a lower level than that available in Sweden, Ireland and the UK. It should be noted, however, that within this crude north/south division further variations exist (Blackman, 2000a, 2000b; and refer to Table 3).

As discussions indicate, the situation in Sweden, Ireland and the UK in relation to formal care services has been subject to change. Recent changes in all three nations indicate a reduction in the future role of the state as a provider of care in old age. Increasingly, both institutional and community care is subject to means testing with large numbers of individuals in need of care services having to rely on their relatives and/or private providers to meet their needs. In this respect the UK (with the possible exception of Scotland), Ireland and even Sweden, appear to be moving towards a model of care for senior citizens where family is increasingly involved in providing or financing the long-term care of older people as the state assumes a residual role. Given the overall contraction of the state's role in northern European countries in this study – and the continuing lack of commitment to a substantive increase in the state's role vis-à-vis older people's care in Italy, Portugal and Greece – it appears that a trend towards a more 'rudimentary' European system of public care for older people is underway. In those countries (Sweden, UK, Ireland) where the state has, in

Table 3: Health/care in the six member states

Dimension	Country					
	Greece	Italy	Portugal	UK	Ireland	Sweden
Free universal access to basic NHS services provided by GPs	Yes	Yes	Yes	Yes	No: free only to those with full eligibility status[a]	No: patient pays between 11 and 15 Euros per visit
Free universal access to basic NHS provided hospital services	Yes	Yes	Yes	Yes	No: free only to those with full eligibility status[b]	No: patient charged up to 8.45 Euros per 24 hrs
Percentage of those aged 65+ in institutional care[c]	<2	<2	<2	5	5	6
Community care. Percentage in receipt of home help services[d]	<1	<1	<1	8	3	17
Availability of places in residential/semi-residential homes, per 100 people aged 65+[e]	0.5	1.91	1.58	9.9	5.14	8.7

Notes:

[a] Those with limited eligibility pay fees directly to doctor.

[b] Persons with limited eligibility pay 32 Euros per night up to a maximum charge of 317 Euros in one year. Those who attend an Accident and Emergency department without prior referral from a doctor are liable to pay a charge of 25 Euros.

[c] Figures from Korpi (1995).

[d] Figures from Korpi (1995).

[e] Figures from Pacolet et al (2000). The figures given by Pacolet et al (2000) for UK and Sweden in this instance are significantly higher than those listed by Korpi (1995). Three factors may account for the difference. First, Pacolet et al are listing availability, while Korpi is listing numbers receiving institutional care. Second, the inclusion of semi-residential element may be influential. Third, as Pacolet et al (2000, p 88) argue, compatible and coherent cross-national data that relates to institutional and residential care is extremely hard to find. Nonetheless, the basic point that levels of formal institutional and community care services are significantly lower in Greece, Portugal and Italy remains.

the recent past, been involved to a limited extent in caring for senior citizens it is trying hard to reduce or opt out of its responsibilities. In Portugal, Greece and Italy, where historically the level of public involvement has been exceptionally low, the state is not particularly interested in taking on additional duties of care. In all the countries under consideration here, the state is increasingly operating as a provider of last resort, stepping in only when, and if, informal and privately purchased services are not an option.

Retirement migration, health/care and well-being

It was noted in Chapter Three that the extent to which the social rights of certain categories of retired EU migrant citizens are formally recognised in European legislation is limited. Discussions above have also highlighted differences in the way that member states look to meet the health/care needs of senior citizens. The qualitative analysis presented later offers grounded insights into the ways in which respondents sought to promote their health and well-being and meet their healthcare needs and the impact that differences in rights and levels of provision available may play. A privileged few are able to exclusively make use of private provision regardless of location, others at different times either choose to, or have to rely on, various rights to public healthcare linked to their status as national and/or European citizens. Decisions about accessing healthcare are not only influenced by a variation in the financial resources available to individuals, but also by disparities at the nation state level in the type and standard of public healthcare services provided in different EU countries. Such judgements are further complicated by the previously noted fact that, in terms of rights to social provision, European citizenship remains very much a differentiated status dependent upon whether migration occurred during, after or without a prior period of engagement with the PLM. What at first may appear to be highly personal choices are in fact decisions taken against a backdrop of the complex institutional, legal and political realities of contemporary European welfare states.

Three approaches to accessing health/care services

Essentially the respondents divide into three groups when the issue of accessing healthcare is considered. The first and smallest group is made up of those respondents (10%) who choose whenever possible to make use of private healthcare services wherever they find themselves located. A second larger group of respondents (24%) also favour private health provisions following migration to a host EU country. This group, however, can be distinguished from the smaller group (who always choose private options) by the fact that significant numbers in this group are keen to retain rights to access public health and care services in their countries of origin. Finally, the largest group (41%) of respondents stated that they ordinarily relied on publicly provided services when resident in other EU states. Approximately two thirds of this group also indicated that they relied on public health provisions in their country of origin.

Choosing private healthcare: money, mobility and the market mentality

A minority of respondents chose to opt out completely from the public healthcare rights available to them as either national or European citizens. Regardless of their location, these individuals use their personal wealth to either directly purchase healthcare or pay into private medical insurance schemes. The following Swedish returnee clearly sees advantages in private healthcare over public provision:

> "If you have enough money to pay for it, I think you'll actually get a better medical treatment abroad than in Sweden.... In Sweden, you have to wait a long time before you'll get treatment, and there's no freedom of choice." (R212)

In terms of the location in which respondents access healthcare, personal wealth has an important impact. The rich may choose to relocate to make use of particular doctors as they feel appropriate. In that context they are exercising their Community law rights to move in order to receive services (see Chapter Three). Those reliant on individual insurance schemes may also choose a policy that enables them to return to their country of origin for treatment, or alternatively, they may have the option of staying put and paying less for an enhanced service. Insurance-based and private schemes thus promote mobility and autonomy. In particular one respondent feels that he gets better value for money by remaining in Portugal and taking advantage of the comparatively cheap costs of private medicine:

> "The insurance price is based on the Portuguese prices; in Holland the health services are much more expensive." (323)

Rights to public healthcare so central to social citizenship at both national and EU levels may be of little concern to such respondents as they have the financial ability to exit collective public welfare arrangements and access private welfare on an individual basis. In terms of healthcare, social citizenship only becomes relevant to such individuals when either their money runs out or an emergency forces them to engage temporarily with public services. It should be noted, however, that private arrangements, particularly those financed by individual insurance schemes, are often of limited use in cases when the need for long-term care becomes a reality. Older people who suffer from progressive chronic diseases associated with the ageing process that require high levels of often expensive nursing care regularly find themselves excluded from private insurance schemes. Apart from the very rich, many will find that ultimately they have little choice but to rely on public healthcare systems, backed up (if they are lucky) by familial care. Retired migrants have, by definition, more limited access to family care and may have to make a further move in order to meet their health/care needs. Chapter Seven examines the relationship between care and mobility in this context and the moves respondents made both in order to provide and receive informal care.

A public/private mix: making choices, maximising benefits

A second, larger group of respondents stated that they made use of private health services when residing abroad. This group mainly comprises migrants from the northern European countries of Sweden, Germany and the UK who had chosen to retire to southern European locations such as Spain, Portugal, Greece or Italy. This mirrors a more general pattern in post-retirement migration in Europe in that such migration is generally northern Europeans migrating south (cf King et al, 1998, 2000; Williams et al, 1997; Warnes et al, 1999); a movement that reflects their level of material advantage and regional inequalities across Europe. Leaving aside the formal legal requirements of Directive 90/364, concerns about poor levels of public provision often prompt such migrants to take out private medical insurance and/or pay privately for minor treatments in order to overcome any perceived deficiencies in host state healthcare services. These comments from a German couple illustrate this approach:

> X: "A prejudice exists about Italy's medical system being very bad."

> Y: "The hospital in Salò is not that good. There's a GP and we've always been quite satisfied, it's just hospitals. I wouldn't like to go to Salò."

> X: "The widespread belief among Germans residing here is that, if you need to go to hospital, you'd better run away from here. They usually go to Bolzano, to Innsbruck or to anywhere in Germany."

> Y: "I always go to private doctors in Italy." (122/123)

Similarly, a Swedish returnee who had lived in Spain noted:

> "It wasn't at all problematic, getting ill in Tenerife, because all the Swedish people had great [private] health insurance. Because of this, they got excellent care.... But only because of their insurance. Public healthcare in Spain is awfully bad. You really need to have a private insurance." (R209)

In the past for some respondents who retired abroad the decision to take out private health insurance was of course not simply a matter of choice but rather necessity. For example, an English returnee whose husband was the driving force behind a decision to retire to Spain (in spite of a past history of health problems) stated:

> "I realised too with the health service, what the pitfalls would be. I was well aware that there was no reciprocity at that point.... We just had private medical

insurance in Spain, because we knew that when we came back we would be on the national health…. One of the pitfalls was that you had to buy yourself in [to private insurance schemes] at some colossal cost." (R015)

The above quotation serves to highlight two issues in relation to debates about national and European social citizenship. First, the importance of the reciprocal agreements that now exist between member states to ensure that EU retired migrants who are resident in another member state have the right to access the public healthcare systems available in their host country. Today respondent R015 would (if she wished) be able to access Spanish public healthcare provisions in the event of illness abroad (Betty and Cahill, 1999; King et al, 2000); although she still retains the *choice* as a private consumer to opt out of Spanish state provisions by purchasing healthcare. The important point to stress is that they would now have a *right*, effectively as European citizens, to call upon public health services to meet their needs wherever they reside within the EU. It should be noted, however, that these European rights are based on a principle of non-discrimination, rather than harmonisation (that is, that individuals have a right to the level of health service provided in the host country) and certain needs may still be ignored. When considering the healthcare rights of EU retired migrants the notion of European social citizenship delivers new rights in a very real manner. National rights that were once limited in their effect to the borders of a particular nation state have become the basis for a second level of social rights that operate beyond national boundaries.

The second significant point to note is the comment "that we knew that when we came back we would be on the national health". Interestingly over half of the respondents who stated that they used private health services while resident abroad also actually made use of, and/or were keen to retain, any rights to public healthcare in the states that they had left behind. They do this by returning temporarily, or sometimes permanently, to their country of origin to access treatment or care available to them because they are able to officially satisfy conditions of nationality or residence as laid down by individual member states. For example:

"I used to come back three or four times a year to collect my prescription. And I carried a slip of paper, authorisation to get me through customs, and then I would have three months supply." (R019; British returnee previously retired in Spain)

Similarly, this Belgian retired migrant who lived in Portugal made sure that she retained residency status in Belgium in order to maintain access to public healthcare.

"We do not have very good experiences in the hospitals, for instance. This is one of the problems. We have a very good doctor here who is Dutch, but I always think if I lose her what am I going to do, I very much dislike the hospitals here … the system doesn't satisfy me I feel insecure. We should be allowed to choose our own doctors wherever we are and the costs should be fully covered [reimbursed] by our national systems."

(This medical doctor is a private one. The respondent is officially living in Belgium in order to access public healthcare there. For instance, she goes back to Belgium twice a year to have her preventive examinations for cancer.) (303)

These respondents continue to make pragmatic use of their status as citizens and/or residents of a particular state in order to claim rights to public health services, rather than exercising any rights they may have at a European level. Returnees permanently relocate back to their country of origin in order to do this. Some retired migrants, who are effectively resident abroad, appear to work the system to their own advantage by retaining a property or a family address in their country of origin. Within our study, 36 northern European respondents identified themselves as 'seasonal migrants' who divided their time between two countries.

At risk of stating the obvious, the study appears to confirm that this trend (to retain health/care rights in the country of origin) is closely linked to perceptions about the extent, quality and (lack of) financial costs of particular European state's public health/care and welfare systems. An analysis of the interviews conducted with Swedish and British returnees, countries whose citizens enjoy rights to extensive, often 'free' (or highly state subsidised) public health and care services, reveals that an entitlement to public health provisions was an important factor in over 80% of decisions to return 'home' on a permanent basis. These respondents widely believed that the public systems, which they retained the right to access on return, could more adequately meet any increasing health/care needs than the services that they relied on in their host states. On numerous occasions Swedish and British returnees clearly expressed the importance that access to quality public health and care services had in their decisions to return. The steps that a British returnee (who had previously been resident in Greece) took to ensure access to the NHS serve to illustrate this:

"One thing was my wife's health – her arthritis improved greatly because of the sun and the dry climate but it started getting worse again, and we realised we wouldn't be able to afford the proper treatment for it in Greece, so we had to re-establish ourselves with an address in England so we could then become recognised by the NHS. We went to live with my step-daughter in Bristol. We wrote to everybody saying we are back, officially we are now English residents." (R017)

The complex relationship between health and mobility reported in the case above was not uncommon. While the climates of southern Europe may constitute a key resource at certain stages in people's lives, the same condition at a later stage may demand access to a different kind of health resource (such as hospital services). At this point the balance may tip in favour of subsequent moves, perhaps temporarily or periodically initially, in order to manage the condition and access acute services. Ultimately, as acute conditions become chronic, the persons concerned may contemplate a more permanent return. This underlines the importance of understanding retirement migration as a fluid and reflexive process.

Many northern European returnees reported concerns about increasing age bringing about failing health and the possible need for some form of long-term care or permanent medical assistance for chronic conditions in the future. As the risk of needing long-term care or frequent medical intervention increases, then the ability to access public provisions assumes a greater importance and is a significant factor in precipitating a return to a setting (usually the country of origin) where such services are seen as being available and/or of a better standard.

"[We returned] because of my husband, he couldn't manage to live in Spain without any help from friends or otherwise, he would have to pay for care. When we moved down to Spain, we were rather young compared to the others; sometimes the difference in age was at least twenty years. Therefore, we noticed what happened to others when they got old. Maybe they had to undergo an operation, and after some time in hospital they had to go back home. At the private hospitals, there were no rehabilitation centres. I remember some particularly good friends of ours. They had to pay for all the care at home, and it cost the earth. The last years in Spain, my husband needed a lot of help. He wasn't able to drive any longer, and he had such terrible pain." (R204)

"But we've noticed that the older one gets, the more one wants to move back to Sweden. It's much more common, we've seen some tragic examples. People who stay in France until it's too late to move back. Then, they don't have the strength to move. And they have a really hard time in France. They really do." (R220)

"[In England] ... a lady came along from the local social services to see what I could do, and provided me with all sorts of gadgets and advice which was very useful – you get this sort of attention. In Portugal there is really nothing, a thing they call the caisca and it's a pathetic thing. People line up there with a doctor, conscientious but not terribly clued up, in attendance, very often he can't get through his patients." (R003)

Evidence in this qualitative study supports the findings of a recent survey by Warnes et al (1999), which found that the two most significant factors in influencing British post-retirement retirees to consider a return home would be "severe incapacity, sufficient to prevent the continued running of a home" (p 717), followed by "significantly worse health" (p 735). Our research suggests that many younger, healthier post-retirement migrants share the concerns of older retirees who had previously returned to their country of origin; indeed there was clear evidence that they too would return home if they were unable to care for themselves in future years.

"Should I enter a nursing home, I would prefer to do that in Germany, simply because nursing homes in Italy are full of old people that can't speak either German or English, so I wouldn't stay in Italy. But, as long as I can take care of myself, I'll stay here." (110; German in Italy)

The proximity of family and the ability to be understood in one's native tongue, just noted, are also contributory factors that combined directly with concerns about failing health in old age and the level and cost of services available in host countries.

Q: "And if you are very old and have to have somebody to look after you, would you prefer to stay here?"

"No, I think not because.... I think, to be honest, we would move back to England.... The experience is that when you begin to get very old, it's better [to return home] because people who are your friends and your connections find it easier to help in your own country." (409; British couple in Greece)

For northern Europeans who have chosen to access private healthcare while resident in southern Europe the continued ability to access a range of quality public services (and in some cases family support) in their country of origin is clearly an important contributory factor in many later permanent return migrations. The opportunity to drop individually purchased private healthcare arrangements in a host country and advantageously move back into collectively organised public healthcare (through return migration) is available exclusively to those migrants who meet three important criteria. First, on retirement they have moved to a country that offers a level of public health/care service below that of the system that they have exited. This enables them to secure some comparative advantage when they eventually return. Second, they have to be able to afford the cost of private treatments or insurance cover in the host country. Third, they must be able to negotiate any residency hurdles in the home state in order to retain their social citizenship status on their return. This may mean retaining private property in that country as a means of satisfying any habitual residence test. Within the context of this study, generally though not exclusively, this translates into a situation in which certain nationals of northern European states are able to retire to southern EU member states in the comfortable knowledge that an extensive range of publicly provided services exists elsewhere for them to fall back on as and when the need arises. To this extent, those who have the material and practical capability to move in and out of public healthcare arrangements in this way may be regarded as privileged citizens in relation to other respondents in the study.

Reliance on rights: accessing public healthcare

A third group of respondents within the study indicated that they were (or had been) to a large extent reliant on public healthcare provisions in host states. Two thirds of this group also stated that they were dependent on public healthcare provisions in their country of origin. When resident in host countries these respondents effectively rely on their rights as European citizens to guarantee them access to the publicly provided treatment and care that they require. There are very few respondents of northern European origin in this group. Typically those who migrate from northern to southern Europe without access to private health services return permanently to their country of origin to make use of what they regard to be better public healthcare services. This is particularly true in cases of long-term or serious illness.

A consideration of the data generated by those respondents who originated from southern European states (that is, returnees from Italy, Portugal and Greece) highlights four important issues relevant to this discussion of health/care rights and citizenship. The first point to note is the almost total absence of privately purchased provision among these returning southern European respondents. There are only two instances when such respondents (Italian interviews; R107/ 8, R121/L110) mention making use of private hospitals in host states. This is of course not surprising given that the principle motivating factor behind the initial movement of southern European respondents was the search for work abroad (usually in more prosperous northern European states), often to escape poverty at home (see previous discussions in Chapter Four). Making use of private healthcare provisions on return to their country of origin is also rare among the southern European returnees interviewed. The few that do regularly use private healthcare cite deficiencies in the available public healthcare systems as the main reason for their decisions to use private services. For example:

> "I regret that here I don't have the same medical assistance that I used to have in France because in Portugal [public] healthcare is very bad.... In Portugal I had to turn to my private doctor ... but my health didn't improve." (R313)

Second, with the exception of the few respondents noted above, the vast majority of southern European respondents are reliant on their rights to public healthcare both when resident abroad and on return to their country of origin. During their time in host countries as migrant workers many were able, under European legislation, to claim access to public healthcare for both themselves and their family on a parity with the nationals of their host state. However, such rights to healthcare are dependent on an individual's status as an EU national migrant worker rather than on nationality. As this Italian returnee notes, in the past these arrangements seriously limited his right to public healthcare when he temporarily returned to Italy.

> "Well, first of all let me say that the Luxembourg NHS is very good. Everything was free.... One was entitled to free services as long as one worked there.

When we finished working in December, we lost any rights to be treated in Luxembourg, but, at the same time we didn't have any rights to be treated in Italy because we were regarded as migrants residing abroad – for four months a year, we weren't entitled to medical assistance anywhere." (R116)

Third, a recurrent perception among southern European returnees is the lack of quality in public healthcare services in their country of origin in comparison to those experienced in their host countries in northern Europe. The prevalence of this view varied according to the state under discussion. Italian returnees on the whole were satisfied with the Italian public healthcare system, although one respondent was critical of the bureaucracy involved and another saw the German system as superior. Many Portuguese (cf R313 previously) and Greek returnees, however, regarded the treatment and coverage that they received in public systems as migrant workers abroad as superior to that which they now have access to 'at home'. Two women were particularly frank in highlighting some of the shortcomings of Greek public healthcare:

"The most important thing that Germany offered to us was the medical care. There is a big difference between here and there. In Germany I was led from one doctor to the other, they would listen to me, here nobody cares. Here in Greece I wouldn't have got a bed in the hospital if my brother hadn't seen a friend and secretly given him extra pay.... When I speak about this, they reproach me that I keep talking about Germany but this is the truth even if it hurts. I love my country that's why I am bitter about it." (R412)

"Here one has to secretly give doctors extra pay to have oneself looked after. You have to wait for hours in the medical services of IKA to be examined by the doctors and nobody gives a damn." (R413)

Fourth, in contrast to their northern European counterparts, concerns about health in general and more particularly accessing public healthcare play only a minor role in precipitating the return movements of southern European respondents (returnees). Reasons given for a return to their country of origin by southern European returnees were usually linked to periods of paid employment ending (due to redundancy or retirement) or a desire to return home for some kind of family reason. Typically, this was to provide informal domestic care for an ageing parent and/or a wish to be near relatives in the homeland (cf King, 1994). On several occasions the onset of poor health or physical impairment (sometimes due to dangerous working conditions and accidents) did force a small number of migrants to return to their country of origin earlier than anticipated. A few were also similarly advised to return to a warmer climate for health reasons.

Although in reality some southern European respondents were permanently resident in their country of origin at the time of interview, a small number of these returnees were also keen to 'work the system' in a similar way to their northern European counterparts, in order to continue to access what they perceive to be the better public healthcare provisions of their previous host country.

> "I have medical care here but officially I do not appear as a permanent resident in Greece. I haven't transferred my rights from Germany. My children live in Germany so officially I appear as living with them there. Sometimes I go and visit them for a couple of months ... when I return from Germany I get a document which entitles me to medical care here. I also have the IKA insurance but I don't use it. I go to Germany for my check-ups. I have been doing this for 13 years now." (R416)

Similarly, this Portuguese couple keep their residency status in France:

> "I have a daughter there and if something happens we have somewhere to stay. But I don't have any intention of going back there [permanently]. If I have worked there and if I have been deducted there [that is, paid contributions] then it's logical that if I have healthcare needs that I will use the French health services."

> "If we need something, an operation for example, we prefer to do it in France than in Portugal and wait 6 or 7 months." (R308; wife's addition)

In time, one Greek returnee plans a more permanent move to Germany:

> "I have thought about it and decided that when I grow very old I will go to Germany and die in a home for the aged there.... The medical care is beyond comparison, it is even better than home. There is always someone to take care of you ... the hospitals are so clean and beautiful." (R407)

Although this practice was not as widespread as among northern European respondents, it more generally emphasises the point that some retired EU migrants are not adverse to claiming false residency and/or making use of family links in past host locations if this enables them to access more comprehensive public health/care systems.

Conclusion: negotiating the mixed economy of health/care across European social space

This chapter should not be seen as an enthusiastic endorsement of the public health and care systems of northern European states when compared to those of southern Europe. Public health and care services continue to evolve in a number of directions across the EU. Recent research (Betty and Cahill, 1999; Warnes et al, 1999) notes an improving Spanish NHS with excellent primary care services that compares well with the presently beleaguered British NHS; however, the continued significance of concerns relating to health and allied care services in the movements of retired EU migrants should not be overlooked.

As discussions at the beginning of this chapter illustrate, the range and quality of care services available for senior citizens continues to vary across the EU and clearly such variations impact upon the migratory decisions of many of the respondents who took part in the research.

In a strict legal sense the right to access public healthcare within individual EU member states often has little to do with citizenship or indeed nationality. As we have seen in Chapter Three, Citizenship of the Union is an exclusive status that effectively privileges certain forms of contribution. There is a direct link between these forms of contribution (in particular via paid work) and residency status, and it is residency status that ultimately determines access to social entitlement and healthcare in the host state.

A considerable number of the retired EU migrants within this study appreciate the importance of the residency issue. Many returning retirees decide to return to reside permanently in their country of origin if they believe such a move will secure for them some advantage in public healthcare provision. Certain other respondents, whether they are (northern European) post-retirement migrants or (southern European) returnee workers, are willing to retain formal residency status in northern EU member states in which to all intents and purposes they are no longer resident in order to gain access to what they perceive to be better public healthcare provisions. While this approach to accessing healthcare rights should perhaps not be applauded it is nonetheless understandable. It is one consequence of the varying levels of entitlement, quality and patient costs that are available to retired EU migrants in the different national healthcare systems of EU member states. It is not the intention of this book to set up a hierarchy of public healthcare systems and criticise the arrangements of individual EU member states as inferior or lacking. Such an approach is not only unhelpful but also fails to take into account that many national health systems in southern Europe were established in the late 1970s and early 1980s (Freeman, 1999). However, for as long as real, or perceived, differences exist to convince retired EU migrants that the public health/care systems of southern European member states are inferior to their northern European counterparts in meeting their needs we should not be surprised if individuals strategically choose to secure the best deal for themselves any way they can. Such tactics are even more understandable given the limits and tensions at the very heart of European citizenship. Rhetorically the EU is committed to reducing social exclusion across Europe, but simultaneously it continues to endorse an exclusive notion of citizenship.

This chapter has identified some tensions in the relationship between the development of citizenship and the promotion of equality in EU social policy. In the first instance, it questions the limitations of the non-discrimination principle as the vehicle for the promotion of equality given the persistence of territorial injustice and regional inequality. The non-discrimination principle is of little value in practice where services and resources are provided on a residual basis or simply fail to exist. In that sense locational issues, or the geography of migration, still determine the social status of Community migrants. To some extent this situation has been exacerbated by EU policy, in the context of monetary union and measures adopted to ensure compliance with convergence criteria. In southern European countries this has typically translated into fiscal measures designed to reduce social expenditure. Efforts to promote a more proactive incursion in the field of EU social policy through progressive interpretation of the subsidiarity principle may promote social harmonisation and secure a more universal distribution of social resources. Action in the context of domestic social policy may not, however, be sufficient to temper the increasing levels of social polarisation resulting from the differential ability of those groups of citizens with access to occupational and private sources of provision to promote their own well-being and exercise autonomy in retirement. To the extent that equality encompasses autonomy and freedom of choice, this raises two linked concerns. Firstly, that mobility constitutes a resource in its own right (the right to move) and occupational and private assets generally facilitate mobility (and have been supported by the EU for this reason) to a far greater extent than social assistance. Secondly, the ability to exercise mobility also provides the recipient with opportunities to manage a portfolio of resources across European social space. In the context of this chapter, we have seen how the differential ability to move shapes health status and well-being (whether this means moving to access warmer climates or family care). In addition, the ability to negotiate their formal status in both sending and receiving countries, through careful management of private resources and residency status, enables them to retain access to key healthcare entitlements in their home state; many are thus 'cushioned' from the risks associated with migration.

Notes

[1] In some instances authors refer to these types of care as home help services.

[2] Recent work has identified these regions as particularly attractive to other forms of intra-Community mobility and 'eco-migrants' (cf Ackers and Stalford, 2002).

[3] Fanning (1999) notes that in 1996, I£80 million was provided by the state to the voluntary and community sector.

[4] In the past up to 70% of senior citizens have been covered by the medical card scheme (Larragy, 1993).

[5] Some social security benefits are available to informal carers. The government has recommended the introduction of a new non-means-tested benefit 'continual care payment' for carers who provide a high level of care. Carers are also allowed a free bus pass (CEC, 2000).

[6] Korpi (1995) notes that under certain special circumstances when medical conditions apply municipalities will pay a relative to care for the elder. These 'workers' have low hourly rates of pay and are typically the daughter or spouse of the person receiving care.

[7] It is important to remember that the majority of senior citizens continue to live in their own homes, but longer lives mean increased numbers may need institutional care and/or support of CC services in the future.

SIX

Money matters

This chapter considers financial security on a number of levels. Initially some basic issues in relation to social security in old age are briefly discussed. A developing hostility to early retirement within the EU is noted and a basic framework for exploring sources of social security in old age is established. The second part of this chapter then moves on to outline the differing pension arrangements for senior citizens within the six countries on which the study is based. Within each member state the relevant reforms of the last decade are noted and their likely impact discussed. Part three looks at the importance of both individual financial circumstances and wider institutional and economic conditions in relation to the migratory movements of the respondents via an analysis of the qualitative data generated in our study. Several topics are explored, including the impact of economic considerations on migratory movements, respondents' strategies for managing their money and the potentially negative impact of gendered life courses and migration on the income of female retired migrants. In conclusion it is noted that while pensions do not precipitate movement to the same extent as concerns about accessing particular health/ care services, economic factors are nonetheless important and maximising the potential of personal finances is an important aspect of retirement migration decision-making.

Social security for senior citizens in the EU: some themes and issues

Faced with the demographic trends noted in Chapter One and fears about the capability of many member states to meet their present pension commitments, the European Commission has made clear its support for increases in the minimum age at which individuals can retire and access their pensions and the abolition of enforced retirement ages (CEC, 1997c, 1999; Hall, 2001). It is also in favour of promoting policies that restrict early exit from the paid labour market as a way of ensuring the future viability of Europe's pension systems: "The most productive and efficient way to counter the threat of ageing to the sustainability of pension systems is to reverse the trend towards early retirement" (CEC, 1999, p 12). The European Commission is keen to promote 'active ageing' policies in the future that entail longer working lives for many individuals. Such changes are of particular relevance to this study because approximately 38% of the respondents are aged 65 years or less with significant numbers taking advantage of early retirement packages. In the UK the New Labour government has stridently proclaimed that work is the best form of welfare (DSS, 1998b). At a basic level the current thrust of the European Commission's thinking appears to indicate that a similar approach is to be pursued at the European level as the way to ensure an adequate standard of living for Europe's senior citizens in retirement. Encouraging or compelling people to have longer working lives may ease the pressures on pension systems (people pay in for longer and potentially draw benefits for fewer years), but it remains to be seen if the general public will support this approach. It would be highly unlikely that those respondents with access to a reasonable level of income through occupational and private pension schemes and/or other personal assets would seek to exchange their 'years in the sun' for a longer period at work unless strictly necessary. When the European Commission (CEC, 1999, p 12) asks, "Does it really make sense for individuals to retire 5-10 years earlier than their parents did, when they are in far better health, generally have easier working conditions and are likely to live 6-8 years longer?", a straightforward answer from many would be, 'yes it does make sense', provided your finances are in a healthy enough state to make early retirement an option. Furthermore, there is no simple link between the length of an individual's working life and their relative prosperity in retirement. A person's location within a highly stratified paid labour market and the knock-on effect that this has in terms of when and how they can access different systems of welfare in later life may be of greater significance (cf Titmuss, 1958). Within the context of this study the different social security systems that operate in each member state and the cost of living in various locations around Europe complicate matters further.

Making sense of the differing systems of social security that operate across Europe is a complex business. Bonoli's (1997, 2000) two-dimensional classification of European welfare states along Bismarckian/Beveridgean lines and high/low aggregate welfare spending (as a percentage of GDP) provides one way forward. Bonoli, states that:

> Bismarckian social policies are concerned with income maintenance for employees ... based on social insurance ... and provide earnings related benefits ... conditional upon a satisfactory contribution record.... Beveridgean social policy aims at the prevention of poverty ... [and is] characterised by universal provision with entitlement based on residence and need. (1997, p 357)

The argument here is that in general terms the provision of social security benefits in old age across Europe can be seen as being governed by two basic principles. Receipt of benefits organised according to a 'social insurance' principle require individuals (usually paid workers) to consistently pay contributions into some form of collective pension scheme in order to be able to receive benefits on retirement from the paid labour market. In contrast benefits that are based on a 'social assistance' principle are conditional on an individual demonstrating a level of need usually through the application of a means test. Such benefits do not take into account an individual's past record of paid work and any linked requirement of financial contribution to collective arrangements.

Although Bonoli accepts that today many EU member states combine elements of both approaches in a two tiered system, his argument is that the dominant basic principle which underpinned the initial provision of pensions in the past continues to have a lingering effect on *how* and *why* contemporary pensions are delivered to different groups within a given national context. Beyond this, consideration of fluctuating levels of social expenditure impact on *how much* welfare is delivered (Bonoli, 2000). Using this approach some light can be shed on how and why contemporary arrangements for the provision of social security in retirement differ across countries. Italian, Greek and Portuguese systems can be classified as Bismarckian due to their emphasis on state run, social insurance type pension schemes in which the level of pension paid to ex-workers is a reflection of their previous position in a highly stratified paid labour market (PLM). This Bismarckian emphasis, coupled with relatively low levels of public expenditure in comparison to other EU states, may go some way to explaining why it is only in recent years that these states have been concerned to provide a basic level of social assistance in old age. In contrast the Swedish, Irish and British systems are seen as being historically rooted in the Beveridgean ideal of poverty prevention in old age. The essential difference between these three states is that Sweden is set apart by its high aggregate level of social expenditure as a percentage of GDP when compared with Ireland and the UK. Consequently, Sweden is able to provide more generous pensions and social assistance benefits than the UK and Ireland, which look to ensure minimal universal coverage but simultaneously contain limited financial resources via the application of means tests[1].

Trying to understand the variety of schemes operating within a single system can be a daunting prospect with any attempt at comparative analysis even more frustrating due to the often differing and complex institutional and administrative arrangements that pertain in different states (Denman, 2000). A useful way forward, particularly in a cross-national context, is to differentiate between various tiers or pillars of pension provision and their relative importance in providing an adequate standard of living for older people (see Figure 3). Each tier is a potential source of income, with the relative importance of differing elements subject to variation dependent on an individual's past position(s) in relation to the paid labour market and the social security systems of their past and present countries of residence. The outline offered in Figure 3 should not be taken as a definitive statement that captures the complexities of current arrangements across the EU, rather it draws together some of the insights offered by a number of commentators (CEC, 1997c; Augusztinovics, 1999; Fanning, 1999; Denman, 2000; Andrietti, 2001) and represents an attempt to outline a basic classification of the various components of income that senior citizens may be able to call on. As Daykin (1998) makes clear, the contrasting institutional arrangements that pertain in different locations are important. For example, the significance of second and third tier pensions in providing retirement income varies greatly across Europe and is usually of most importance in those countries where statutory provision is minimal. The quality and quantity of benefits available from different tiers in the mixed economy of retirement income have a further significance when considering IRM in the EU. As noted in Chapter

Figure 3: The mixed economy of retirement income

Tier	Typical characteristics/elements
First tier	Statutory pensions regulated and provided by the state Three types of scheme: **Non-contributory** 1) Social assistance pensions or minimum income guarantees: universal, flat rate, means tested **Contributory** – this includes two elements: 2) Flat rate contributory pensions 3) Supplementary earnings related pensions (state run occupational pension schemes)
Second tier	**Occupational pensions** Voluntary supplementary pensions provided by employers or through collective agreements
Third tier	**Personal pensions** Individual savings plans for retirement offered by banks, insurance companies and other private financial institutions
Fourth tier	**Non-pension income** Income earned 'post-retirement' from work Personal wealth, savings, investments and assets (eg property)

Two sole reliance on non-contributory, first tier pensions means not only a limited income in retirement but also effectively denies the recipients of such benefits the rights to mobility and residence in retirement enjoyed by other more affluent European citizens.

Recent reforms: pension systems in Greece, Italy, Portugal, the UK, Ireland and Sweden

The ways in which distinct schemes within tiers one to three are financed and managed fluctuates according to differing national legislation and regulation (Denman, 2000). Variations in approach across the six member states from which respondents are drawn are discussed in the next section which looks at how each of the national pension systems functions. Recent reforms of pension systems in each country are also noted and their likely effects discussed.

Greece

Greece has been characterised as a 'pensioner's welfare state' (Symeonidou, 1996). Due to a combination of early retirement, demographic ageing and the numbers claiming disability pensions it has a higher percentage of pensioners within its population than any other country in the EU and pensions remain the biggest single item of social expenditure for the state (Papadopoulos, 1997).

The overwhelming majority of workers are covered by a state run, but highly fragmented and complex, social insurance based pension system. In 1995 there were over 236 different pension funds, the most important of which are managed by the Institute for Social Security (IKA) and the Agricultural Insurance Organisation (OGA). Pensions are generally financed on a pay as you go (PAYG)[2] principle, via a combination of employer and employee contributions, with a limited number of funds (for example, farmers and seamen) also benefiting to a certain extent from direct state funding. These state run social insurance schemes provide for the majority of pensioners with only a small minority receiving supplementary pensions while private pensions remain scarce (Symeonidou, 1996; Papadopoulos, 1997). In addition, since 1996, insured pensioners with a low income can claim a 'pensioners' social solidarity benefit' (EKAS), provided that they have paid contributions for at least 13½ years. This benefit, which is reduced as income rises to avoid perverse incentives, is paid to just under 3% of the population and is worth 7.36% of the national minimum wage (Matsaganis, 2000).

The basic problem with the Greek pension system is not so much the number of schemes in operation but the way the system operates. Arguably, the level of state financial support that a certain fund attracts can depend more on political influence than the needs of different funds to supply adequate benefits for their members. A clientelistic tradition still prevails in which certain privileged groups look to maintain their position in relation to pension entitlements (Guillén and Matsaganis, 2000; Featherstone et al, 2001). Consequently, there are very big variations in the levels of pension enjoyed by different groups of pensioners. "The inequalities in the labour market and the privileges institutionalised within the social insurance system are maintained in the pensions system" (Papadopoulos, 1997, p 186).

Throughout the 1980s, with the socialist PASOK government in power, the state pension system in Greece expanded alongside other sectors of the welfare state (see Guillén and Matsaganis, 2000, for details). More recently, however, reforms to the pension system have been concerned with retrenchment rather than expansion. The number of people claiming from funds almost doubled in the period 1977-94, simultaneously, the number of individuals working in the paid labour market and funding the pension system has fallen (Symeonidou, 1996). It is estimated that there will be a 21% rise in pension expenditure by 2030 (Papadopoulos, 1997). Alongside these demographic pressures attempts to reform the pension system have been influenced by the need for the Greek state to balance its books in order to meet the economic criteria laid down for entry into European Monetary Union (EMU). The pension system is seen as an obstacle that needs to be addressed if the Greek social welfare system is to remain viable (cf OECD, 2000). Arguing that the present system remains "a huge fiscal burden on a weak state [is] socially unjust in its allocation of privileges and grossly inefficient in its bureaucratic fragmentation" (2001, p 463) Featherstone et al note that the reforms of the 1990s are an attempt by the Greek state to make the state run public pension system sustainable in the short term, while also looking for private and occupational pensions to play an increased role in future provisions.

The past decade has seen the introduction of a series of measures aimed at cutting future pension levels, increasing retirement ages and promoting disincentives for early retirement. In 1992 Law 2084/92 introduced some radical changes to the social insurance system. The retirement age for both sexes was raised to 65 years; national insurance contributions for both employers and employees were increased by 3.65%; and a reduction was made in the maximum percentage of salary payable as a pension on exit from the PLM from 80% to 60%[3]. Following these measures the semi-autonomous 'Spraos Committee' was convened by the government to further explore the pensions problem. Their main findings, published in October 1997, did not make for easy reading. Arguing that the pension system was full of 'overblown promises' and would be unsustainable by 2010, the committee went on to attack the continuing clientelistic culture and fragmented nature of a system that allowed the interests of certain privileged groups of workers to prevail. To remedy these problems the report went on to identify 30 areas where action was required and outlined a range of policy options. In the light of a hostile reception from the press and consequently the general public, however, the government distanced itself from the report and ducked the issue of fundamental reform, putting it aside until after a general election (Featherstone et al, 2001).

A further series of reforms were instigated in 1998. First, in an attempt to ensure future financial stability the various insurance funds of certain self-employed groups have been merged together. Second, the employment opportunities of retired pensioners have been curtailed: from 2001 those aged 55 plus who start work again will have their pension suspended. Third, stricter conditions for the payment of survivor's pensions have been introduced and finally, a new basic contributory scheme of farmers insurance has been set up to ensure retired farmers a level of pension equal to the wider urban population (CEC, 2000).

Overall the reforms of the last decade, when combined with the increasing numbers of senior citizens, have led to a deterioration in the standard of living for the majority of Greek pensioners. This situation is expected to worsen in future as the full burden of the reforms, many of which have been phased in over time, impact fully on future generations of workers (Symeonidou, 1996). In spite of recent retrenchment, however, many of the structural problems at the heart of the Greek pension system remain unresolved. Certain privileged groups (professionals, electricity workers, the military) continue to be exempted from the reforms and maintain their advantageous position. For the majority of the population pensions remain low especially for those who are reliant on basic social assistance type benefits.

In comparison to insurance type benefits, social assistance plays a relatively minor role within the Greek welfare state accounting for approximately 6.3% of social security expenditure in 1997 (Matsaganis, 2000). Pensioners without sufficient contributions have to rely on a very low rate means-tested social pension funded out of general taxation (Katrougalos, 1996). Within the Greek system there is little tapering of benefits and most social assistance type benefits are withdrawn once a certain income threshold is reached. This basic 'social pension' has a value of 23.14% of minimum wage and is paid to approximately 0.33% of the population, that is 32,685 people. In addition female pensioners who have four or more children are entitled to receive a special 'mothers of many children' supplement. This is worth 15.69% of the minimum wage and is paid to 222,225 women, a number of whom will be senior citizens (Matsaganis, 2000). Older people reliant on social pensions remain very much the poor cousins among their fellow senior citizens. Levels of payment remain low and those on the best social insurance pensions can draw a pension worth up to 23 times as much as the national social assistance minimum (Papadopoulos, 1997, quoting 1994 figures).

Italy

According to Ascoli (1996) the Italian pension system reflects some of the main characteristics of the wider welfare state. It is a diverse and discretionary client based system in which various groups of workers (public/private, self-employed/ employees, industrial/agricultural, and so on) pay into different funds which enable them to access differing levels of pension on retirement. It is, therefore, a system in which widespread inequality of provision exists between different groups (Ascoli, 1996). Virtually all retirement income is paid out through the state run social security system with private pension funds traditionally playing a very small role. The majority of people are insured with the Italian National Social Security Institute (IPNS), which administers four major schemes alongside some 40 minor ones. Pensions are earnings related and based on compulsory, contributory PAYG principles (Ascoli, 1996; Brugiavani, 1998; Taylor-Gooby, 1999).

Prior to the reforms of the last decade the Italian pension system was one of the most costly and generous in Europe (Bonoli, 2000). The net result of a generous formula for calculating and index linking workers pensions (to increases in earnings) was a system in which private sector workers could expect to draw a pension worth 80% of average annual pay in their last five years, with some local authority employees drawing up to 100%. At the beginning of the 1990s, however, a combination of wider economic crises, one of the lowest fertility rates in the developed world, a growing early retirement culture among well placed public employees and the anticipated increasing costs of funding the pension system in the future forced reform onto the agenda (Ascoli, 1996).

The 'Amato reforms' of 1992 were the first in a series of attempts to reduce public expenditure on pensions (Niero, 1996; Taylor-Gooby, 1999). An individuated contribution based system was largely maintained, but a number of changes aimed at curbing the generosity of the Italian state were introduced. First, a gradual five-year rise in the retirement age of private sector workers (to 65 for men, 60 for women) was approved. Second, it was agreed that in future, pensions were to be updated in relation to prices rather than wages. Third, contribution levels were increased, the minimum contribution period necessary to qualify for a pension was increased from 15 to 20 years and the basis for calculating average earnings doubled to 10 years (Ascoli, 1996; Niero, 1996; Brugiavani, 1998; Taylor-Gooby, 1999; Ferrera and Gualmini, 2000).

It has been argued that the reforms of 1992 "reduced pension outlays and ironed out major differences between various sectors" (Brugiavani, 1998, p 205). Nonetheless, Ascoli (1996) notes that while in general terms some groups of employees are treated more equally certain "old inequalities remain while new ones arise" (p 117). Post-1992 public sector workers maintained an advantageous position as the reforms to their pension schemes will be phased in over a longer period of time. Generally the level of public protection offered is also reduced with the young, many women[4], and those on the margins of the paid labour market losing most because of increases in the minimum contribution period. Ascoli further condemns the reforms because he sees them as failing to take account of increased labour market flexibility and contemporary migratory trends.

In an attempt to encourage the development of the private pension sector, the government introduced a voluntary, complementary pension plan (1993). Funded by either employer or employee contributions, individuals are now able to invest up to 10% of their annual wage in long-term schemes managed by private investors (Niero, 1996; Ferrera and Gualmini, 2000). Potentially the development of private pensions is seen as a way of reducing the burdens on the public purse, however, Ascoli (1996) argues that figures from the IPNS suggest that the combination of new complementary pension plans and social security will fail to guarantee the level of provision previously available under the state run system.

The 1995 'Dini reforms' took Italian pension reform a step further. First, the method of calculating entitlements to state pensions was fundamentally altered. The defined benefit method (that is, where a pension is linked to previous earnings) was dropped and a defined contribution approach, in which a tight link is established between a workers past contributions and level of benefit received was adopted[5]. Furthermore, it was decided that factors such as an individual's age on retirement, aggregate number of pensioners and wider national economic performance would also be taken into account in future benefit calculations. Second, in an attempt to curb early retirement, a flexible retirement period was introduced with 57 established as the minimum age for pension entitlement (Brugiavani, 1998; Taylor-Gooby, 1999; Bonoli, 2000).

The Dini reforms, described as a 'revolution' in the Italian social security system (Brugiavani, 1998), appear to have set the tone for the future. New initiatives introduced in 1998 look to speed up the phased introduction of the more rigid contribution rules announced in 1995 (CEC, 2000). While arguably the series of reforms enacted throughout the 1990s have stabilised pension expenditure in the short term, it appears that prospective generations of pensioners will bear the full long-term costs of such moves. As Ascoli (1996) predicted, in future Italian workers will pay more to receive less in retirement.

Those pensioners with poor employment records are able to access state financed social assistance benefits. In the past the social pension (*pensions sociale*) guaranteed access to a minimal state pension for those without adequate means or sufficient contributions to access a state social insurance type pension. Many of the recipients of social assistance benefits in old age are women whose role as informal familial carers has limited their activity in the paid labour market (Ascoli, 1996). Indeed, it is estimated that approximately 80% of those drawing social pensions are female (Mirabile, 1999).

Recent reforms (1998) of the Italian social assistance system have seen the introduction of a minimum income guarantee to be administered by local government. In the case of old age this takes the form of a new basic provision, the *assegno sociale* (CEC, 2000). This benefit is available to all senior citizens aged 65 plus, but importantly, it is now subject to stricter means-testing criteria that will take account of the income and the assets of a claimant and their spouse (Ferrera and Gualmini, 2000). Furthermore, Farigon (1996) reports that as minimum income schemes are administered at a regional level the social assistance available to older Italians may vary according to geographical location. In central and northern Italy the needs of senior citizens are high on the agenda, whereas in the south social assistance schemes are focused primarily on the relief of unemployment and poverty.

Portugal

Pensions are the largest single item of social security expenditure in Portugal. The system is centred on a compulsory, state run, contributory insurance scheme for all salaried workers. In common with certain other southern European welfare states (Greece and Italy) preferential schemes continue to provide decent occupational pensions for a minority of well placed groups (for example, civil servants), while the majority of workers are less well provided for in retirement (Guibentif, 1996; Bruto da Costa et al, 1997; Hampson, 1997b; Cardoso et al, 1999). Since 1993 a number of significant reforms have been established that effectively constrain public pensions. The retirement age for women is being raised progressively to 65 years of age to bring it in line with men; the minimum period of contribution required in order to access a state insurance based pension has been tripled to 15 years; and pension entitlement is now calculated on the basis of an individual's contributions over their entire working life rather than, as previously, a more limited 'best years' principle. Rules also stipulate that the final pension cannot be lower than 30% nor exceed 80% of past earnings. In contrast to the recent general tightening up of the pension system, pensions are now index linked to prices. This means that in future pensions will at least rise in line with inflation, something that did not necessarily happen pre-1993 when increases were at the discretion of the government. In spite of this change, however, the overall aim of pension system reform in Portugal can be seen as an attempt to reduce the future burden on the state. Increases in individual contributions and a simultaneous reduction in entitlement are the most probable outcomes of this process in the future (Hampson, 1997b). A more active role for voluntary, supplementary occupational and private (that is, second and third tier) pension funds is also likely to be a feature of 21st century pension provision (Guibentif, 1996; Ferreira, 1997).

Older people aged 65 plus of limited means who are not covered by contributory schemes are entitled to a low level old age social pension (*pensão social de velhice*). This state funded pension was worth a meagre PTE 23,600 (E118) per month in 1999 (Baptista, 1999). In order to qualify for this benefit (established in 1980 by statutory order 464/80) an individual's income must not exceed 30% of the national minimum and a couple's must not be in excess of 50%. In 1996 the social pension was worth 37% of the national minimum wage and was collected by some 41,130 people in 1997 (Hampson, 1997b; CEC, 2000). In addition a new national minimum income guarantee (MIG) is about to be instigated. Benefits under this scheme will be means tested, and variable according to household composition.

United Kingdom

In common with the other states in this study the UK pension system is built around a number of different schemes. Aside from social assistance (discussed later) the state operates a compulsory, flat rate pension scheme financed by workers' contributions. In addition, individuals in paid employment must also have supplementary coverage from either an approved occupational scheme, the State Earnings Related Pension Scheme (SERPS) and/or a private personal pension (Twine, 1992; Johnson and Rake, 1999; Bonoli, 2000, Chapter Three; CEC, 2000). All of the above, public/state schemes are financed on a PAYG basis. Legal retirement age currently stands at 65 years for men and 60 years for women; between 2010 and 2020 the retirement age for women will gradually rise so that it too is 65 years (CEC, 2000).

In the last two decades the importance of the state as a provider of income in old age has been undermined most notably by the reforms of the Thatcherite administrations in the 1980s. Faced with the prospects of rising costs due to an increasingly ageing population, and the first payments under the SERPS scheme instigated in 1975, the Conservative government set about reforming the pension system. Citing the inflexibility of the existing system and drawing on New Right thinking (see George and Wilding, 1994), a major shift from state to market provision of pensions was introduced in the 1986 Social Security Act. Under this legislation the basis on which SERPS pensions were calculated was tightened up and widows entitlements reduced by half so that they would only be able to draw 50% of their late spouse's benefits. Importantly, a 2% tax incentive was offered to employees who chose to opt out of SERPS and take up a privately funded personal pension scheme (Bonoli, 2000).

The impact of these reforms should not be underestimated. Taylor-Gooby (1999) has argued that the 1986 Act is an example of systemic retrenchment (see Pierson, 1995)[6] and that even if New Labour, in future, wished to revive the basic state and SERPS schemes it would find this a difficult task to achieve. As Bonoli (2000) points out, the value of both have been systematically undermined in terms of what an individual actually receives and also in relation to the other options now available. Since 1980 when a decision was taken to increase the basic pension in line with prices rather than earnings its value fell from 32% (1983) to 22% of average male earnings in 1993 and it continues to decrease in value relative to wages. Furthermore, while employees continue to need compulsory secondary coverage they are no longer tied to SERPS. Opt out proved to be popular; by 1992 over five million people had taken advantage of the substantial national insurance rebates on offer, left SERPS and entered into contracted out private pensions (Bonoli, 2000). SERPS thus had fewer people contributing to it, which in turn reduced its capacity to meet the needs of those who remained. Certainly, the reforms of the 1980s helped to exacerbate the inequality of provision that was previously a feature of the pension system. People in part-time work, with interrupted career patterns and/or on low pay (a large proportion of whom are female) tend to remain heavily reliant on the state schemes. Consequently they have lost out in two ways; firstly, they have not enjoyed the fiscal benefits accessed by other sectors of the workforce; and secondly, the value of their pensions has declined leaving them at real risk of poverty in retirement.

As Bonoli (2000) notes the 1986 Social Security Act has had a significant long-term impact. By encouraging people to opt out of the state system and reducing the value of SERPS, the state substantially reduced its future funding costs to the extent that any 'demographic time bomb' has now effectively been defused. However, this has not been achieved without considerable costs. The problems of poor advice and misselling in relation to private schemes saw a number of people opt out of occupational schemes and into less beneficial personal ones. Private pensions are also of least benefit to the low paid due to their cost and, as previously discussed, the shift from state to market has been achieved at a cost to the value of state pensions. The key contemporary problem for UK governments is no longer meeting the cost of pensions but ensuring adequate provision for all in retirement (Johnson and Rake, 1999).

More recently reform of the pension system has been part of New Labour's commitment to build a 21st century welfare state (Blair, 1997, 1999). As Rake et al (2000) note, the government, in outlining its approach (DSS, 1998a) has chosen to build on, rather than challenge, the policies of its Conservative predecessors (cf Araki, 2000). There are to be four elements to the UK pension system in the future. First, the basic flat rate pension will remain with payments to all who make the required contributions. Second, a means-tested MIG will also be available (see later section). Third, state run 'secondary pensions' are to be introduced gradually. These are aimed at low earners (up to £9,000 per annum) unable to access occupational or personal pension schemes and will ultimately replace SERPS, which will be phased out. Fourth, an expanded role for private provision is proposed with the introduction of the Stakeholder pension scheme (Blair, 1999). Targeted at those earning between £9,000 and £18,500 these pensions are to be regulated by government, feature low charges and have guaranteed portability.

Rake et al (2000) argue that the interplay between the four elements is crucial as they need to provide incentives for people to keep working and thus contributing to a combination of the schemes on offer in order to meet their financial needs in retirement. Using a simulation model approach to predict the returns on investments in the differing elements for various individuals and couples, the authors argue that their findings offer illustrative case studies for people with low earnings, interrupted contribution histories and periods of part-time work. Their findings make for interesting reading. Those individuals who rely on a combination of the flat rate basic pension and the state run secondary pension will, in retirement, have pensions very near the level of those without sufficient contributions who rely on the MIG option. It appears that New Labour's proposals will only provide an income significantly greater than that of the non-contributory MIG option for low-income couples in permanent partnerships with complete working histories; such couples are likely to be limited in number due to commonplace events like child rearing, divorce and unemployment. Rake et al (2000) conclude that New Labour's reforms offer little leeway for individuals to recoup entitlement losses for time out of the paid labour market to bring up children or enter training and education. The question has to be asked, therefore, how the present pension proposals for the lower paid fit with New Labour's wider aims of 'making work pay' and the promotion of 'lifelong learning'. It is argued that the second state pension will not become a replacement for SERPS but will, in combination with the basic pension, form the basis of a new pension provision for poor people. It is likely that such reforms will increase the complexity of an already complicated system and create an increased role for means-tested provision in the future (Rake et al, 2000).

From April 2001 pensioners aged 60 plus in the UK with limited income in retirement will be able to claim a means-tested MIG. This will be paid in the form of income support and qualifying couples will be entitled to £140.55 per week. In order to be eligible a single pensioner must have less than £6,000 in savings and an income lower than £92.15 per week. (The corresponding figures for couples are £12,000 in savings and £121.95 per week income.) In addition pensioners on limited income can apply for help to meet the cost of their rent and/or council (local) tax. Provided that they meet qualifying criteria, and that funds are available in their area, poor pensioners are also able to apply for various loans under the rules governing the Social Fund. The majority of all people aged 60 or over who are resident in England and Wales (including those on income support) also qualify for a one-off annual winter fuel payment worth £200 to help offset heating costs. Those who qualify for the MIG may also be able to claim additional support under the cold weather payment scheme that pays out benefits to eligible claimants during specified periods of extremely cold weather. All pensioners also qualify for a single annual Christmas bonus payable in December (DSS, 2001). Rake et al (2000) remain sceptical about the naming of this new form of means-tested social assistance for pensioners, pointing out that the minimum income is far from guaranteed as individuals have to actively apply for benefit rather than receiving it directly as a result of living in poverty. This ruling may further exacerbate the more general problem of low take up associated with many means-tested benefits.

Ireland

The Pensions Board established in the 1990 Pensions Act regulates and supervises the pension system in the Irish Republic (Fanning, 1999). The state continues to play a role in providing a level of income in retirement through its provision of the pay-related social insurance pensions (PRSI)[7]. Organised on a PAYG basis this benefit is financed by compulsory contributions from employers (two thirds) and employees (one third) (Fitzgerald, 2000). Individuals are able to draw their benefit from the age of 66 onwards, with flat rate supplements available to those living alone and/or aged 80 plus (CEC, 2000). Worth 28.5% of average gross manual wages (O'Leary, G.G., 1999), alone the state contributory pension is unlikely to meet the financial needs of retired senior citizens. Consequently, the state has encouraged employers to provide additional supplementary provision for their employees in fully funded occupational schemes and it also provides a number of tax concessions for self-employed workers if they take out pensions with the private sector. Membership of occupational and private schemes is voluntary and coverage remains patchy. Not all companies provide schemes and there are wide disparities in membership levels between different sectors of the workforce, with temporary or part-time workers least likely to be involved. In 1995 52% of employees, 27% of the self-employed and 12% of farmers were covered by voluntary supplementary occupational or private schemes (see Fanning, 1999).

Although the demographic pressures on the Irish pension system are not as immediate as some of those faced in other EU countries[8], predictions of a rapid rise in the economic dependency ratio after 2011 (O'Carroll, 1998), concerns about the low levels of income for those reliant solely on PRSI or social assistance pensions and fears about the ability of the state to meet its future commitments (Fanning, 1999), have forced pension reform on to the agenda in recent years. In 1996 a National Pensions Policy Initiative was set up to stimulate debate and gather input on future pensions provision from interested parties. In 1998, following consultations and a report by the Pensions Board (Carroll, 1999), the government set out its vision for the future. A commitment to the retention of the contributory PRSI pension was accompanied by a recognition that in order to avoid poverty in retirement, it should be extended to more vulnerable groups of workers and be worth a minimum of I£100 by 2002 (Fitzgerald, 2000). Alongside continued support for the state scheme the government emphasised the need for a substantial extension in supplementary occupational and private provision. Compulsory membership of such schemes (though not ruled out in the future) was rejected in favour of voluntary entry in the hope that 70% coverage of all working people aged 30 years plus can be achieved in the near future.

In order to stimulate this process, and in a move to simplify the current schemes, in 2000 the government introduced new Personal Retirement Saving Accounts (PRSA) supported by tax incentives and linked to a flexible retirement age of between 55 and 70. In effect PRSAs are named individual savings accounts with benefits based on defined contributions. PRSA providers are to be approved and regulated by the Pensions Board, both employers and employees will be able to contribute to accounts and individuals will be able to transfer in assets from previous arrangements. It is hoped that the new scheme will open up opportunities for smaller companies and individuals not yet covered by occupational schemes (Finucane and Kelly, 1998; O'Callaghan, 1998; O'Carroll, 1998). It is argued that the overall objective of the recent pension reforms is to increase the extent and quality of pensions available to all retired persons in Ireland (O'Carroll, 1998), but others believe that the reforms do not go far enough. G.G. O'Leary (1999) for example, believes that only compulsory, privately managed pension accounts will enable all workers to supplement the modest incomes available from the state run PRSI schemes. At present he concludes that only a comparatively wealthy sector of the workforce benefits from private and occupational coverage and that the recent reforms will do little to address this situation. Whatever the eventual outcome of the voluntary/compulsory debate it appears that in future the financial market will play the key role in providing a decent pension. In line with developments elsewhere, the only option available to most individuals will be defined contribution schemes in which eventual pension payments are linked closely to past contributions and subject to the vagaries of the investment market (O'Carroll, 1998). This may not be an approach that will work particularly well for those on the margins of the paid labour market.

For those with inadequate contribution records the state provides a means-tested non-contributory pension that is funded out of general taxation. Drawn by 98,835 people in 1997 there are again additional allowances (set at the same level as for the PRSI pension) available to pensioners living alone and/or aged 80 plus years. Those on means-tested benefit may also qualify for a TV licence, telephone, fuel and electricity allowances and free travel (O'Leary, G.G., 1999; CEC, 2000). Worth 23.8% of the gross average industrial wage in 1994, 18.6% of households receiving the social assistance pension and 37% of those dependent on the allied non-contributory widows benefit are said to be living in poverty (Fanning, 1999).

Sweden

Described as "the worlds most impressive system of state welfare" (Gould, 1996, p 73) it should come as no surprise that retirement pensions in Sweden are some of the most generous in Europe. An established, compulsory state run social insurance system is the main provider of income in old age with pensions accounting for 53% of social insurance expenditure in 1997 (RFV, 1999). Essentially two principles underpin the Swedish pension system. First, there is a right to basic social security in old age organised according to social assistance principles (see below) and second, there is a national supplementary pension based on the principle of compensating individuals for loss of earned income in retirement (Ståhlberg, 1995). In addition to these two elements a number of negotiated occupational pension schemes exist and most Swedish pensioners are able to call upon a combination of income from various sources. The further option, of taking out an individual private pension scheme is proving to be increasingly popular. As Gould (2001) notes, approximately 25% of Swedish adults had private pensions in 1996 compared to 5% in 1984. The market rather than the state may have a more central role for many in the future. The Swedish state's pension system has not escaped totally unscathed from the significant economic pressures that came to bear on the Swedish state with the recession of the early 1990s. Faced with these pressures and increasing numbers of people aged 65 years plus in the near future[9] the setting up of a new state pensions system was agreed by parliament in 1998.

The first pensions to be paid under the new system were paid out in 2001. The new scheme of state social insurance remains compulsory and universality is retained, but an element of means testing has been introduced in some areas (Kuhnle, 2000). The old earnings related element, the ATP, is to be gradually replaced with a new scheme the *inkomstgrunded älderspension*. This is a PAYG earnings related pension with fixed contributions of 16% of pensionable earnings up to a ceiling of 7.5 base amounts[10]. Importantly the scheme has shifted from one based on defined benefits to one of defined contributions. The benefits payable to future pensioners will be calculated on the basis of lifetime contributions (rather than, as previously, the best 15 years) and be linked to changes in wages and the projected life expectancy rates of a particular cohort of pensioners. A minimum age limit, of 61, has been established for the right to draw the pension and there are to be only a few exceptions (students, those caring for young children or in military service) where pension rights will accrue and be financed out of general taxation rather than individual contributions (Ståhlberg, 1995; Bonoli, 2000; CEC, 2000; Kuhnle, 2000). Although, generally, the Swedes will remain the wealthiest of Europe's pensioners (Gould, 1996), the reforms will effectively decrease the value of their standard state pensions by some 5% so that they will be worth around 60% of previous gross earnings (Bonoli, 2000).

Potentially this loss may, however, be offset by the introduction of the *premierservsystem*, which is the second element of the newly introduced earnings related scheme. In addition to the 16% contributions previously noted (which meet the cost of current pension provision) a further 2.5% contribution will be taken and invested in fully funded personal accounts organised around conventional insurance principles. The idea is that these individuated accounts will accumulate funds that each worker can access as and when they retire in the future (RFV, 1999; CEC, 2000). Although the Swedish state retains its major role as a provider of retirement income and the recent reforms appear to have broad based support (Ståhlberg, 1995; Kuhnle, 2000), arguably, once again the pensioners of the future will be less well off than their present day counterparts (Gould, 1996). Certainly if wages fall in the future and more pensioners live longer, then the value of the pension will decrease (Bonoli, 2000). In line with many other states across Europe there appears to be a general shift of the future potential burden from the state to individuals (Bonoli, 2000). As Ploug and Kvist (1996, p 82) argue, the Swedish pension system has been "transformed into a less generous system, emphasising less state responsibility, and more scope for the market".

Those senior citizens who have low, incomplete or no contribution records are reliant on a national basic pension, the *garantipension* for income in old age. Financed according to PAYG principles it is available to individuals who have been resident in Sweden for a minimum of three years. This guaranteed basic pension is adjusted annually and payable to Swedish citizens aged 65 years plus, and is available to those resident in Sweden or European Economic Area (EEA) countries. In order to draw the full amount available a person must have been resident in Sweden for 40 years. Its level is set by reference to the *basbelopp* (base amount) and currently the maximum basic pension is worth 2.13 base amounts, with benefits reduced on a sliding scale system depending on levels of income from earnings related schemes. In addition poorer pensioners in Sweden are able to draw two means-tested supplements *pensionstillskott* (pension supplement available to those with very low incomes) and *bostadstillägg*, a housing supplement which meets up to 85% of housing costs (CEC, 2000).

Towards an EU approach? Convergence of security provision in old age

In recent years debates about the provision of social security in old age have assumed a greater priority in Europe as a number of pressures have come to bear. Changes in the demographic profile of the European population, which in future may lead to increasing numbers of pensioners being supported by fewer workers, have also helped to fuel fears that certain member states will not be able to meet the financial commitments of their public pension schemes into the 21st century (Denman, 2000; Hantrais, 2000). These fears, in combination with the strains placed on member state economies by the recession of the late 1980s and early 1990s, and in some cases the criteria laid out for entry into EMU (Bonoli, 2000; Ferrera and Gualmini, 2000), have led to a situation in which pension policy has been dominated by wider economic priorities. While these pressures have resulted in a range of state-specific responses, the "clearest general pattern is one of retrenchment in benefits ... efforts to raise additional income" combined with "a debate about the restructuring of provision and the redirection of responsibility, mainly towards the market" (Taylor-Gooby, 1996, pp 216-17). The reforms of the past decade have certainly constrained future public pension provision and may mark the beginning of more systemic reforms. It is important to realise that many reforms have been phased in over a long period of time and as yet their full impact has not been felt in the majority of the countries under consideration (particularly in Italy, Greece and Portugal, where state run social insurance schemes continue to play a major role). As the reductions in levels of benefit available from state schemes begin to bite it seems unlikely that people will simply be content with lower standards of living in retirement. The UK may provide an insight into likely developments. As the ability of British state pensions to provide an adequate standard of living has been reduced, people have increasingly turned to privately purchased alternatives. Two points are worthy of consideration

Table 4: Outline of non-contributory social assistance benefits for senior citizens in the six member states[a]

Country dimension	Country					
	Greece	Italy	Portugal	UK	Ireland	Sweden
Name	Social pension	Assegno sociale	Pensão social de velhice	From 2001 MIG paid as 'income support'	Old age non-contributory pension	From 2001 garantipension
Eligibility criteria	Age 65 Uninsured, no income from other means	Age 66 Annual income not to exceed (s)[b] € 3,405	Age 66 Income not to exceed (s) € 6,811 (s) 30% or (c) 50% of minimum wage	Age 60 Savings of less than (s) £6,000 (c) £12,000. No entitlement to higher rate pension	Age 66 Subject to means test	Age 65 Subject to means test
Financing mechanism	100% state	100% state	100% state	100% state	100% state	State/PAYG
Annual value in Euros (€)	€ 1,775[c]	€ 3,405	€ 1,416	€ 2,860	Up to € 4,784	Up to € 8,523[d]

Notes:

[a] All details are taken or calculated from information in CEC (2000) and relate to the situation in 1999, unless otherwise stated.

[b] (s) denotes single person, (c) denotes figure relevant to a couple.

[c] We are grateful to Dr Dimitri Papadimitriou for information here in relation to Greece.

[d] This figure is based on our own calculations. Relevant information was accessed at www.pension.nu and the sum refers to the full, guaranteed pension available to a single person in 1999 (ie SEK 77,532 pa). Currency rate applied was 1€ = SEK 9.09.

Table 5: Outline of statutory supplementary pensions for senior citizens in the six member states[d]

	Country					
	Greece	Italy	Portugal	UK	Ireland	Sweden
Scheme/schemes	Multitude of occupational schemes, majority run by IKA/OGA	4 main schemes, 40+ minor ones run by IPNS	206 schemes overseen by National Pensions Office[a]	Two elements to UK scheme: Basic pension (BP) State earnings related pension scheme (SERPS)[b]	Two elements to PRSI: Retirement pension (RP) Old age (contributory) pension (OACP)[c]	Two elements to new scheme Inkomstgrunded alderpension (IA)
Minimum contribution period to be eligible for benefit	4,500 working days	20 years from 1/1/01	15 years	10 years (BP) Earnings in excess of lower earnings limit in at least 1 year since 1978 (SERPS)	156 weeks contributions (RP/OACP) Annual average of 24 weeks contributions (RP). Annual average of 10 weeks contributions (OACP)	None for the earnings-related element
Contribution period necessary to draw full pension	35 years	40 years	40 years	44 years contributions (male) 39 years contributions (female)	156 weeks contributions (RP/ OACP) Annual average of 48 weeks contributions (RP/ OACP)	Not applicable. A full pension does not exist in this scheme. Pension will be based on lifetime earnings reported from age 16. No upper age limit
Minimum age requirement	65 (60 for women insured 31/12/92)	65 male/60 female	65	65 male/60 female Both 65 by 2020	65 (RP) 66 (OACP)	61
Minimum annual value in Euros	€17,992 (those insured before 31/12/92) €9,724 (those insured after 1/1/93)	€4,764 No minimum for persons insured since 1/1/96	€8,476 or 30% of past earnings if higher	€1,196 (BP)	€5,148 (RP) €2,756 (OACP)	Up to €8,523, ie the level of garantipension
Maximum annual value in Euros	€100,932	No maximum	Variable but not more than 80% of past earnings	€4,732 (BP) €8,788 (SERPS)	€5,460 (RP/OACP)	Variable
Financing mechanism	PAYG	PAYG	PAYG	PAYG	PAYG	PAYG/fully funded
Compulsory membership?	Yes for all employees	Yes if salaried workers	Yes if salaried	(BP) Yes for workers (SERPS) No if in other occupational or private scheme	Yes for paid workers/ self-employed	Yes

Notes:

[a] Figure refers to 1993 and is taken from Ferreira (1997).

[b] SERPS is to be phased out gradually and replaced by state run secondary pensions, see text.

[c] To qualify for a 'Retirement pension' you must have been insured before the age of 55. The 'old age (contributory) pension' requires that you become insured before age 66.

[d] Details from CEC (2000), unless otherwise indicated.

here. First, as Johnson and Rake (1999) argue, saving in old age becomes less solidaristic and increasingly individualistic in future generations. Second, private options, while fine for those who are able to afford them, work less well for those excluded from well-paid, full-time employment (Twine, 1992). Overall, pension reforms in the six countries under consideration have the potential to create more losers than winners, an effect that is exaggerated when considering women's pensions (Ginn and Arber, 1994; Ginn et al, 2001; Leitner, 2001).

The UK, Ireland, Italy and Sweden have, to varying degrees, already embraced the market. It appears that in both Greece and Portugal greater reliance on private supplementary pensions, with a parallel reduction in the part played by state schemes will also be a feature of 21st century provision (Guibentif, 1996). For those pensioners with poor contribution records in compulsory state run, flat rate/occupational (first tier) schemes who lack additional cover in voluntary membership in other occupational and private alternatives (second and third tier) the outlook is bleak. The recent introduction of MIG schemes in Portugal, Italy, the UK (see Coutinho, 1998; Ferrera and Gualmini, 2000; DSS, 2001) and its ongoing consideration in Greece (Matsaganis, 2000), mark an important step forward, however, this does not disguise the fact that social assistance benefits in all the countries studied (with the possible exception of Sweden) fail to adequately meet the financial needs of those who are reliant on them in retirement.

Money and movement: maximising benefits?

Systems of social protection for senior citizens across Europe continue to differ in terms of their organisation and structure. Although the majority of EU member states combine elements of statutory basic pension schemes (tier one) with supplementary ones, usually occupational or private schemes (tiers two and three), there are significant differences in the rules, regulations and taxation levels to which pensions are subject in various national locations (Walker and Maltby, 1997; Eurolink Age, 1999; Denman, 2000). At EU level, Regulation 1408/71 effectively makes the aggregated pension rights of workers, retired workers and qualifying family members portable should they wish to relocate to another member state; provided that they have paid national insurance contributions (or equivalent) in an EU or EEA country (Stalford, 2000). The effective outcome of this regulation is that an EU citizen's pension rights are personal and to some extent portable, therefore, both post-retirement migrants and returning (or remaining) workers are legally able to relocate or remain once a period of paid employment has ceased. However, the intention of Regulation 1408/71 is to coordinate rather than harmonise different national pension systems so significant inequalities in the monetary value of retirement pensions remain a feature of provision at a national level. Other factors, such as fluctuating exchange rates and the cost of living in one EU member state relative to another also have an impact on the purchasing power of an individual's pension. Furthermore, as Warnes (1993) notes when discussing post-retirement migration, "people only move if they have the resources to finance the change and if institutional and political conditions permit relocation" (p 453). Given that the EU allows for the free movement and residence of post-retirement migrants (who are also citizens of a member state) provided that, as economically inactive persons, they meet the resources requirement of Directive 90/364 Article 1 (1) (OJ, 1990, L180/26) (refer to Chapter Three), the ability to exit paid employment and then access a decent standard of pension/income effectively becomes a prerequisite for movement post-retirement[11]. Retired EU citizens are thus expected to be able to support themselves if they choose to live abroad. As one respondent succinctly put it:

> "I don't think they would accept any 'oldies'. When we moved there [France], we had to prove that we had enough money to support ourselves." (R211)

As the data presented below illustrate, although relatively few respondents cited lower living costs as central to their migration decisions (see Figure 2, Chapter Four) many were keen to maximise the potential financial advantages that relocation could offer.

Exporting advantage

Discussions in Chapter Four have already indicated that a combination of factors are often important in influencing migratory decisions in retirement, however, the significance of economic considerations should not be dismissed lightly. Analysis of the data indicates that northern European post-retirement migrants were aware of the financial advantages to be gained by migrating to southern European states. Many of these respondents were able to call upon significant funds in retirement due to their previous membership of various occupational and private pension schemes. In one sense, therefore, they can be regarded as enjoying considerable advantages over less wealthy compatriots who are reliant on basic state pension schemes in retirement. Migration to another (usually southern) member state with a lower cost of living allows them effectively to export and build on their relatively privileged financial situation. As long as significant differences in wages, pensions and the cost of living remain across the EU, those with sufficient financial resources will be able to exploit such differences by moving advantageously in retirement. For those with a choice, the location that a person ultimately chooses to reside in when retired can affect a pension's value in much the same way that options and decisions about how and where to accumulate it can.

> "I'm better off here [Corfu] with this pension I can manage twice as well as in France." (427; French male)

> "With German money it is easy to live here [Corfu]." (420)

> "It's cheaper to live in Greece than it is in England. Quite a lot cheaper." (418)

"You see I was sort of forced to live here by my wife's health problems.... Now you see, the cost of living in Italy is much lower than in Germany and I won't be so foolish as to go back now!" (103)

"When someone comes [to Portugal] with a Belgian pension, they can settle here and have a good life." (319A; Belgian couple)

"Retirement has effected my income positively because of the lower tax here [Greece]." (425; Dutch male)

"I get the state pension and the civil service pension. In Portugal that was more than adequate, here [UK] I just about hang on." (R001)

As the data above indicate, for those from northern Europe, decisions to migrate south in retirement offer real economic benefits. Perhaps the clearest indication of the potential for such moves to enhance a persons economic position comes from the small number of northern European post–retirement migrants who spoke of being able to live to a better standard in southern Europe even when relying exclusively on a state pension from their country of origin:

"I had to have benefits back there to live on my pension. But out here I can manage comfortably on my pension. There it was a case of housing benefits and things like that. Here my rent is low, I can manage comfortably.... Actually if you want a laugh I got £20 for the cold winter added to my pension.... Of course it wasn't cold here, but I didn't tell them that!" (414; British man in Greece)

The variations in housing costs noted by respondent 414 were also a factor in a number of decisions to relocate. When considering the cost of purchasing property, variations between prices in the UK and other member states geographically located in both northern and southern Europe were great enough to encourage people to migrate to other countries.

"Well yes there were other options Wales, Borders, but we found property was expensive and it wasn't what we wanted, and my husband really liked the West coast of Ireland." (R517)

"I had the money which I got when I sold the house in England, and that is what bought this house and paid for all the structural changes and I still have a little bit left." (502; British female in Ireland)

"I have a great quality of life in Portugal. I would hardly have a house like this in England. This is because the land was bought years ago and the house slowly built. Today I don't know if I could have such a house even in Portugal." (314A)

> "I bought for 5 million [escudo] and sold for 13.5 million ten years later. A
> marvellous investment. I don't think you could do that nowadays." (R006;
> Briton who had retired to Portugal)

The evidence presented so far illustrates that many respondents continue to
enjoy substantial economic benefits when living abroad; but as respondents
314A and R006 confirm, the passage of time can change things. It would be
wrong to suggest that people can always manipulate the different regional
living costs within the EU to their advantage. Economic conditions are subject
to (sometimes sudden) alteration and in the wrong fiscal climate any advantage
can soon disappear, even when based on prudent planning.

> "Well, we just felt that we couldn't afford anywhere in England, and we didn't
> have much money between us, and we felt 'Well, if we don't do something
> now we never will', and it seemed like a good idea at the time and we saw
> these properties advertised and they seemed very reasonable.... We heard
> about it first of all through friends who enquired and dropped the idea, and
> I'd always had a great affinity for France and the Continent – I had been
> going since 1947, and so we thought it would be an adventure which we
> could afford, and certainly when we did all the planning I was an accountant
> so I went in great detail over the figures. When we worked it all out it was
> quite a beneficial proposition – we would still have had enough money over
> here to give us a bit of interest and the pensions would have been enough to
> live on, we could manage. But what we didn't take into account was ERM
> and the withdrawal, we had no sooner gone over there and signed the
> agreement to buy and we got back and we had Black Wednesday, and we
> watched the pound fall and fall and fall." (R020)

> "Oh yes, every day the pound dropped – when we first went over it was ten
> Francs to the Pound, when we actually moved it was down to eight, and there
> was a time when we were over there when it dropped below seven. And of
> course our pensions were just dropping, there was slight inflation, and in
> effect our pensions were about half the value that they were when we went
> out. Had we paid the full amount of the property price at first we would have
> done better, but we didn't, we still owed the balance. The difficulty was that
> we were living on a pension which was approximately half the French pension."
> (R014)

While it can be argued that the crisis of 1987 was a one-off, another British
respondent who had weighed up the financial advantages of retirement to
southern Europe decided to return home in the face of unfavourable economic
circumstances and concerns about the cost of his wife's healthcare (see previous
quote in Chapter Five).

> "The second thing was my pension – we were living on my teacher's pension
> and the success of John Major in keeping inflation down whereas the Greek

rate went up and up, so we thought we'd better cut our losses and get back to England or we'll find ourselves stuck." (R017)

The three respondents above serve as a reminder that while people may be actively engaged in pursuing strategies, including migration, in order to enhance their financial position in later life, wider economic conditions and policy changes are to a great extent beyond the control of ordinary citizens.

Up to this point analysis of the data indicates that it is northern European respondents who cited the financial advantage to be gained by migrating south as a significant factor in their movements. Indeed, it would be hard to imagine someone reliant on a basic Portuguese state pension relocating to Britain in order to enjoy the advantages noted previously by respondent 414. Money, however, or more correctly a lack of it was the main motivating factor in the majority of southern European respondents' initial migratory movements into northern Europe to look for work in order to escape poverty (refer to discussions in Chapter Four). In retirement, although southern European returnee workers did not discuss maximising their pensions in the same way as northern Europeans, a legacy of their earlier migratory movements as workers is that they are often able to enjoy significant financial advantages over their non-migrant compatriots.

"They gave me a fair pension and they've never left me without money. As soon as I could retire I came back and now they send me my pension every month and they're always punctual, never any delays.... Everything is fine, I have a very good pension, enough for me to even have savings, I have everything.... If I had stayed in Greece, I would be entitled now to a farmer's pension. Would it be enough? I don't think so. I would have to live on beans I think that now, thank God, I am fine." (R418)

"We are happy because my husband through his contributions record in France has a reasonable retirement pension.... We worked a lot and we suffered a lot but going to France was good for us in terms of our old age." (R317; Portuguese returnee)

"So we worked a lot there but now we can enjoy a good pension, because, at that time, we paid a lot of taxes there ... people complain about taxes in Italy but you should have seen Luxembourg, they would give us our wages with one hand and take it back from us with the other! It is sent very punctually every month. Luxembourg is very well organised. The pension system works much better than in Italy." (R116)

"In Luxembourg I worked for 777 days and my pension from Luxembourg is higher than my Italian pension! 15 years! 15 years of hard work and what I am rewarded now with? Peanuts! That's what our government does!... Living on one's Italian pension is just impossible." (R115; Italian couple)

Many of the southern respondents who moved north for work were engaged in heavy industrial or manual work. One feature of their narratives was the number of industrial injuries suffered while working abroad. Ironically, suffering an injury while working in a host country also had its benefits. Respondent R400 was injured while working in a German foundry and, following extensive treatment, was able to return to Greece with a degree of prosperity.

> "It happened there [Germany], I almost lost my eye ... the whole procedure with my eye and the hospitals took me six months, I was paid and didn't go to work. Then I started again but at the end of the year they told me that I could take compensation and leave if I wanted. It was a lot of money, I took it voluntarily and came back to Greece. I had lived there for 18 years. I came to the village, I bought a shop in #### and an apartment and I rent them till now.... I also bought a tractor with my savings, I enlarged my stores and I work my land well. I am okay, I also have my pension now I am insured in OGA 1." (R400)

Moving to northern European member states and accruing pension rights while working in such locations appears to have boosted the retirement incomes of many southern European returnees. Due to the fact that the majority of them were originally on the margins of the paid labour market in their homelands (and therefore would have been poorly placed to reap substantial benefits from the highly stratified state run occupational systems that dominate in southern Europe) it is likely that if they had not migrated in the first instance then they would now be considerably less well off financially in retirement.

Rodriguez et al (1998) report that many northern European post-retirement migrants have been attracted in the past to the Costa del Sol by a combination of the low costs of living and the higher purchasing power of their pensions in southern Europe. The data presented in this section confirms that the financial benefits of relocation in retirement play a significant part in attracting northern Europeans to southern European countries. This research also emphasises that while northern European post-retirement migrants are basically able to export their pensions to some advantage, southern European returnee workers who choose to move back to their country of origin on retirement may also be able to import financial advantage in the form of improved pensions in retirement. Differences in the types and patterns of previous employment between these two particular groups in the study (that is, northern European post-retirement migrants and southern European returning workers) and the impact that this may have on their pension entitlements should not, however, be overlooked. King (1994) has suggested that in relation to labour migration: "Motives for return generally have less to do with unemployment and recession in the receiving countries, and more to do with a variety of social and psychological factors such as nostalgia, family obligations [for instance to ageing parents; see Chapter Seven], and the desire to enjoy nouveau riche status back home" (p 231). While southern European returnee workers may be the nouveau riche in terms of some of their compatriots, they remain poor cousins when compared to many post-retirement migrants from northern Europe who have taken up residence beside them.

Managing money

The capacity to finance and sustain a move by drawing on quite substantial occupational and/or private pensions was a feature among the respondents; one Swedish man noting:

> "It's true that it's cheaper to live in Spain but you still have to have a certain amount of money to be able to settle down there.... I've never met any poor people. They have all tended to be rather wealthy." (R217)

The majority of northern European post-retirement migrants who moved to southern Europe could call on a number of sources of income in retirement. This should not be too surprising given Warnes' (1993) previously noted observation that individuals must have sufficient financial resources in order to finance a successful move.

> "My pension at this moment is fully private, until I'm 60 years of age when I will also get part of my occupational pension." (430; Dutch man in Greece)

> "My pension comes from England. My husband died one month before I was 60 so they wrote to me.... I chose to have the widow's pension so I get that from the government and then my husband always paid so that I could get a pension from the railway." (302; British woman in Portugal)

It has already been noted in Chapter Four that 69 respondents were 'multiple movers' who had experience of migration prior to retirement. Many of these people's financial arrangements were further complicated by the fact that they drew pensions from a number of different countries. Nonetheless, the majority of respondents were more than capable of arranging their finances in order to ensure that they got the best deal possible. For example:

> "I'll surprise you by saying that I'm actually receiving three pensions because the German company also provided a private pension scheme. The Italian National Institute for Social Security doesn't know about it, and I'm not so fool as to tell them!... The Italian pension is directly credited to me through my bank as well as the private pension, whereas the German pension is sent to Parma first, then the Commercial Bank in Parma sends a cheque to the Commercial Bank in Trieste and I have to go and fetch it."

> Q: "Do you pay taxes on your German pension?"

"No, of course I don't, because nobody knows about it, or they know it but they can't be bothered to do anything about it … and I'm not going to remind them about it you can be sure of that!" (103; German living in Italy)

As the above quotation illustrates, pensions in an era of electronic international banking are easily transferable. While there was a minority of respondents who complained about relatively small currency conversion charges being applied when they drew their pensions at foreign banks, the majority (like respondent 103 above) experienced no problems and used a variety of methods to access their money in order to promote their personal well-being.

"The pension is transferable anyway. If we were to live here permanently, if we registered as resident, we could get our pension paid here. But I think most expatriates tend to keep their pensions in pounds, in the bank in England, unless they don't live there. The pound is susceptible to fluctuation, but at the same time, only living here six months, we just have it paid straight into the bank [in England], and if I need money I either use a cash card in the machine, or I ring them up and say transfer the money across. So there's no great problems." (413)

"I just decided I'd keep banking in the UK. My pension is paid in there, it's easy enough to put your card in the slot and out it comes." (414)

"I don't have my money sent here. I go home to Britain three times a year. I bring a lump sum out and put it in my bank here. It saves a lot of complications." (419)

"Very straightforward. We just contacted the pensions people and they sent us a form. We had a bank in the nearest little village and they paid in every month. We never had any trouble." (R007; British woman)

The positive impact of lower levels of taxation in certain member states can also be seen as a factor in a number of relocations, particularly for Swedish respondents. The first of the following quotations was offered by a wealthy Swedish woman who was officially registered as resident in France, but who was in reality a seasonal migrant who, along with her husband, owned two further properties in Sweden, which they frequented particularly in summer. In her case tax avoidance was a major factor in the decision to 'live' in France. Saving money by reducing taxation levels is also important to respondent R210 and his past occupation had given him enough insight to 'play' the system so that he could retain a home in Sweden to which he eventually returned.

"I wouldn't call us tax dodgers, but of course it's a great advantage, in the case of his pension I think we are paying 20% less [in France] so that is quite a large difference." (R218)

"We were registered in Spain. From the fiscal point of view if you are registered in another country you are not really allowed to own a house in Sweden, but since I was dealing in property this was not really a problem." (R210)

Sweden has some of the highest levels of taxation in Europe and so such moves may be expected to a certain extent. Financial gains may, however, come with certain potential costs.

"I know a lot of people who are registering themselves in Spain, mostly they are doing it because of the taxes but I suppose it will be more difficult for dodgers in the future due to the European Union ... but then its important to consider the fact that if you register in Spain you no longer have the right to medical treatment in Sweden.... When we're complaining about the taxes you have to remember that they also give us some great advantages." (R217)

The most forthright expression of the tax avoidance benefits that ensued by relocating in retirement from northern to southern Europe came from a British returnee who recalled a golden era in which it was possible to live abroad almost tax free and, simultaneously, dramatically improve the purchasing power of their pension, provided that individuals were willing to take some chances and illegally import money.

"There was all sorts of trouble when Spain joined the EC and everyone was saying oh no they mustn't join the EC because they would have to pay taxes and they never paid taxes. You see that's why it was wonderful to live in Spain, because there was no taxation, no income tax or things like that, we were official residents, and we paid our tax, but we'd go into Malaga to pay it and it would be about five pounds a year! We were living very well and it was fantastic! Of course now everything has VAT on and everyone has to have a fiscal number and there are thousands out there on the Costa del Sol fiddling the government for millions of pounds! They weren't paying tax in Britain because they had an offshore address and they weren't paying tax in Spain and of course they were in luxury ... but then things began to change. Before if you put sterling into Spanish banks the interest was fantastic, because it was their way of getting sterling.... I used to take it sticky taped all over me, and put it in the bags because a sterling account would earn fantastic interest. You know, it was heaven, it really was!" (R018)

While these respondents were able to exploit differences in taxation regimes in a positive manner, some less fortunate (or perhaps resourceful) people believed that they were penalised by taxation arrangements relating to pensions earned in different countries.

"That's the scandal. One has to pay taxes, I do pay my taxes, I'm honest about the pension I receive and I have to pay 34% of it. But this is due to German and Italian pensions being worked out in different ways. In Germany pensions are worked out on the basis of a formula whereby pensions are not subject to taxation.... That is why German pensions are generally lower than Italian pensions, or pension taxation is not envisaged. On the contrary, the Italian formula envisages pension taxation, which accounts for pensions being higher in Italy, for you know that part of your pension will go back to the state. The result is that I pay taxes twice, once in Germany, because we receive a pension from which taxes have already been deducted, and then in Italy as well." (R101; Italian man who moved for work)

"The non existence of a 'tax agreement' between Portugal and Holland makes things difficult for the Dutch to live in Portugal. That forces people to pay taxes in Holland even if they are citizens in Portugal. Hopefully, I don't have to pay taxes here. No one ever asked me. What I am very curious about is when we will have European [monetary] Union, very, very shortly ... whether it's going to change, because the taxes in Holland are much higher than they are here. [I know] ... people who live in Spain and pay Spanish taxes which are much lower so, they are much better off.... For me, it's a bit funny to pay taxes in a country where you do not live and not pay taxes in a country you do live in." (322A)

The current taxation arrangements between different member states can be problematic for some, but this research indicates that most respondents are more than capable of understanding and manipulating tax and residence rules to their advantage. For the majority, the management of money while living in host countries was relatively unproblematic, indeed, for a good number relocation in retirement promised considerable financial benefits. Recent changes at EU level are likely to simplify taxation matters in the future. The European Commission (CEC, 1997c) has been aware of the complex nature of bilateral taxation agreements between member states for some time and has acted by implementing Directive 98/49/EC to safeguard the supplementary pension rights of workers moving within the EU (Eurolink Age, 1999; Andrietti, 2001)[12]. Interestingly, in the very long-term, developments in EU economic policy may remove many of the financial problems and advantages that have been noted by respondents. The introduction of a common European currency and emerging debates about the future harmonisation of tax regimes across all member states are likely to reduce the present financial advantages of IRM noted by many northern European post-retirement migrants.

Gender issues

Recent works have begun to highlight the issue of gender discrimination in the workings of European pension systems. This developing literature has pointed to the negative impact that discriminatory pay differentials, the gendered paid labour market and unpaid domestic care responsibilities have on the pension rights of many women (see Ginn and Arber, 1994; Ginn et al, 2001; Leitner, 2001). In addition it has been noted that the current trend towards a greater role for occupational and private pensions in future provision (see previous discussions) will serve to exacerbate the existing gender inequalities.

> Pension systems where the state provides minimal pensions, leaving private occupational pensions to play a major role, are particularly detrimental to women's acquisition of their own pension. Without state intervention those with domestic responsibilities (mainly women) are substantially disadvantaged in their earning power and in their employment patterns, and hence in their ability to provide for their own retirement through pension contributions. (Ginn and Arber, 1994, p 81)

Although the majority of our respondents (both male and female) indicated that they were happy with their financial situation in retirement (with some able to draw on substantial income and assets), a small number of the women who we interviewed indicated that they had problems in relation to the adequacy of their income in retirement. The most extreme example of poverty that we came across was the case of respondent 305 who was a widow, aged 79, unhappily living in Portugal who cared for her son who had been labelled as having Down's Syndrome. A person with dual Belgian/Portuguese nationality, she had previously followed her husband to the Belgian Congo and the couple had lost most of their substantial wealth at the time of the former colony's war of independence. As the following extract from the interviewer's notes indicate, she had fallen on hard times and had found it necessary to weave rugs in order to make ends meet[13].

> "Nowadays, she practically lives from those tapestry orders and also from a social pension which she receives due to her son's disease. Nowadays besides these revenues, she also has a social pension due to her son's disease. She has looked for several supports without success. But finally Sintra's social assistance, with the help of some girls who also buy her tapestries, has helped her a lot. The husband used to receive a social pension of PTE 16,000 paid by the Portuguese government." (305, extract from interviewers notes)

Widowhood had also had an adverse effect on the incomes of a number of women. Both of the female respondents featured below relied on their husband's pensions/benefits prior to their partner's death. Respondent 508, a British woman who was widowed following migration to Ireland, was working to help meet her needs and respondent 105 (a German woman resident in Italy) was engaged in a battle with bureaucracy to secure her widows pension.

> "For the moment I clean the boats just down the road, and I am going to start working for Bill and Ben, doing the bedding plants ... lots to do, and I am sixty now so I will get a pension. They carried on here paying Joe's invalidity pension for six weeks after he died, then they put me on a means-tested pension until my own comes through they were very good.... I could claim widow's pension you see ... so I am fine, and I don't pay rates here and I pay

£120 to have the turf cut and that will last me nearly two years. When I get to 66 I might qualify for a travel pass." (508)

"Please note I've been a widow for 18 months now and I haven't received a penny yet from Germany ... I worked for a very limited number of years in Germany and I have never reached the amount of contributions necessary to become entitled to a proper pension so when we decided to move [back to her former husband's homeland] I had the very small amount of money I managed to become entitled to paid directly to me." (105)

A lack of contributing years and the fact that she had chosen to cash in her limited contributions on leaving Germany meant that accessing her widow's pension was fast becoming a necessity. A lack of individual pension rights due to inadequate contribution records and/or the cashing in of limited contributions was mentioned by several women.

"I don't receive any pension [from Germany] because when I left I asked to be paid all the money that would have made up my pension to be paid immediately." (107; separated German woman)

"Although I started working when I was 8 years old I never made any contributions in Portugal." [Interviewer's comments: She tried to get her retirement pension when she was 60 but didn't get it because she did not have a full record of contributions to social security] (R317)

As the previous quotation cited by respondent R317 (see the section in this chapter on Exporting advantage) indicates, this woman was content enough to rely on her husband's pension. For those women whose relationships had ended the picture was not quite as rosy.

"I receive a certain amount of money from Britain, very little as I said. The Italian state intervenes by adding an amount of money to the British pension known as *pensione integrativa* [a pension integrating another one to enable it to reach the minimum level of acceptability]. The Italian National Institute for Social Security integrates my British pension with the amount of money needed to reach the lowest pension in Italy." (R104; Italian/British woman separated from spouse)

"My ex-husband never declared to the finance board that I was working for him. I could have been entitled to a pension now if he had done so." (118; Austrian woman who has suffered at the hands of various men and is now poor)

Leitner (2001) has observed that retired women are more likely to be reliant on means-tested social assistance benefits than their male counterparts. Ginn et al (2001) have also noted the importance to widows and divorced women of rights to retirement income derived from a former husband's pension contribution. Analysis of our data tends to support both assertions. It is also likely that migration leads to extra complications; women who are trying to access pensions derived from their status as the wives and widows of former partners can be faced with the extra difficulty of understanding their rights in relation to a complex array of differing national rules and regulations.

The benefits of being a 'pensioner' in Ireland

As previous discussions have indicated, exiting from the paid labour market and drawing a retirement pension can bring certain fringe benefits (subsidised travel, and so on) on achievement of 'pensioner' status. Analysis of the interviews with respondents who had migrated to retire to Ireland indicated that in relation to travel and accessing free medical services Ireland was particularly generous in its welfare provisions to post-retirement migrants.

"I have this minute British pension for the years I worked in England.... That qualified me for the best present that I've ever had. It's under £5 a week but it doesn't matter how much a British pension amounts to if you have one you are entitled to an Irish medical card, which entitles me to totally free medical attention. That British pension is worth a great deal of money, because I've had one or two big operations since I came over. I would see the advantage as being enormous to my not having a small Irish pension, because the worth of the British pension in terms of being eligible for the medical card – I mean doctors are £20 a visit. I have developed asthma since I came home and I am on permanent asthmatic medication, so my medical bills would be considerable it would have been financially extremely difficult for me to meet those bills."

Q: "An Irish pensioner would have had to meet them?"

"If they have less than £70 a week then they get a medical card, but if they have a little bit more than that, you are sort of between a rock and a hard place." (R501; Irish woman who returned to homeland post-break up of second marriage)

"Yes – we have to wait until 9.45 in the morning before we can use it. The bus pass is more than a bus pass, it's a travel pass, and it's valid even in Northern Ireland, I can go to Belfast if I want to for nothing, or even the Aran islands." (501)

"I have a free travel pass, and I am going to visit a friend in Clare after Christmas and that won't cost me a penny its very good. I have a medical card as well.... I applied for it and they said 'how much money have you got? where do you get it from?' and I listed it and they gave me the card. And because I am 66 I get so many free units of electricity." (502)

Individuals who are ordinarily resident in Ireland and receiving a social security pension from another EU or EEA member state are exempt from the means test that is applicable to Irish citizens and automatically qualify for a category one medical, which entitles them to free medical care (Comhairle, 2001a). The advantages of this rule can be, as respondent R501 indicates, quite substantial.

Conclusions

Potentially, international retirement migration within the EU offers significant financial benefits to those who choose to relocate to another member state. The extent to which individuals are able to secure such benefits is dependent on a number of factors. A person's previous location within the paid labour market is important. The financial advantages of secure, full-time, well-paid employment and the consequent occupational and/or private pension entitlements that often accrue are in many ways a prerequisite for moves to other member states in retirement. Continuing differences in the organisation, regulation and level of pensions in different member states across the EU similarly remain significant. Many northern European post-retirement migrants are able to enhance the purchasing power of their pensions by relocating to areas of southern Europe with lower living costs. Gender has a more negative impact. Women who have taken on the role of informal family carers, or have disrupted their employment records due to their partners mobility, often lack the contributions required to access adequate individual retirement incomes and are dependent on rights derived from their partners contributions to various pension schemes. Such arrangements leave female retired migrants particularly susceptible to poverty, especially when loss of their partner occurs due to death, divorce or separation.

In comparison to health/care provisions pensions play a less significant role in migratory decisions; this may be for two reasons. First, pension rights are individuated (in the sense that levels of payment vary according to previous contributions and employment record) and exportable across national boundaries in a way that the health/care services of different member states are not. Second, most cases of IRM in the EU involve an initial movement that secures some level of financial advantage in retirement. What should not be overlooked is the fact that many respondents were keen to maximise the potential of their retirement income and were aware of the positive economic benefits that relocation to certain other member states could bring. By exploiting their right as European citizens to reside in another (usually southern European) member state, with lower living costs and/or levels of taxation, northern European post-retirement migrants are able to secure a substantial boost to the purchasing power of their pensions. Likewise, many southern European workers returning home following a period of work in northern European states can retire in relative comfort thanks to the pensions that they have accrued while working abroad. Respondents generally, are creative in the way that they go about managing their money in order to maximise its potential and secure the best deal for themselves. Some will become officially resident in a host country if it is in their best interests, while others, who to all intents and purposes are resident in host countries, decline to formally declare residence and retain bank accounts and/or property and assets in their country of origin, or elsewhere, if such arrangements best suit their needs. Many respondents are well aware of the potential of international migration to enhance their financial situation in retirement and certain individuals are not adverse to manipulating tax and residency regulations for their own benefit if they think they can get away with it.

Notes

[1] This is a simple classification but nonetheless one that has some value. See Ploug and Kvist (1996) and Chapter Seven of this text for a more complex classification.

[2] In PAYG schemes an implicit intergenerational contract exists in that the contributions paid by current workers are immediately paid out to finance current pensions. In funded schemes, the contributions of current workers are invested to finance the future pension of those making contributions. Most state schemes are financed according to PAYG principles and the majority of private ones are of the funded type.

[3] This figure relates only to primary pensions and is applicable only to those who entered the labour market after 1993. For those who entered earlier there is no cap. For those who entered after 1993 an overall cap of 80% of replacement ratio – 60% primary and 20% supplementary – was introduced. We are grateful to Dr Dimitri Papadimitriou for this information.

[4] Women also lose out in another way. The criteria for entitlement to a minimum pension was changed in 1992 so that a spouses earnings would be taken into account when assessing eligibility.

[5] In defined benefit schemes the employer promises that on retirement the pension payable will be a certain proportion of final earnings. Under such schemes the employer takes the risk in guaranteeing a certain percentage of past earnings will be paid out in retirement. In contrast with defined contribution schemes there is no guarantee of a certain level of pension benefits. The employer only agrees to pay a contribution (usually a percentage of wages) into a pension fund. The risks are carried by the employee as the level of pension depends on the amount paid in contributions and how the pension fund then performs on the investment market.

[6] Pierson (1995) describes systemic retrenchment as policy changes that alter the context of future spending decisions. As such they contrast with what he describes as programmatic change, that is cutbacks that can always be reversed because the overall framework for future welfare spending has not been altered.

[7] There are two elements to this, the retirement pension and the old age contributory pension. See Table 5 for details.

[8] The Irish population has a younger age profile than most other EU member states with the economic dependency ratio peaking in the 1980s. More recently, the vibrant economy, increased female participation in the paid labour market and the rise in inward worker migration, as the boom continues, have improved the exchequers funds (see Connell and Stewart, 1997; Fanning, 1999; O'Leary, G.G., 1999).

[9] Gould (1996) reports that 20% of the population will be over 65 years of age by 2020.

[10] The *basbelopp* or base amount "is used to calculate the income that forms the basis for pensions.... [It is] an amount of Swedish krona, fixed for one year at a time.... The link to the base amount allows many payments made by the social insurance system to retain their real value when the general level of prices change" (RFV, 1999, p 21). Certain other Swedish welfare benefits are calculated according to the base amount. In 1994 the base amount was roughly equivalent to 20% gross of the average manual worker's wage (Ståhlberg, 1995).

[11] While resident abroad, migrant workers and their families are able to claim rights, including rights to healthcare and social provisions, under Directive 68/360 (OJ Sp Ed, 1968, No L 257/13) on a parity with those nationals of the host state in which they are working.

[12] From 2001 Council Directive 98/49/EC instructs member states to implement legislation that makes supplementary pensions schemes "payable across the EU net of tax and transaction charges applicable" (Eurolink Age, 1999, p 3). Prior to this date a worker who moved to another member state had to take out an occupational or supplementary scheme that was approved in the host state and bear the tax burden (or benefit) of such moves.

[13] For a fuller consideration of this respondent's situation see case 3 in Chapter Seven.

SEVEN

Moving and caring

Introduction

We have already rehearsed some of the legal consequences of different forms of social contribution, and in particular unpaid, caring work on the formal citizenship status and welfare entitlement of retirement migrants. Chapter Three referred to the impact of care on the labour market participation of women and the long-term implications of this in terms of post-retirement choices and autonomy within marriage. It also discussed the extent to which stereotypical conceptions of ageing have informed the evolution of Community citizenship entitlement, particularly the association of retirement with dependency and passivity and of unilateral flows of caring resources. This limited and static perception of old age as an homogeneous life course phase with the retired population apparently sharing a common experience of progressively evolving dependency fails to recognise the fact that the population of retired persons encompasses two generations (Warnes, 1993) and that relationships within those two generations are characterised by a reciprocity of care giving and receipt. The failure to acknowledge the important social and economic contribution that retired people make, as care providers and consumers, reinforces their conceptualisation in Community law as a potential 'burden' on welfare systems, legitimising their more circumscribed entitlement under the free movement provisions.

The interviews with retired migrants included a range of questions around migration motivations and the impact of moving on the spread of family resources, caring needs and the dislocation of family relationships over geographical and legal spaces. The responses of the different groups of retirees interviewed (post-retirement migrants, returnees and returning workers) indicated a clustering of different experiences, although common themes emerged. This chapter focuses on the relationship between care and mobility and the ways in which the interviewees managed transnational kinship.

International migration research rarely considers the issue of care as a factor precipitating or shaping mobility. Indeed, the focus within most migration research on economic factors and profit maximisation by definition underplays the importance of care. While recent years have seen increased interest in the impact of family on mobility, in general the concern is with children and concerns around family formation as a barrier to mobility (Ackers, 1998; Ackers and Stalford, 2002). One reason for the lack of attention to care has been the focus on mobility during people's working lives. However, recent interest in international retirement migration would also appear to 'play down' the relationship between care and migration. O'Reilly's work on the British on the Costa del Sol (2000a, 2000b) and King et al's (2000) study of British retirement migration to the Mediterranean make little reference to informal care as a determinant of mobility. King et al do make reference to the lack of community and palliative care services (reflecting the 'custom and expectation of family care in Southern Europe') which is 'keenly appreciated in the expatriate community' as an issue shaping the experience of this population of retired persons. O'Reilly further refers to the importance of geographical reasoning in location decisions:

> ... many [retirees] had made a conscious decision to retire somewhere near to home. The closeness of home, and the possibility to fly back to see relatives, and for relatives to be able to visit, were important factors. (2000b, p 191)

The limited consideration of care as a factor affecting mobility in these two studies perhaps reflects the specific focus of the research on the movement of British retirees to southern European locations. As such they do not encompass the issue of return, both in terms of returning workers and returning post-retirement migrants.

Gail Wilson's recent work does consider the relationship between migration and ageing. While noting that "migration studies usually concentrate on migrants of working age" (2000, p 71), she outlines four 'overlapping types of migration'. The first of these refers to what she calls 'lifestyle' migrants (otherwise known as amenity migrants); the second to returning economic migrants; the third to those frail older people moving to access family care; and finally, those older persons displaced by wars and famine. While her reference to the importance of return migration among economic migrants is welcome, Wilson emphasises the prevalence of moves to access care (from family in the main) and particularly among the second and third of her groups and makes no reference to retirement mobility triggered by the need or desire to provide care. A study by the National Council for the Elderly (Malcolm, 1996) focusing on the specific situation of older return migration from Britain to Ireland, on the other hand, found that, "the main reason for return was a desire to be near family and friends or to care for relatives.... 84 per cent of interviewees returned to their home towns and 74 per cent actually to their parents' house" (Malcolm, 1996, p 27).

The relevance of considering return is important not only in terms of understanding the different factors that may come into play in a second or subsequent migration episode but in conceptualising migration as a more fluid, transient, process. We have already referred to the peripatetic nature of retirement migration (in common with most forms of migration in fact). In order to understand the relationship between family, care and mobility we need to analyse decision-making processes in the widest possible sense. Each life course change may precipitate a reconsideration of location and, on some occasions, may impede mobility rather than facilitate it. We also need to distinguish between the decisions about whether to move, when to move (shaping the temporal nature of mobility) and where to move (the location decisions shaping the geography of moves). Concerns around care may intervene in any of these processes in a more subtle fashion than traditional approaches to migration theory suggest. Ackers' previous research on women and migration included work on migrant women's experiences of 'caring at a distance' (see Ackers, 1998, Chapters Five and Eight). Interestingly, a review of this work specifically refers to the inclusion of a chapter on care as, "unusual in a book on migration" (*Journal of Ethnic and Migration Studies*, 2000, p 553).

While the literature on international retirement migration has generally made little reference to the impact of care on migration decisions, more consideration has been given to this issue in work on interregional mobility. Mason, for example, explores the relationship between kinship and geographical reasoning arguing that, "geography and kinship are inextricably linked, yet also negotiable in their relationship, and subject to change" (1998, p 2). She suggests that the geographical discourse of kinship is likely to become an increasing feature of everyday life as mobility increases and family and kinship relationships become more complex and less predictable. Mason identifies a number of factors shaping attitudes to distance. These include gender, legitimacy of purpose, access to resources, social class, encouragement of relatives (in terms of migration decisions) and the need for practical support on the part of themselves and also of their kin. Mason shows how attitudes and responses to separation are not an immediate function of physical distance, however, as some people respond in different ways to distance:

> ... living away from kin does not mean that kin relationships are insignificant, and there is a very real sense in which many people are prepared to contemplate, and to put into practice, long distance kinship. (1998, p 30)

Negotiating care across geographical space necessarily involves some 'distortion' of 'normal' relationships. Mason refers to the difficulties of morally and emotionally loaded visits when compared to the 'more casual and relaxed relations' between neighbouring relatives. In the context of transnational space, these relationships are rarefied as practical considerations often mean jumping from relatively limited and more impersonal contact (by telephone and letters, for example) to co-residence. So, one might be living in another country one day and in the same house the next!

Rogerson et al similarly point to the effect of children's sex, marital status, employment status and number of siblings on the geographical proximity between parents and their adult children, while noting that, "distance is the strongest predictor of assistance exchanges among family members that require a physical presence" (1997, p 122).

The relationship between care and mobility is raised, in a slightly different context, in a report by Eurolink Age on caring for older people in Europe. Echoing Mason's concerns around the complexity of family relationships, the report refers to changes in family structure as "adult children move away from their parents and with marriages more frequently ending in divorce and subsequent remarriage" (Eurolink Age, 1995b, p 8). This raises interesting questions about the nature of caring obligations and the morality of care in such dispersed and reconstituted families. Here the emphasis is on the movement of young people away from rural areas on the potential supply and demand for informal care. Perhaps unwittingly reinforcing the association between age and dependency and the assumption of a homogeneity of experience among the retired, the report nevertheless raises important issues around the valuation of care and the problems of achieving work–life balance. In an interesting twist so relevant to legal status, the report talks of the importance of "older women's care for their grandchildren as an important facilitator of the labour market participation of younger women" (Eurolink Age, 1995b, p 8).

We have already considered the impact of taking time out of paid work in order to care on the long-term legal status and autonomy of retired migrant women. The reliance of daughters on the support of mothers in enabling them to continue in paid employment suggests another form of vulnerability in the life course loop of those women unable to access the care of grandparents due to migration. These are all issues raised by respondents in the course of the interviews although, in many cases, the challenges posed by transnational kinship reflect the migration decisions of retired people themselves and not simply those of their children.

Reciprocity and interdependence: retired migrants as care providers and recipients

The following section presents some of the findings from the interviews as the basis for a discussion of the relationship between care and mobility in the lives of retired migrants. The narratives explored challenge the stereotypical perception of retirement as a period of dependency, passivity and 'receipt', presenting instead an image of retirement as a period characterised by reciprocity and constant shifts in the relations of care. We have already seen in Chapter Four how care figured in the migration motivations of respondents, not so much in order to access caring support themselves (although this was an issue) but rather to provide care for family members. In the majority of cases respondents were neither in receipt of care themselves nor did they use distance as a means of escaping caring obligations. A picture emerges of the tenacity of caring obligations across geographical space.

The section begins with a discussion of the numerically more significant circumstances of those persons who reported having moved in order to provide care. This is followed by some cases in which respondents reported having moved in order to access care themselves (although by no means only family care). The sample of care providers is divided into two sections, the first of which concerns moves to support children and grandchildren and the second, moves to provide care to parents and other adult relatives.

Moving to care

In the main when parents moved to support their children it usually meant helping them to look after grandchildren and run the home in order to enable their children (especially daughters) to work and develop their careers. There has been increasing recognition in recent years of the role of grandparents in the care of grandchildren and also in supporting working mothers to manage the work-life balance. While the comparative social policy literature would suggest that this is a phenomena specifically associated with the 'mother-daughter' economies of southern Europe, in practice, it is also very common in other areas of the European Union and was referred to in our interviews by British and Scandinavian respondents. Rogerson et al identify a similar trend in the US:

> Research shows that informal support and care giving flows in both directions
> ... with the increase over time in two-worker households has come an increase
> in the amount of childcare provided by grandparents. (1997, p 121)

Interestingly Rogerson et al also comment on the role of parents in 'crisis' situations, citing unemployment and marital disruption as examples of circumstances in which parental care may be sought. Liselotte Wilk makes a similar point in a paper on intergenerational relationships arguing that while:

> ... economic development has cut the 'vital connections' (ie time and
> proximity) of a good relationship between grandparents and grandchildren
> ... the instability of marriages and partnerships has turned grandparents into
> important representatives of stability and continuity. (2000 p 26)

Grandchildren, she adds, "give meaning to their grandparents' lives" (p 27).

The contribution of retired parents to the care of adult children is evident in some of the examples referred to below, particularly in cases of marital breakdown echoing Rogerson's and Wilk's work, but also in the context of disability and physical and mental illness. The cases presented here highlight some specific concerns around the mobility of disabled citizens and their carers[1]. The following subsection begins with the presentation of three case studies that illustrate a number of the issues referred to previously. The introduction of a few case studies in this final empirical chapter, also serves to illustrate the relationship between many of the issues we have previously discussed in the experiences and decision-making processes of retired migrants.

Case 1: Vassiliki and Stavros

Vassiliki and Stavros had moved to Germany in order to work leaving their two young children in Greece to be cared for by their grandparents. During this time the couple financially supported themselves, their children and both sets of grandparents back in Greece. The children subsequently joined their parents

in Germany. Some years later Vassiliki and Stavros returned to Greece taking
early retirement due to ill health allegedly caused by the nature of their work
there. Their son subsequently suffered a serious car accident in Germany losing
both legs, which resulted in a series of moves too and from Germany to support
him (he subsequently returned to Greece). Vassiliki describes the situation as
follows:

> "Everybody was leaving so I said: Why not us? My husband went there and
> he found an easy, good and well-paid job and stayed. After 10 months I went
> as well. Our children came two years later. It was very difficult to find a
> house at the beginning. When we said we had a child they would give us a
> small apartment and later they would throw us out of it. Anyway, I worked
> for 16 years and then I stopped because I couldn't work anymore. My husband
> worked for 20 years. Life there is good, one can earn money and I mean it ...
> we sent to the village as many marks as we could, and this is how we made a
> fortune. On this money we lived, five persons in Germany and our parents –
> four persons – in Greece. We helped them as well.... My son was five years
> old at the time we left. When I left for Germany as well, we used to come
> back every year to see our child. It was a hardship for both our child and
> ourselves.... Later two of our children came to Germany as well.... Now, it
> is my eldest son that I help more. He is an invalid due to a car accident. He
> has no legs, I help him a lot." (R409)

Case 2: Paul and Mary

Paul and Mary had lived abroad all their lives. Mary had moved regularly with
Paul's job. They paid to have a house built for themselves in Portugal for their
retirement. The plans went wrong, however, and the house was not built to
their specifications. In practice this restricted their ability to care for the husband's
mother. The couple subsequently returned home to support their son and
grandchildren following a marriage breakdown. The wife then became ill
herself and is currently on dialysis:

> "The thing that upset me more than anything was the fact that it was now
> not going to be possible to have his mother come for a holiday because she
> was disabled and my plan was, she'd come and stay with us wherever we'd
> been, and have a nice holiday and she was dying, dying of cancer but we
> wanted to have her for a holiday and it wasn't possible because of the way the
> house was built."

> Q: "What made you return to England?"

> "Well, we've got four children and they've all had divorces, now we find that
> very hard because we've been married forty odd years, forty five years, so we

find that extremely hard ... now the final straw came ... I needed to be back here and see what was happening."

"One [divorce] was when we were still in Malaysia, the second was eight years ago, nearly nine years ago, that was traumatic, and I thought if only I'd been there perhaps I could have done something. You probably couldn't have done but that's how a mother feels about her kids ... bearing in mind that our children have all been to boarding school, so ... I don't care what anybody says you have a little feeling of guilt that you sent them away ... and then my youngest son phoned us up and his wife had left him with three young children, two years of age, six years of age, and seven years of age. Now that was the end as far as I was concerned, and I said to Paul, 'I'm going to England tomorrow, you can go and get me a ticket, I'm going'. I really came home, to be perfectly honest, thinking I could wave the magic wand over my daughter-in-law, and make her see sense about leaving the children, which doesn't work, but I tried. What I thought was, 'if I'm here in [England], I'll look after the children a few days, or a few evenings, and you and Dave can go out together and try and find what you had originally', but she wouldn't listen, she said 'No, I've changed'."

"I've always been there for my grandchildren because my eldest daughter divorced her husband here because he was cruel, and she divorced him, took the children and went to her sister ... and since then she's found her own feet and she's gone to university and the eldest boy's working. But I'm always there for them, it they've got a problem. Like the eldest grandson, he's about to be a daddy. Now he didn't want his mum to tell me, he phoned me up and talked to me, because we've been very close ... and then one of the daughters, the youngest, she had to have a cancer operation, now I came home for that to help out."

[Mary then refers to a deterioration in her own health]

"I said to Paul, I don't think I'm going to be able to go back, there's too much going on, and I just don't feel well, and he said 'Oh, well, we'll see, we'll see what the doctors think'. Anyway the next thing I went to the hospital and the doctor turned round to my husband and said, 'Your wife should have been in hospital yesterday, not tomorrow or today, she's got renal failure and she needs a blood transfusion right now'. Paul immediately, without me saying one word, put the house on the market and I said to him 'I quite understand if you go back, and you can come over for holidays, you know' but he refused." (R010)

Case 3: Anna

The 79-year-old respondent in the next case had delayed her own planned return, following her widowhood, in order to continue to care for her disabled son. Anna came originally from Belgium and married a Portuguese man before moving with him to the Congo. Since 1961 she has lived in Portugal. Her husband died three years ago and since then she has lived on a very meagre income (her husband left bad business debts and was unable to retrieve capital from the Congo), supplemented by Portuguese health and social support. The Portuguese interviewer describes the situation as follows:

> The interview took place in Anna's house, which shows us some economic difficulties having nothing in common with our other interviewees' situations. In order to lessen those difficulties she makes beautiful tapestries, real masterpieces, which she showed me during the interview. She sells these to her friends and to other people who order from her and she works 8 to 10 hours a day. Nowadays besides these revenues she also has a social pension due to her son's disease. She hasn't any private insurance. She considers herself in a very difficult situation:

> "I have been living very poorly with the money I managed to obtain from my husband's business in the Congo. In Portugal, fish is very expensive and for almost a year I was eating a tin of sardines and rice everyday."

> Anna refers to the difficulties that she had to take care of her son, aged 51, who has Down's syndrome:

> "It was difficult, much too difficult to take care of him at my age by myself. I am too old to have so much responsibility for my son. He couldn't do anything alone. My son was totally dependent on me. I didn't know anything about Portugal and social care here. And we had economic difficulties. It was a very hard time. Now it's a little better."

> The husband used to receive a social pension of PTE 16,000 per month paid by the Portuguese government. At this moment, with the help of a friend who is a lawyer, she manages to receive a social pension. She has sold everything she has to ensure her son's support. She makes tapestries because she wants to leave a retirement pension to her son when she dies. Finally, she managed some financial support to help pay her son's residential expenses in a private institution costing PTE 53,000 a month. A friend advised her to write to Queen Fabíola of Belgium requesting her help:

> "Some time later the Queen answered me. She wrote saying that a social assistant would be in touch with me. And so she was. We made an appointment at Ritz's Hotel. The lady informed me that it was possible to help us – me and my son – if we moved to Belgium. Until then we couldn't have Belgian benefits. We would have to change our residence to have the Belgian social pension for my son's disease. But I couldn't do that. I really couldn't because, finally he was so well integrated here. I really couldn't make that decision

[she cries a lot]. If my son stayed there alone, I would have always felt that I abandoned him." [She cries again.] (315)

These three cases illustrate the kinds of reciprocities that characterise many family relationships and the flux of moves families made in response to care. In the first example, the respondent left her children to be cared for by her parents in order to enable her and her partner to establish themselves and earn the money that they could then remit home to support their parents and children. The story of family separation witnessed here with children living apart from parents for extended periods of time is a typical feature of the lives of many EU migrant families, particularly those from southern countries who moved north to find work (Ackers, 2001; Ackers and Stalford, 2002). Although the respondent returned 'home' because of her own ill health at the time of the interview, she was also involved in caring, in a fairly intensive way, for her disabled son.

The second case also evidences the number of moves many retirees made over the life course and the web of interdependencies or reciprocities that form the cycle of care in their lives. Having initially planned to bring her mother-in-law over to care for her in the host state (as she was entitled under Community law) the couple then moved back to the UK temporarily in response to a series of family crises affecting their three children. In particular they spent time caring for their grandchildren. In practice they never returned to Portugal as the respondent herself became seriously ill and they were forced to remain in the UK. With echoes of other stories related to us in the course of this research, the interviewee also talks of the guilt that she experienced in leaving family behind earlier in her working life.

Finally, the third case tells the painful story of a very old woman who was widowed in the host state. The case illustrates the heterogeneous nature of the retired migrant population, the unpredictability of life courses and the genuine economic need faced by some irrespective of their pre-retirement financial status. It also illustrates the difficulty of translating formal legal rights (in this case to return home with her son and benefit from the social care system in Belgium) into practical benefits. While in this case it was the son's disability and his emotional needs that constituted a barrier to her mobility, preventing her return, in other cases involving care for older dependants, respondents cited the onset of dementias and similar degenerative conditions as barriers to the simple exercise of legal rights. In material terms the respondent would have been in a stronger position had she exercised her national citizenship entitlement and returned home with her son to claim the superior benefits open to her in Belgium. While her Community law entitlement does furnish her with the right to access Portuguese services (which she is now exercising), in practice, as seen in Chapters Five and Six, the level of provision is quite limited.

This clearly illustrates the limitations of the right to non-discrimination in the face of significant diversity and inequality in provision. Of course, in future this woman may need care herself. If and when this situation arises, the woman will find herself entirely isolated from family and the benefits of her home welfare system, with limited personal resources and potentially torn between remaining in Portugal for her son's benefit and returning to Belgium for her own.

In one quite unusual case illustrating the link between care and mobility, a Portuguese couple had moved to France to support their son who had fled from Portugal in 1974 as a political refugee, to avoid conscription. Some years later they went to France to visit him:

> "I didn't like what I saw. My son wasn't well dressed. I said to my wife, there's nothing else to do. I'll stay here. You must return to Portugal and manage our things and then you may come here. I'll stay here with our son, otherwise he may be lost. What made us migrate wasn't the lack of work or the need for money. It was our son's situation. He was young and he could be lost. I only returned to Portugal when I saw his life straightened and when he got married [three years later]." (R306)

Other respondents reported restrictions on their mobility (preventing a return 'home') as a consequence of caring obligations. In one case (R504), a widow delayed her return in order to support her daughter, while in another a woman reported having remained in the UK much longer than she had wished in order to meet her husband's caring obligations towards his mother (as an only child). Soon after her husband's death, she returned home to Ireland (R510). These two cases, in common with Anna's story (case 3 previously), underline the importance of taking a broad and sensitive approach to the relationship between care and mobility. Care in that context may not be so much a factor shaping migration, but rather tying respondents to certain locations inhibiting or delaying planned return moves.

A far greater number of respondents mentioned the need to move, typically returning home at least temporarily, in order to support their own older parents or parents-in-law. Nineteen respondents referred to such moves, illustrating the importance of conceptualising retirement as a demographic period encompassing two generations. In practice these two generations are quite different not least in terms of dependency and their role in providing care. Discussions in Chapter Six have indicated that return migration is often precipitated by the evolving dependency of the retired migrant themselves. These cases also evidence the extent to which such moves are made in response to the needs of other family members and the importance of recognising the contribution of retired people to the care of the very old and infirm.

This contribution may take the form of spousal care or care for older, frail, ascendant relatives. Many of the respondents in the following cases cited issues concerning care giving and receiving between spouses and of concerns around mutual care as factors determining migration decisions. Much of the established literature on the issue of elder care focuses on the gendered nature of care giving. While not denying the importance of gender relationships in care-giving, the kind of marked gender differences identified in the course of previous research (Ackers, 1998) may reflect the focus on women of working age. Indeed,

Rose and Bruce (1995) make the point that much of the debate about gender and informal care has focused on the caring expectations placed on white younger and middle-aged women and the impact of this on labour market participation, career progression and financial autonomy. Rose and Bruce refer to the:

> ... high theoretical and political price of attributing agency only to this single valorised group, leaving elderly [sic] people – both women and men – to be conceptualised as passive objects. (1995, p 115)

In the process, it erased the contribution of male carers who were themselves senior citizens. Their findings indicate a much higher prevalence of 'mutual care' among older couples at particular stages in their lives, perhaps before intensive personal care is required, as "gender divisions of care which had operated earlier in the life course hold less rigidly" (p 117) than previous research suggests. On the other hand, it underwrites the persistence of the "long and deforming fingers of gender" (p 128). Ungerson also identifies the limitations of feminist perspectives on informal care, which "overemphasised the intergenerational aspects of care at the cost of ignoring care between spouses" (2000, p 624).

The situation of many older couples in a migration context places further pressure for mutual care given the limited access to other family members and daughters in particular. Notwithstanding the greater involvement of male partners in spousal care, the interviews also lend weight to Rose and Bruce's concerns around the role of men as gatekeepers, effectively controlling the lives of women (and making key decisions about care options). In that sense, the following interviews reinforce the arguments discussed in Chapter Four and previous research on the determinative role of men in migration decision-making processes (Ackers and Stalford, 2002).

In addition to the contribution of our older respondents via 'mutual' spousal care, the research has identified a cohort of older people, including both men and women, who moved in order to provide care for frail relatives. This phenomenon is rarely reported in the extensive literature on elder care. Even that literature which does take an intergenerational perspective tends in the main to focus on the relationships between older people and their adult children and grandchildren. Chris Phillipson (1996), in his input to an important contribution on intergenerational relations (Walker, 1996), criticises the tendency of policy, in the context of demographic change, to depict older people as a burden on society. Arguing that generational relations need to be seen "from the standpoint of the life course as a whole", he refers to evidence of "giving and receiving throughout the life course: both within and across generations" (p 216). Citing Cheal (1987, p 216) he contends that, "it is the propensity of the elderly [sic] to give, rather than their necessity to receive that requires sociological explanation at this time" (p 141). Unfortunately, however, the ensuing discussion tends to characterise intergenerational relations in terms of relationships between adult children and aged parents (or between 'workers' and 'pensioners'). As such it fails to acknowledge the 'two generation' issue and the reciprocity of intergenerational support that takes place within the retired population.

These concerns remain completely absent from international migration theory. The next case to be discussed describes a fairly typical picture of ongoing mobility triggered by caring needs and, as such, calls into question the validity and explanatory potential of mainstream migration theory which characterises migration decision-making in terms of discrete, often unilateral, international moves. In common with many of the families who moved from southern Europe in the 1960s, often several members of the same family moved. In this case Sonia's father moved first and was followed two years later by his wife and their children. They remained in the UK for over 40 years during which time Sonia met her Italian partner who was also working in the UK and they had two sons, one of whom now lives in Italy and the other in the UK with his three children. The return moves of Sonia, her husband, her father and her grandfather before him were all triggered by the need to care:

> "My father had to come back to Italy when my grandmother died because there was his brother who needed caring for. While here he fell ill too, he got cancer, so my mother and I had to come back too, and I would take care of him during the day whereas she would watch him at night."

Sonia expressed a strong desire to return to the UK, mainly to be near her grandchildren who she used to see 'every single night'. Her husband recognises Sonia's desire to return, saying that she would "go back to England on foot" if necessary. On their return to Italy, however, and in order to support their son in the UK, they suggested that he move into their property, reducing their own ability to return:

> "The future is a problem, you see, my son and his family are living in our house now.... God, one makes so many mistakes!... It was mainly our fault, we told him 'go and live there now'." (R106)

In addition to moves triggered by the need to provide personal, 'hands–on' care and support grandchildren and other family carers, this case illustrates another important dimension of family care, so often overlooked in the academic literature, namely the exchange of economic resources within families. The respondent in the previous example has provided her son with a property (effectively restricting her own mobility). Elsewhere financial assistance took the form of income or payments for care. This case, along with many others, also underlines the unpredictability of life courses and in that context the limitations of conceptions of citizenship based on static and simplistic legal categories and limited notions of contribution.

The couple in the next example moved to Greece after taking early retirement in the UK. Their situation and the circumstances leading to their return echo those of other respondents. While respondents sometimes referred to the relationship between climate and health (in improving certain chronic conditions) as a precursor to migration, subsequent deterioration of the same condition often results in a subsequent return to access formal health/care services (see Chapter Five). Furthermore, the example highlights the extent to which migratory pressures, or the attraction of migration, 'runs in families' with other siblings moving also, often to other locations, resulting in the geographical dislocation of caring resources and obligations. In such situations a whole range of variables come into play when a particular crisis arises. These include the issues of distance and access, but also the number and gender of siblings. The results of our previous research on gender and migration, with its empirical focus on women of working age, highlighted the pressure on daughters in particular to take on caring roles, even in situations where a son lived nearby (Ackers, 1998, pp 294-6). In the current project we have found less evidence that gender makes a difference, perhaps because of the increasing propensity for spousal care in the retired population.

The first of the following cases provides an example of the relationship between mobility and health (or care needs) over the post-retirement life course. The respondent notes how the initial move to southern Europe was motivated by concerns to improve his wife's health. Once her condition had deteriorated beyond a certain point, however, and access to quality healthcare became an issue, the balance tipped in favour of a return move. Other factors affecting the migration decision, however, included the need to care for an ageing mother. In this context the respondent raises a couple of other important factors affecting their migration decision; firstly the migration of other family members on the availability of care and secondly, the availability and ability of sibling support:

> "One thing was my wife's health – her arthritis improved greatly because of the sun and the dry climate ... but it started getting worse again, and we realised we wouldn't be able to afford the proper treatment for it in Greece.... The other reason for coming back, I should say, is my mother's health, she's almost totally blind, and just at the moment she is going through a crisis – she's 93 and she's very stubborn. My sister died of a brain tumour, she was five years younger than me, living in Australia and after that I was the only member of the family alive in Greece, and I really felt under an obligation to be a bit closer." (R107)

Migration clearly is, as Wilson argues, "a process that emphasises the importance of a life course perspective" (2000, p 71). In the next example, the Portuguese respondent had initially migrated to France for work and then made a series of repeated returns, firstly to care for her mother-in-law and then for her own mother. These decisions would appear to have been made jointly with her husband who subsequently died in Portugal. She was then unable to return to her life in France due to the deterioration in her own health. The Portuguese interviewer describes the situation as follows:

Maria's stay was interrupted because of family reasons. She stayed for one year and then returned to France for one and a half years due to her mother-in-law's health. But due to her own mother's health she decided to return permanently:

"I thought I shouldn't be there and my mother here alone; she made so many sacrifices to raise us. My sister was in Lisbon, the other brother in Angola and so I thought, it's not fair, knowing that she's suffering and we are each one going our own way and she, here, alone. And that's why I said: 'let's go back'."

The following Italian family was similarly dispersed, placing pressure on the respondent to return to support her sister in caring for their mother:

"The situation got worse, because my father back here had grown very old now and would catch pneumonia every single winter, you can imagine.... My sister was married and lived here, the other sister was in Switzerland and my brother was still in France. My sister here, she had to look after her own family and take care of our parents too, it wasn't really fair on her. We'd had the baby for three months now and we had to decide whether he should grow up in France or Italy. So we decided to come back. And that way we could lend a hand to my sister." (R107/8)

The powerful sense of 'obligation' to move in order to support sibling carers, as much as to provide care directly themselves, was a feature of women's lives reported in a previous project (Ackers, 1998). In the following example the woman interviewed expresses a strong sense of guilt at being unable to return to support her ageing parents in Scotland and her sister-in-law who, in her absence, had taken on the prime responsibility for care. The case is interesting as it illustrates the tensions within many migrant families, particularly following family breakdown and remarriage. Linda had originally moved to Italy in the 1960s on a short-term basis following completion of her degree. Having met an Italian man she then remained. Following the breakdown of that relationship Linda met another Italian partner (whom she did not marry) who had a son and daughter (and grandchildren) from a previous marriage. In this case, the spread of family resources and competing kinship obligations mean that Linda is unable to provide care for her parents:

"I miss my parents, because they're very old now. They're beginning to have problems and I do feel a guilt-complex for not being there to help out.... My sister-in-law takes the bulk of the responsibility, and my brother too, I can only visit on certain occasions."

Q: "Would you be able to go back to Scotland should they need you?"

"No. No, unfortunately I have to say no. If I were alone, if I were single yes, I could say yes, I could leave my job for an amount of time and I could go, but not being single with my partner.... He wouldn't accept it. Obviously for a short time he would, for a few weeks no problem but on a long-term basis no, it would be very difficult. I feel torn actually. That's a problem, something that nags on my mind but there's nothing I can do about it. I must take things as they come." (L101)

Similar pressures came to bear in the next example involving an Italian couple who moved repeatedly throughout their married life in response to the husband's employment. While the wife accepted the expediency of these moves for work, she has in recent years grown to resent her inability to return to Italy to care for her mother. Their three children were all born in different countries and now two live in Portugal where they married Portuguese men, while the other has moved to Venezuela. The case also illustrates the quite typical dominance of the husband in migration decision-making (see Ackers, 1998, 2001; Ackers and Stalford, 2002):

"[Analisa never worked] I had three children and a husband whose profession implied travelling. We almost went around the world. My daughter stayed here (in Portugal) because she was working. After that my husband retired, so we came back to Portugal, selfishly [tone of resentment] for he has no more family back in Italy. He recalled Portugal as being a country in which it was cheaper to live, in which one could lead a good life. Our daughter was here and now we have two grandchildren, besides he enjoys playing golf. I would rather go back to Italy because my mother is old and she needs company. All my family is there, it would only be natural for me to go back, but my husband was glad to come back to Portugal, more than I was."

"[Living in Portugal] wasn't my choice. It is my husband's preference. Really I had preferred to go back to Italy. There, I have my family, but my husband didn't want to because his relatives have already died and he thinks he has more quality and more freedom here, in Portugal.... Right now my husband is absent for one of our son's could not find a job in Portugal, so our younger son went to Caracas and my husband went with him to help him start a business. My husband and son have been in Venezuela for the last three months. If my husband dies I will surely return to Italy. And I will come to visit my children often." (324)

The majority of cases discussed in the previous section have involved return moves in order to provide care. This pattern fits to some extent with the 'model' proposed by Litwak and Longino (1987) as a framework for studying intergenerational proximity. This 'developmental' model predicts that moves made by older people may be classified into three categories (arranged chronologically):

- amenity-related moves following retirement;
- return moves to be closer to friends and family members following a decline in health or following the death of a spouse;
- moves to institutions.

Our findings support to some extent the importance of 'amenity' in initial post-retirement moves (although this is less of a factor among the returning workers). The association of the second phase of return migration with increasing dependency is, however, less clear-cut. Litwak and Longino infer (although it is not clear) that such moves are made in response to the increasing dependency of the migrant themselves and some evidence of this and the final category of moves to access institutional care is provided later. The material presented in this section, on the other hand, presents a somewhat different picture of the relationship between evolving dependency and mobility as the migrant retiree returns in order to support dependent relatives back home.

We have seen, in the examples given, how the process of moving rarely implies a disinterest in, or a neglect of, caring responsibilities in the home state. One alternative to the prospect of returning to care lies in the exercise of legal rights under Community law, to take ascendant and dependent relatives with them or to bring them over to join them. In the second of the previous case studies, Mary noted how her mother-in-law had, 'stayed with us wherever we had been' but sadly the plans to convert their accommodation in order to support a very sick relative proved unsuccessful and they were forced to return home to care. This provides yet another example of the difficulties of moving around with disabled dependants. In practice the findings of this study echo those of the gender and migration research in this regard; exercising the legal right to be joined by ascendant relatives is often simply not practically possible or, necessarily in the best interests of the persons concerned. It is often difficult for such very elderly or perhaps confused persons to settle and integrate in the host state. Where such moves do take place the pressure on carers is enormous as other social and support networks are dislocated, significantly increasing dependency.

In a small number of cases respondents reported having taken older dependants with them to the host state in order to be able to continue to care while also fulfilling their own needs (in terms of healthcare, and so on) and wishes to move. The following example illustrates the kind of situation that arises: the mother-in-law had already become 'dependent' and was living with the respondent in the UK prior to their move and moved with them to Spain, partly to promote her health and that of the respondent (in that sense the respondent was both carer and in need of care). Faced with more serious ill health (typically more acute problems) the family return with the intention of moving again once the caring relationship comes to an end:

> "It really started because I had a problem with my chest, lung trouble, and the doctor said a warmer climate would help, and Mark's mother, who lives with us, had had a stroke. A warm climate would help her health also.... We didn't

stop to think about it, underneath there was a garage and it had been dug out and we thought it would make a marvellous opportunity for Mark's mother to have a self-contained flat under there."

[They returned when her mother-in-law's health deteriorated]

"We'd be off tomorrow if we could but we are stuck for the moment with Mark's mother's failing health, which really we're in abeyance. What we've done, we've bought a little caravan, which is on the side of the property, and a sort of plan is that once we are free and able to ... we'd take the caravan over to Spain and stay with friends." (R102)

The arrangements made, in this case, to enable the couple to return and continue to support Mark's mother raise some of the issues discussed in Chapter Three. What are the legal implications of living in a caravan on their return, for example? Would this be adequate to satisfy the habitual residence test or are they, by taking such steps, effectively disentitling themselves to citizenship claims in the UK? Certainly, as previously noted, those persons with the financial resources to maintain a proper residence in the home state are at an advantage in this respect and can more easily massage the system to maximise their access to benefits.

The problems we have already discussed of moving dependent and confused family members presented itself in the next case but in a rather different and interesting context. Here the person in need of care had already migrated from the UK to Spain earlier in her retirement and was now quite frail and unable or unwilling to return home in order to be cared for by her family. Her retired son and his wife therefore moved out to live in Spain in order to look after her. In terms of formal legal rights, the son in this case is unable to claim the full citizenship available to the children of migrant workers as his mother had never worked in the host state. As he is not himself undertaking paid work in the host state, but rather caring, his residence is contingent on his ability to satisfy the resources requirement and eschew any claims to social citizenship in the host state. It is situations like this that challenge the validity and equity of legal distinctions and the concept of economic contribution. The man concerned is clearly reducing the burden that his mother would otherwise place on the host state and, in that sense, making a genuine economic contribution while, in the process, restricting his own economic and citizenship status and the welfare claims he is able to make in the host state[2]. While both he and his mother may be entitled in the UK to disability and carer's benefits, social security benefits designed to support carers are, in general, not transportable. A similar situation was considered by the Court of Justice in *Snares*. In this case a British worker with severely impaired mobility following an accident at work was in receipt of disability living allowance in the UK. He decided to settle in Tenerife in order to be cared for by his mother. Following his move, the UK authorities set aside his disability living allowance on the grounds that he was no longer resident in the UK. The Court of Justice found that this was not contrary to Regulation 1408/71 as certain forms of social security benefit were not transportable[3].

These cases raise some interesting issues and may represent an increasingly common situation as the population of retirement migrants begins to age. While legal rights exist to move frail and disabled relatives to join their family abroad, in practice this often proves difficult to exercise. On the other hand, the benefits available at domestic level to support these persons and their carers are not transportable. The 'option' of moving to support dependent relatives in the host state is likely to become increasingly prevalent as the population of retired migrants age. Another example of this kind of situation is provided next.

Oliver's mother had initially moved in with him in England, following the death of her husband. When Oliver's job demanded a move to Singapore, the mother moved to Spain accompanying her brother and sister-in-law who were moving out there to live. There she stayed for some 20 years until she became ill. By this time her brother had sold up and returned. Oliver then took early retirement at the age of 54 and moved with his wife to Spain to support his mother who refused to return to the UK. Finally, they brought her back to the UK as they were no longer able to provide the level of care she needed:

"She was, by the time I retired, the age of 82, and she was becoming infirm, and it had been for the last year or so up to that time a case of her being ill and we had to go out there, drop everything and organise ourselves. So there she was, getting infirm, and we couldn't see how we could, on retirement, be able to keep popping over there, because it's quite an expensive business, and that among other things decided us that we would go and spend a few years, we thought, in the first place, which we thought would see her out, and then we would come back. Well, she was my responsibility, there was no-one else to share it, and it seemed to be a reasonable way to have a couple of years of sunshine and sangria, if you like, and at the same time attend to her needs because it was thought then that she had only a year or two to live. It was really aimed at being a short-term venture, a couple of years, but it didn't turn out like that because she lived until she was 89. So that took us into our seventh year there."

"[At the age of 89] ... the local doctor said that we really ought to do something about it because she's going to have to go into some sort of care and the care there was pretty Dickensian, so we made arrangements to get her into a nursing home back in England, and that's where she spent the last nine months of her life. She fought against it in the first place, and I understood that it was a very difficult decision to have to make and I'd been more or less responsible for her at that time for something over thirty years, and one wanted to do what was best, but at the same time it had got to the stage where we were getting old, we couldn't do all the things that we ought to be able to do, when she was ill we couldn't lift her out of the bed and to the bathroom and things like that." (R002)

Once again this case emphasises the 'two generation' issue and the importance of recognising the contribution of younger retired persons in the care of frail older relatives. The examples presented in the previous section evidence the relationship between care and mobility in the context of movements to provide care. The experiences of this group of retired citizen-carers underlines the problem of existing legal categories and the characterisation of retired persons as dependent and in need of support. Many older retired people move in order to support family members and, in the process, make a significant economic contribution by taking pressure off domestic welfare systems and supporting their adult children to continue in employment.

The research also identified a number of cases in which mobility was precipitated by the need to access care themselves, typically in the later phases of retirement. To some extent the following stories evidence the weaknesses of host society welfare systems, particularly in the provision of nursing and community care, raising broader questions about welfare diversity and territorial justice across the EU. The quality of formal provision is, however, only a part of the story and in many cases respondents talked of their emotional need to be near family and 'home' at this stage in their lives.

Moving for care

We referred in Chapter Four to the importance of retirement planning. Part of the overall retirement 'plan' for many older people involved the idea of a subsequent return 'home' at the point at which they needed support or when either partner died (as Litwak and Longino, 1987, predict). In all, 23 respondents said that they either had or would consider returning home for care. In some cases this was not a plan as such but presented itself as something of a crisis, whereas for others it was carefully anticipated. The reasons for returning can be divided into two groups. The first group emphasised their desire to be nearer to family and their children in particular when they need support. The second, on the other hand, argued quite strongly against reliance on family, either because they felt that this was an undue burden on their children or that it undermined their own autonomy. Instead, they planned to locate themselves in some form of sheltered or residential care. In other words this latter group were moving, in keeping with Litwak and Longino's model, to access institutional care.

We have already referred to the geography of retirement migration and the fact that flows are typically away from the more socialised systems of care associated with northern Europe and in the direction of the 'mother-daughter' economies of the southern European countries in which families play a significant role in the provision of care for older relatives. In that sense it is not so much that they are denied legal access to state provision but simply that little in the way of community services or residential provision exists. Indeed, in an example that blurs the distinction between formal and informal care, the following respondent spoke of the problems in accessing public medical care as an older person with no family living nearby in Greece:

"In cases of major surgery and after-nursing care, which is important, we've seen that Greek people are forced to bring in relatives or their own nurses which they pay for." (403)

In another case a man, now aged 68, had married a much younger woman with the intention of them both moving to Corfu. At the time of the interview the wife had, however, returned in order to care for her father (aged 87) and also to return to work as a care assistant in a residential home. Reflecting on his own situation and the potential need for support in the future, he expresses a wish for his wife to move to Greece to care for him. In the event that she would not do so he feels he would be forced to return.

"[My wife] only comes in the summer for three weeks. I did go back last October but she's working and she's very, very, busy and it is difficult. She works for an agency but she's self-employed, and it's unbelievable. You don't realise how many people there are that can't help themselves, or need help. It's amazing. So, if I got to that stage, I hope she'd come and look after me but if she didn't, then I would have a problem and I would probably have to go back to England. Obviously, here, there wouldn't be that facility." (426)

It comes as no surprise, therefore, that a number of key informants interviewed in the receiving countries referred to the pressures on older retirees to return home when faced with the need for support. The following examples are all provided by Greek or Portuguese key informants.

"I guess the biggest worry is the medical problems. What will happen if the people are getting older and hospitalised? I think it could be a very big problem in the future. I think that the British Council is very worried about, extremely worried about, the people in their 50s who in another 20 years may not be in a condition to look after themselves anymore and it's a time bomb because we don't have the facilities for old age persons [in Greece]. That is going to be a problem. People in their 50s are still active, they don't think that in 20 years life could be different. Some of them [will return], some of them stay as long as they can. But you have to remember as well that people who left children in England, maybe they will have to return sometime. Someone has to look after them." (K405)

"When they can no longer take care of themselves, who is going to do that here in Greece? They prefer to go back home so the state will take care of them again. They all end up back in their countries." (K400)

"Corfu is not so well organised to offer global services to foreign people who have a lot of needs. They will return to their countries of origin if they experience difficulties, for instance medical difficulties. They go to old people's homes or close to their children. The majority will return." (K406)

"As for support services to older people, either Portuguese or foreigners, they are very few, especially in terms of residential care." (K305)

"They are people who make very discreet lives. Therefore, it is why we don't notice them … when their life conditions get worse they go back to their country. They stay in Portugal only in some hard cases." (L312)

The key informants' analyses of the situation do not suggest that the population of retired migrants place an undue burden on host social security systems, but rather (as argued in Chapter Five) that, when need arises, they return home to access family care or the support of their home welfare system.

The right of the dependent ascendant relatives of Community migrant workers to join their children in the host state has already been discussed. The following example provides a case in point illustrating the complex dynamics and negotiations taking place across geographical and social spaces that characterise the 'doing' of transnational kinship. The interviewee visited Italy on holiday with her parents, met a young Italian man and moved to Italy to marry him. She has remained there ever since despite the breakdown of her marriage:

"Even when I got separated I never thought of going back to France – my daughters are Italian, my life is here, the most important things I've done in my life are here.… My sister is in France, but my brother is gradually moving here and I think he'll soon decide to stop here for good. On the other hand I've moved my parents to Italy. My mother died two years ago. They had already been living here for some time and my father lives [nearby] now. It wasn't easy to convince them because my father was already old and they only accepted to come because I was here." (L106)

The following case is cited in some detail to give an impression of the relationship between care and mobility. The couple's moves, since retirement, have been very much motivated by different and competing ideas around care. In the first instance they left Sweden in order to make fiscal gains, but with the intention of returning to claim a return on past contributions. The way they describe the situation is interesting as they talk initially about moves to effectively evade Swedish taxation but later refer to return moves in order to access the benefits they have contributed towards during their working lives. This is precisely the kind of deliberation referred to in Chapters Five and Six when we talked about the differential ability of retired migrants to tailor a citizenship package optimising their access to benefits across the mixed economy of welfare and global social and economic space (see also Dwyer, 2000a, 2000b, 2001).

The respondents refer to the importance of care in their migration decision, their role as care providers for their divorced daughter and her children and the importance of this to their own sense of purpose and their daughter's ability to work. In that sense they clearly feel it is important to them to be making a useful contribution to society. They also talk of their own care needs in the future.

[Wife] "Swedes usually move because of financial reasons. When we moved to France, you really gained a lot of money, because of the taxes. When we decided to go abroad, we were planning to stay one year.... But that year turned into two years, and five years, and finally thirteen years. If you've been living in Sweden for a major part of your life, like we have, and a lot of other Swedes who are now living in France.... Then, you've contributed with a lot of money to the Swedish society, and you want to get some use of this money as well. If you move to another country, you have to pay a lot of money yourself. But if you choose to return to Sweden, you will get at least some of that money back...."

"We have four children. And one reason why we moved back to Sweden ... or rather why we moved back right then, and to this place.... One of our daughters is living just next door. She's divorced and she's got two small children. When we moved to Sweden our grandson was one year old and our granddaughter four years old. Today, we're quite busy baby-sitting. We pick them up at the day-care centre and ... it's great. In case she needs a baby-sitter we can be there within a minute. And there's another advantage.... When our children left home and built their own families they all left Stockholm. Therefore, we've never been living that close to our grandchildren. Altogether, we've got ten grandchildren and the oldest ones are practically grown-ups. But today, two of them are living just on the other side of the street and that's great. And at the same time, we're helping our daughter so that she can keep her job.... Actually, I felt that way during our last years in France, because I knew that she was going through a hard time, and that she needed our help. And that was one of the reasons why we decided to move back to Sweden."

[Husband] "Yes, and I think it's important to stress that.... If you're planning to move to another country, it's important to make sure that you have something to spend your time with.... To have some kind of meaningful task, to make sure that you're actually needed. That's really important. We had decided that we wanted to move back because of social reasons. We didn't want to stay in France until one of us passed away.... We both wanted to go home, while we were still able to walk upright. We totally agreed on this. But we've noticed that the older one gets, the more one wants to move back to Sweden. It's much more common.... Because ... we've seen some tragic examples ... people who stay in France until it's too late to move back.... Then, they don't have the strength to move. And they have a really hard time in France.... They really do. Yes, and even though the safety net improves all the time, these people are very much depending on other Swedes. Naturally, French people don't care that much about the safety of foreigners...."

[Wife] "Yes, there are some options.... But imagine yourself as the only Swede in a home for elderly [sic] people, where everybody speaks nothing but French. Even though you originally have a good command of French ... the older one gets, the more one loses.... When you're really old, you can't speak any language fluently apart from your home language. And then, you're really vulnerable. We didn't want to end up in a situation like this." (R220)

The case outlined above illustrates the limitations of mainstream migration theory and its tendency to identify a single, typically economic, determinative factor as central to the shaping of migration decisions. The problems with this approach can be seen in the sheer complexity of many decisions as the individuals concerned weigh up a number of different economic and other quality of life factors. It also illustrates the importance of understanding migration decision-making as an ongoing process evolving over the life course in response to both predictable and serendipitous events rather than a single, atemporal decision.

The respondents in this case clearly understand the importance of the whole range of welfare services to their well-being, including the statutory sector, fiscal benefits, family care and, interestingly, the voluntary sector. The importance of the expatriate communities both in terms of direct provision of care and also in advocacy and stimulating the development of voluntary services is remarked on by King et al (2000) who cite examples of the development of a hospice movement in Spain and cancer services, including palliative care services, a previously 'alien' tradition in southern Europe (cf Betty and Cahill, 1999; O'Reilly, 2000b). The respondent's comments about the value of the Swedish expatriate community and the concerns around language and residential care are repeated in some of the following examples. In a number of cases alternative arrangements had been made in order to enable the respondents to remain in the host state and avoid reliance on family care. The previous case discussed at some length (R220) suggests that returning retirees may be motivated not so much by the supply of informal care in the home state but rather by the existence of community and residential facilities.

Notwithstanding the criticisms, in terms of methodology and theoretical assumptions, the selection of partner countries for this research was based loosely on the literature on comparative social policy and 'welfare regimes' as the basis for effective contextualisation. The point about the direction of migration flows away from more institutionalised welfare systems and into more rudimentary systems based on family care has already been made and has important implications in terms of the material value of Community rights. The interviews with retirees suggest that this approach was useful, not only in identifying gaps in welfare provision (the paucity of community nursing in southern Europe, for example), but also in understanding the values and moral standpoints shaping the use of services and, in this context, migration decisions. The sample of Swedish returnees thus talked far more positively about the prospect of returning to Sweden in order to access residential and sheltered care, while southern European returnees spoke disparagingly of the erosion of family values and the lack of family support for senior citizens in northern Europe and their fears of institutional care. This material reminds us of the importance of going beyond a simple enumeration of the levels and quality of services to try to understand culturally transmitted values and perceptions of alternative care arrangements (although of course the two are linked) and the 'proper thing to do'. The research thus suggests a link between 'cultures of care' and migration decisions.

In the next example, the respondent, now aged 86, specifically suggests that she returned in order to avoid putting pressure on her daughter to care. The woman first moved to the UK in her twenties as an au pair and married a British man some years older than herself. He later developed Parkinson's disease and she spent several years looking after him before he died. Then, aged 52, she did not immediately consider a return to Sweden as her daughter had just got married and she didn't want to leave her in England. She also wasn't sure whether she would be able to support herself in Sweden. She subsequently met a new partner but they did not marry as this would have meant her losing her widow's pension[4]:

> "We lived together for a couple of years without being married. And this wasn't always that easy.... We couldn't get married, because then I would have lost my pension. We really wanted it though.... But it was impossible, since he was a widower and I was a widow. But if we'd got married, I would have lost my pension. And after his death, I wouldn't have got his pension either. That was the law.... It was a shame...."

The man was 14 years older than the interviewed woman and once again passed away. She then moved to live near her daughter for a while, before returning on her own to Sweden at the age of 82.

> "I remember thinking, I can't live in England because I don't know anyone. I didn't know the surroundings or anything. I felt very lonely. And then I got the opportunity to get to a place like this, where I had friends and ... so ... I thought that moving back home was the best thing that I could do. I had longed for Sweden a lot. The older one gets, one feels much more.... It becomes much more important where you're born. I think so. They are a lot freer now, because they don't have to think about me. My mother-in-law stayed with us for eight years, after we got married. So I know ... exactly what it's like having a mother-in-law in the house. I wouldn't like to repeat it. I didn't take care of my own mother though. She came to visit us once every year, but she had her home in Sweden. I didn't have to bother. But as I've told you, I know exactly what it's like, and I don't want my daughter to have the same kind of trouble."

> "A close friend of mine had a sister-in-law who was originally from Hungary. And when she got old, she became a bit senile. And then she forgot all about her life in England. She couldn't even speak the English language. She didn't fit in at all anymore. And I wouldn't like to be in that position.... There is a home for elderly [sic] people in London, close to the Swedish church. But I didn't want to move there, because they only spoke English." (R206)

The interviewed woman is clearly acutely aware of the kinds of tensions caused within families as a result of intensive care giving and is keen to ensure that she does not become a 'burden' on her own family. She speaks very positively about her decision to return and the opportunity to move to a special kind of sheltered scheme for older women (provided by the Queen and staffed by Polish nuns).

The desire to maintain autonomy and cushion family from the implications of dependency also motivates the following woman who, in common with the previous three respondents, effectively organises for herself some form of institutional care in the home state. Maria has been widowed twice (firstly at the age of only 23). Her second marriage to a retired man, at the age of 50, precipitated the move from Portugal to Holland. They lived together for seven years before he died and then she remained in Holland for a further nine years before returning to Portugal to be with her family. Maria said that her family (she has no children) had asked her to live with them but, "I'd rather keep my independence and I don't want to disturb anybody". She now lives in a residential home provided by the Salvation Army (R318).

Other respondents were attracted to return by what they understood to be better levels of community support provided in northern and western European countries. The following couple moved to Germany and then the UK for work reasons leaving their two adult daughters in Sweden. Following a period of some 26 years in the UK the wife developed an eye disorder that eventually resulted in the loss of her sight. Her husband also became ill.

> "We started to wind up the business, and I really wanted to go back to Sweden. In Sweden, it's a lot easier to get help. They didn't offer me any home-help service or anything. I had to pay for it privately. I don't mean to complain, but they didn't have that much to offer to visually handicapped people. And then, I had to undergo several surgeries and ... it was really difficult. In 1988, we moved back to Sweden. By that time, I was sixty-eight years old, and my husband was sixty-nine. We found this apartment, a three-room flat at the ground-level. And this is where I live today as well."

> "In Sweden, the support for visually impaired people is much more developed. Today, I suppose it's a bit different, but then ... they couldn't offer me any help at all. Unless you can afford it, and it's very expensive. And I don't think they have a lot of service flats [residential care] either. In Sweden, they are building a lot of places like this. In Sweden, I think the care for elderly [sic] people is much more organised. We had [planned to return to Sweden]. Even though we were living abroad we were longing to be back in our home-country. I think most people do.... And since we had a daughter living in Sweden and another one in Copenhagen." (R216)

In addition to the point about residential care as a factor shaping return decisions, this case echoes the concerns raised elsewhere around the mobility of people with disabilities and the limited value of rights based on non-discrimination in the context of uneven provision.

The man in the next example told of how, while the majority of Swedish retirees returned home when they needed support, some of his friends employed private 'carers' in Spain. In this case the couple actually returned because they were attracted to a type of sheltered scheme. The Swedish interviewer sets the scene:

> The housing is quite special, since they live in an area with exclusively elderly [sic] people. In the same area, there are houses, apartments, nursing homes and all kinds of facilities. In Sweden, it's rather uncommon with all these facilities gathered in a small area. The establishment was originally founded by the Swedish church, at the beginning of this century. A few years ago, the woman had a cerebral haemorrhage, and since then she has got some difficulties with her memory. Furthermore, she has some problems with her hips, and she uses a wheelchair. The couple moved repeatedly in the diplomatic service and have lived in [twelve countries] and most recently, in Tenerife:

> "During our time in Tenerife, we met a family who had applied to this place. Actually, there are three families living here who used to live in Tenerife. So that's the reason why we applied to this place. If we hadn't got the offer to move here, we might have stayed abroad. Actually, I think we would have. Or I don't really know.... In one way, I think we've always planned to return to Sweden. And I suppose that's the way it is; when you get old, you want to return to your home country. There, you have your family and your roots. I don't know a lot of people who've decided to stay abroad.... Most of them return to Sweden. When we considered staying abroad, we didn't think about the medical service or.... We just thought that it would be nice because of the climate and things like that. I only know of three Swedish families who have decided to stay in Tenerife. The rest of them were moving back to Sweden, when they started to get old. All of them.... One of the Swedish women who decided to stay in Tenerife, she has employed a girl who is looking after her. And another one, she has a [paid carer]. They are old, they really are.... They have employed two Swedish girls to look after them. But they are married to Spanish men, these girls." (R209)

The cases discussed above have all involved a return move in order to access statutory support services as a means of insulating family from the obligation to take on full responsibility for their care. The respondent in the last example also talks of the less formal arrangements some retirees made for their care, effectively 'importing' Swedish women to look after them, as one might use an au pair[5]. It would be interesting to discuss with such people the reasons for their preference for Swedish employees. This may reflect the concerns other respondents have raised about a decline in linguistic competence with old age. In the following case, unique in this study but perhaps not so in the broader context of elder care, a German bachelor living alone in Italy had made arrangements to 'employ' a young Russian woman, on an 'informal' basis, as a housekeeper/carer.

> "By chance I met a Russian woman who came here some time ago. She stayed in Italy for a month and I put her up for a week and when she was here she cleaned my house, she cleaned it so well, that it became absolutely spotless! Perfect! I bought her a lot of things, a coat, shoes, skirts, and so on – she was very happy too – and she said she will come back.... I received a letter from her the other day. She is trying to obtain all the necessary papers to come here again as a tourist and I told her 'If it's necessary I'll marry you to enable you to stay here' because I need her to stay here. She is an orphan, her parents died when she was 14. I have no problems. If she wants to, I'll marry her. She's 31, she's a young woman. I told her 'You've seen where I live, if you want to come down, you're welcome', because I need a woman to keep me company and to keep my house." (R102)

This case raises some complex and difficult issues around gender relations, care and migration that fall beyond the scope of this book. What the respondent describes as a mutually convenient and apparently consensual agreement clearly imposes a severe restraint on the young woman concerned. Nevertheless, it illustrates the problem some retired migrants face growing old in isolation, away from sources of family and statutory support and the range of responses to this.

Conclusions

Generally speaking, the literature on international migration emphasises the dynamic of work and economic imperatives over and above all other factors, rarely if ever examining life course and caring as components of migration decisions. The domination of economic-determinism in migration theory predicts a predominantly linear process perhaps in two stages with family reunion following the initial 'pioneering' move of the migrant worker motivated almost exclusively by profit-maximisation. The material presented above emphasises the importance of understanding retirement migration as a process in constant flux. The close link between life course events and the progressive unfolding of caring relationships means that, in practice, people are involved in a series of migration decisions and an almost constant reappraisal of their situation. International moves may thus be precipitated by the need to care or the need for care and, in many cases, such considerations figure in location decisions and also 'non-decisions' – in other words delaying planned moves. In this context return moves are particularly indicative and it is no surprise that the majority of respondents selected in this chapter are in fact returnees (those cases in which the document number is prefaced with an 'R'). It is thus absolutely essential, in order to promote a comprehensive understanding of retirement migration decision-making and the role of care in this process, to conceptualise such mobility in terms of a succession of decisions encompassing return moves and to develop research approaches that capture this.

Understanding the implications of migration on the distribution of caring obligations and resources also demands recognition of the dispersal of families across international space. It is far too simplistic to assume a 'two location' context with the migrant person leaving his or her family in the home state. Evidence of the effects of migration on family structures and the dislocation of kinship networks and caring resources has been referred to in the author's work on gender and migration (Ackers, 1998), the mobility of researchers (Ackers, 2001) and children (Ackers and Stalford, 2002). These studies have all identified a common tendency within families with some history of migration for a more complex dispersal of parents and siblings, often to different international locations. This phenomenon may reflect the nature of 'chain' migrations associated with the economic migration of workers from southern to northern Europe in search of work and economic improvement. Indeed, many of the respondents in Italy, Greece and Portugal reported the dislocation of entire communities and villages[6].

The effect of this geographical dispersion of families on subsequent mobility is evident from the interviews. In a number of cases, typically involving that group of Community migrant workers who returned home following retirement, the return was precipitated by the needs of older dependants in the home state. Quite often, however, the children of these returnees were born in the host state or moved to join their parents following a period of being cared for by grandparents in the preschool years and remained in the host state. The retiree is thus faced with the prospect of leaving their children in the host state in order to return to care. In the longer term they may well face the decision of whether to return again to the host state to access the support of their own children in their later years.

On the other hand, it seems that the movement of one sibling or parent often creates an appetite and generates the confidence required for mobility. In such cases, rather than dealing with two locations, the family may be spread across a number of countries both within the EU and beyond and mobility may be ongoing, making it difficult for the retired migrant to anticipate the consequences of a move to join their children when their children may themselves move again!

The experiences of the respondents interviewed in this piece of research challenge the narrowly stereotypical perceptions of retirement and old age that form the basis of concepts of dependency and residency rights. The emerging picture of a fluid and responsive reciprocity of care giving and receiving over the life course draws attention to the active and meaningful contribution made by older people to the citizenship status of others, both young and old. To that extent the hard and fast distinctions that determine personal entitlement under Community law bear little relation to the social reality of mutual care and interdependency that characterises the lives of older people.

On another scale, the findings of this research raise fundamental questions about the limits of formal, legal citizenship in the context of globalisation and, more specifically, the freedom of movement throughout European social space. They indicate the importance of understanding citizenship as the function of a complex negotiation of legal, social and economic spaces, as those with the know how and financial backing are able, through careful orchestration of their residency status, to maximise their own material benefit and access to welfare.

Notes

[1] The free movement rights of people with disabilities and their carers (including paid personal assistants) forms the basis of a developing new study being developed within the Centre for the Study of Law in Europe.

[2] Social security benefits designed to support carers are, in general, not transportable.

[3] This point is discussed in Chapter Three and is also raised by Warnes (2002, p 143).

[4] This case illustrates some of the points about spousal rights discussed in Chapter Three.

[5] Ungerson (2000) notes, "paid formal care is far more gender skewed than unpaid informal care" (p 625) and refers to the bifurcation of the labour markets for domiciliary care. On the one hand there is the more regulated public sector, while on the other contains 'women workers on very low wages with poor working conditions', often finding work through private agencies. Both Ungerson and Williams (2001) refer to the importance of female migrant labour in this sector.

[6] The effect of previous mobility on proximity of kin is also noted by Warnes (1986).

EIGHT

Conclusions: retirement migration: the challenge to social citizenship?

The introductory chapter set out the research objectives underpinning the research on which this book is based. The retirement migration research together with a series of 'linked' studies of subgroups of intra-Community migrants represents a commitment to the evaluation of the development of Citizenship of the Union. More specifically, by focusing on Community nationals, we have sought to critique the presumption of universalism implied in the concept that all Community nationals share an equivalent status and experience. While other authors have referred to the ways in which Citizenship of the Union has created new forms of stratification (Kleinman, 2002), the level, complexity and justification for status differentiation within the population of European citizens has rarely been dealt with in any detail and in an empirical context[1].

The focus of this book has been on the status and experiences of retirement migrants within the European Union. As we have seen, this population does not represent a homogeneous group. From a legal point of view, it comprises a number of subgroups, which can be distinguished on the basis of their formal status. The movement of retired people thus provides an interesting and relevant case study for the examination of status differentiation. On the one hand it reveals important distinctions based on the quality and geography of legally significant forms of contribution. So contributing in the home state during ones working life and then migrating on retirement has different implications to moving during working life and then retiring in situ. Subsequent return also has legal implications. Furthermore, for those persons (mainly women) who have either taken time out of the labour market to care for families prior to moving or whose labour market participation has been disrupted as a consequence of their partner's employment, mobility may give rise to a less advantageous, derived status. Accompanying partners and family who fall outside Community definitions of family or dependency may be further disadvantaged. The evolution of family relationships, economic roles and migration trajectories over the life course thus shapes the legal entitlement of retired migrants. That entitlement translates into a differential ability to 'plug' into domestic welfare systems and claim social resources. These categories bear *no relation to demonstrable need*, but rather reflect the incremental way in which social citizenship rights have evolved, tracing and teasing away at the parameters of Community competence. Chapter Three set out these distinctions in formal status in some detail to illustrate the level of status differentiation and the discriminatory effect of Community law even within this population of retired Community nationals. European citizenship, at least in terms of formal legal rights, is by no means universal.

Chapter Two considered the relationship between Citizenship of the Union and concepts of equality. Formal equality in the context of Community law rests on the principle of non-discrimination. The scope of this principle demands some consideration if we are to make sense of the complex tiering of entitlement outlined previously. Article 39 EC echoes the provisions of Article 12 EC (the original non-discrimination clause) and refers simply to the abolition of discrimination on grounds of *nationality*. The EU's citizenship provisions suggest a broader approach and more inclusive status, however. While it restates the importance of nationality as a condition of membership, it goes on to state that, "Citizens of the Union shall enjoy the rights conferred by this Treaty". There is no suggestion here that the group of qualifying Community nationals might be further divided into distinct subcategories.

The introduction of a much wider non-discrimination clause in the Treaty of Amsterdam (Article 13) marked the development of a new legal base for action to "combat discrimination based on sex, racial or ethnic origin, religion or belief, disability, age or sexual orientation". Craig and de Búrca comment that,

> the existence of the new Article ends the uncertainty over the existence of Community competence to legislate in and actually to regulate (rather than merely adopting support measures in) such fields, and presumably will lead to the use of stronger legal measures and instruments than has hitherto been the practice. (1998, p 366)

To what extent can the kind of status differentiation we have identified be justified in the context of this new and more progressive commitment to non-discrimination? The reference to age in the text is clearly of immediate interest and calls into question the existence of a Community instrument that institutionalises a specific and contingent status for persons who have "ceased their occupational activity" (Council Directive 90/365/EC). The discussion in Chapter Three and the subsequent chapters detailing the status and experiences of retired migrants do not suggest that age discrimination is a key dimension of discrimination in this context, however. The primary concern would seem to focus around concepts of work (and 'valid' economic contribution), the legal valuation of certain forms of unpaid work (principally in the provision of informal care), the specific conceptualisations of family and dependency and the long-term impact of these over the life course.

Dependency and disability

The prohibition of discrimination on grounds of disability[2] perhaps presents a more fertile basis on which to challenge some aspects of status differentiation within our population. Increasing levels of impairment (Priestley, 2002), particularly in the 'fourth age', were evident in the material discussed in Chapter

Five, raising important issues about the relationship between mobility and care. The resources requirement contained in Council Directive 90/365 echoes these concerns around the movement of 'dependent' persons and the responsibility for their care and support. They must not, in the words of the Directive, "become an *unreasonable burden* on the public finances of the host member state". Residence is thus conditional on the persons concerned demonstrating that they have sufficient resources to render them ineligible for social assistance in the host state, "taking into account the personal circumstances of persons". Article 3 states that the right of residence shall remain for as long as the beneficiaries fulfil these conditions. What this would seem to imply is that an emerging impairment, perhaps some years following settlement in the host state, involving care needs that stretch the resources of the persons concerned taking them below the prescribed threshold, might extinguish their residency status. We have already noted the fact that social entitlement in Community law bears no relation to need; in the context of the previous discussion it would appear that legal rights to welfare bear an inverse relation to need – as needs evolve, rights wane. In this respect, EU legislation can be seen as disablist in its outcomes. The introduction of habitual residence tests in the home country may further restrict the social entitlement of those older people suffering from ill health and impairment on return.

In addition to the 'normal' process of ageing and the progressive evolution of dependency, we have seen evidence among our sample of returning southern European Community workers of welfare externalities in the form of work-related debilitating conditions and disabilities (see Chapter Four). This evidence underlines, in a very tangible fashion, the inequalities inherent in the notion of contribution. The costs of contributing, via paid work, fall unevenly; in some circumstances rather than giving rise to social rights as the basis of well-being and autonomy they generate new forms of impairment (and health inequalities), which may even precipitate premature exit from the PLM.

The concept of dependency also forms the basis of the interpretation of family in Community law and the rationale for the extension of citizenship entitlement to the families of Community migrants. It has been argued elsewhere that this conceptualisation presumes and reinforces relationships of dependency within families, between working and non-working spouses, parents and children (Ackers and Stalford, 1999), and migrants and ascendant relatives (Scheiwe, 1994; Ackers, 1998; Szyszczak and Moebius, 1998; McGlynn, 2000). Directive 90/365/EEC echoes the language of Council Directive 1612/68, in the context of the rights of retired migrants' families:

> Whereas that right can only be exercised if it is also granted to members of the family. The following shall, irrespective of their nationality, have the right to install themselves in another Member state with the holder of the right of residence:

> [a] his or her spouse and their descendants who are dependants

[b] dependent relatives in the ascendant line of the holder of the right of residence and his or her spouse.

The privileging of legal marriage, in this context, clearly renders non-working and particularly third country national spouses vulnerable to relationship breakdown, which potentially extinguishes access to social rights and, in the latter case, residence itself. It also raises questions around the legal status and autonomy of family members and their ability to remain in the host state should the status-holding citizen decide to leave the country.

The legal valuation of unpaid work

The privileging of paid work over and above other forms of contribution as the basis of social claims raises perhaps the most serious concerns. It is widely recognised that welfare states are heavily reliant on the contribution of informal carers (Pateman, 1992; Pascall, 1997). Nevertheless, growing concerns that, in the context of demographic change, measures may need to be taken to promote the role of this sector and actively stimulate the provision of family and voluntary care, to date this has not translated into proposals to regularise the legal status of care providers.

Before examining the definition of employment itself, and the extent to which the emphasis on paid work devalues other forms of social contribution that are not specifically economic (although they doubtless have financial implications for both the persons concerned and welfare systems), it is worth considering the justification for this emphasis on employment as economic contribution. Justification for the scope of legal competency in European Union policy making typically refers to the essentially free market foundations of the Treaty of Rome and the primacy attached, at least in the early stages, to economic union and competition policy. In that context, social policy was generally interpreted as falling outside the scope of Community law. Nevertheless, issues around the funding of member state social policy raise key economic questions of immediate relevance to the European project.

Social planning at domestic level generally assumes a relatively fixed population of contributors and recipients. Faist refers to citizenship as "the institutionalisation of generalised reciprocity and diffuse solidarity of members in a community" (2001, p 40). This notion of reciprocity so central to the functioning of welfare systems is, however, spatially delimited as fiscal considerations and actuarial processes presume a more or less static and boundaried populace and a progressive evolution of contribution followed by claim as the 'normal' life course unfolds and dependency ensues. Mobility increasingly challenges this mechanism in a very profound way. In a strict sense, the conditional status of post-retirement migrants could be justified on the basis that they have not made a spatially significant contribution (in the host state) against which to base a claim.

Contribution via national insurance and income tax is not, however, the sole means by which social citizenship is financed. Consumption and forms of consumption-related taxation (such as value added tax) form an increasing component of social income. VAT is 'footloose' and moves with the purchaser, and many retired migrants and returnees[3] make a significant financial contribution to the local economies in which they reside, many of which were previously characterised by depopulation and economic decline. It is interesting that this form of direct economic contribution, so important to the stimulation of peripheral coastal regions, does not provide access to citizenship in the same way as work does. Indeed, the Community law definition of work provides full access to host welfare systems to persons who, in practice, make a minimal economic contribution and even in situations where their residency is to the economic detriment of the host state. This was the case in *Kempf (v Staatsecretaris van Justitie)* where the 'worker's' income from part-time music lessons fell below the level of income triggering entitlement to income support (cf Chapter Three). The worker in this case would not be able to satisfy the resources requirement contained in Council Directive 90/365/EC. What distinguishes the moral claim of such a person from that of a retired person living in Corfu and purchasing goods and services in the local economy? The development of measures promoting the right to move in order to receive services specifically acknowledges the relationship between mobility and consumption and provides some limited protection to those moving on this basis; they do not, however, give rise to the social advantages attached to status of 'privileged aliens'.

In addition to the discrimination implied in favouring forms of direct income-related taxation as economic contribution there is the difficult question of the valuation of care and the respective claims of the citizen-carer and citizen-worker. Many studies have attempted to quantify the economic value of care work both in terms of the costs to carers (as a consequence of labour market withdrawal or limited career progression) and the savings to the exchequer (see Chapter Seven). This issue has taken on increasing salience in recent years with concerns over demographic change, population ageing, shifting dependency ratios and the pressures these imply for social services. And, of course, carers are also consumers! Arguably, the issue of the status of care and the impact of care on labour market participation (and hence the ability to make the most privileged form of contribution) should fall within Community competency in relation to the prohibition of discrimination on grounds of sex (to the extent that it effects mainly, but not exclusively, female carers). The distribution of caring roles within the family and the persistence of gender roles within the home seriously limit the opportunity of many women – at least at certain phases over the life course, and particularly those with migration histories – to undertake paid work and thus achieve full, independent, citizenship status. In that sense there is a profound inequality in the ability to make legally significant forms of contribution. The result of this is dependency.

Concerns around the reconciliation of work and family life have featured in European Commission policy agendas for many years now. Although legal competence has focused attention on the regulation of sex discrimination in the workplace, there is increasing recognition of the limitations of this formalistic approach to gender equality and a move towards a more substantive approach.

Szyszczak and Moebius note, in the context of the legal valuation of care, the potential of the new legal base (in Article 13) for a more holistic approach to equal treatment legislation that goes beyond the previous strengths in relation to equal pay, access to employment and occupational social security (1998, p 156). In addition they point to the commitment to mainstreaming equal opportunities in the new Employment Guidelines and the reference to family friendly policies, parental leave schemes and high quality care for children and other dependants as evidence of this new approach to equality. A recent programme designed to evaluate the impact of equal pay strategy on gender equality has taken these concerns on board and supported a detailed study of the legal valuation of unpaid work, gendered use of time and the consequences in terms of the achievement of equal pay[4]. With reference to Article 141 and the commitment to gender equality, Barnard (1999) asks the question as to whether there now exists a free-standing fundamental right to equality in Community law. For the time being she concludes that, "for the principle of equality to apply there must be some other Community law for the principle to bite on" (1999, p 232). Article 13 perhaps provides such an opportunity.

Szyszczak and Moebius (1998) outline a number of alternative approaches to deal with the current situation and the devaluation of care. These include a proposal by Scheiwe (1994) that interruptions in labour market participation arising from caring responsibilities for a specified period (she suggests a period of three years after the birth of the youngest child) should not be taken as 'dropping out' of the labour market. Alternatively, they suggest that breaks in paid work for care could be considered to fall within the concept of *involuntary unemployment* (cf Chapter Three). Such persons would therefore continue to fall within the definition of the working population. Lister raises some problems with these kinds of citizen–carer approaches as potentially institutionalising an inferior status for carers and reinforcing gendered boundaries, "locking women further into a caring role" (1997, p 187). She concludes with the proposal that rather than replacing the citizen–worker with the citizen–carer, the conditions need to be created in which citizen–worker/carer and carer/earner can flourish in a non–gendered way (1997, p 201). The key challenge here lies in the domestic division of labour and the politics of time-use. Szyszczak and Moebius (1998) come to a similar conclusion that "it is necessary to translate the economic value of care into legal terms and to extend the notion of the market to include unpaid care work and the notion of the 'worker' to include all persons who provided such care" (p 21). This approach, they suggest, would have a number of advantages. Firstly, it taps directly into the dominant economic discourse and is therefore more likely to be successful. Secondly, it has the advantage of providing a uniform and more inclusive concept of the 'market' and 'worker' in Community law, "one that applies equally to the free movement provisions as to Community equal treatment law" (1998, p 156).

This latter approach might also have the benefit of taking a much wider view of the contribution of care. Measures proposed by Scheiwe (1994) would have an important impact on younger women with children; care is a life course issue and many women and men are caring for older and/or disabled persons. In that context, tying the extension of entitlement to a specific parenting period may prove to be an inadequate and exclusive approach. Thinking specifically about our sample, it could broaden the focus away from a concern simply with childcare and acknowledge the contribution of senior citizens who are carers. Recent developments in the Court of Justice suggest a movement in a similar direction, albeit with impetus coming from another source, as the concept of citizenship is tied more closely to the emergent human rights discourse at Community level.

Citizenship and human rights

The exclusionary tendencies of citizenship at both EU and member state level have led some (for example, Turner, 1993) to consider the more positive potential of an approach to meeting needs centred around the concept of human rights. Lister also contends that human rights "provide a potential tool for sculpting a more inclusionary model of citizenship" (1997, p 60). The extension of social citizenship rights to migrant workers has been justified in recent cases, not solely on the grounds of labour mobility, but on the grounds of freedom and justice. Advocate General Jacob expressed this view in *Konstantinidis* (*v Stadt Altensteig-Standesamt*), demonstrating the important relationship between European citizenship and notions of freedom and dignity:

> Community law ... regards [the migrant worker] as a human being who is entitled to live in that State 'in freedom and dignity' (see the Fifth recital in the Preamble to Regulation 1612/68 on freedom of movement for workers within the Community) and to be spared any difference in treatment which would render his life less comfortable physically or psychologically than the lives of the native population. (paras 24 and 25)

The argument for the extension of social rights on the grounds that they safeguard dignity and freedom makes it hard to justify current distinctions in the rights of retired migrant workers and indeed other mobile citizens. In the context of family members and concerns around derived or adjectival rights, O'Leary (1998) presents a 'fundamental rights' case for the extension of an independent right of entitlement to family members. She criticises the Court's decision in *Diatta* (a case concerned with the impact of divorce on spousal rights and discussed in Chapter Three) on the basis that it fails to identify the fundamental rights concerned. More specifically, the Court did not address the Commission's claims that it would be contrary to fundamental rights if the Regulation enabled a worker to "remove, unilaterally and arbitrarily, the protection accorded by Community law to the members of his [or her] family". The Court, according to O'Leary, had two options:

> ... either to construe the Community measure in such a way that it does not conflict with human rights norms or to strike the Community measure down.

In failing to do so:

> Community law has left spouses and family members of migrant workers in a particularly vulnerable position.... The Court's decisions have endorsed a dependent condition for the spouses of Community workers. By failing to address whether they may rely on fundamental human rights to support their residence in a Member State and not simply their derivative and highly circumscribed Community rights, the Court has not offered the legal protection which it could, and should, have done. (1998, p 263)

The arguments from substantive equality and human rights perspectives, respectively, have thus been used to justify a more substantial incursion into areas of domestic social policy previously caught by the subsidiarity principle as areas of concurrent or shared competence.

Fixed laws, fluid lives

We have referred so far to the problems of status differentiation in terms of the justification for the categories themselves and the basis on which certain people have been excluded. Chapter Three considered these issues in some depth but also went beyond this to consider the problems of status differentiation – and 'fixed categories' – in the context of social reality. The clear distinction in status between persons on the basis of migration, marital and family/dependency status presume the existence of relatively static and predictable life courses and relationships. In practice the population of retired migrants, in common with most populations, is characterised rather by diversity, fluidity and flux. Retirement migrants do not represent a homogeneous group; the flows of people who move in later life include a wide range of personal and economic situations. In many cases migration decisions evolve in an incremental fashion resulting in a series of outward and return moves in response to their own and their families' needs. At one end of the scale migration is indistinguishable from tourism and seasonal migration, while at the other it amounts to full residency. The migration trajectories of many individuals are characterised by a shifting in and out of these diverse forms of mobility (each conveying a specific legal status) as their lives unfold, perhaps triggered by an enjoyable vacation experience, shifting into a period of seasonal or 'snowbird' tourism, then purchasing or renting a property and moving more or less permanently for a time before contemplating a phased return 'home' (see Chapter Four).

In another context, the experiences of the respondents interviewed in this piece of research challenge the narrowly stereotypical perceptions of retirement and old age that form the basis of concepts of dependency and residency rights. The emerging picture of a fluid and responsive reciprocity of care giving and receiving over the life course draws attention to the active and meaningful contribution made by older people to the citizenship status of others, both young and old. As in any migrant population, it includes persons who have divorced, cohabited and experienced widowhood since the initial move. All of these 'issues' shift the person concerned into and out of specific legal categories, shaping in important ways the basis on which they can make welfare claims in the host and home state, and providing another example of the lack of relationship between rights and needs. The hard and fast distinctions that determine personal entitlement under Community law bear little relation to the social reality of reciprocity and interdependency in the lives of older people. They also raise questions around legal certainty and the enforcement and exercise of legal rights.

This picture of diversity and flux and transnational care chains adds weight to arguments for a more inclusive concept of Citizenship of the Union. The existing situation is both discriminatory (in terms of the categories themselves) and inefficient (in the light of repeated and unpredictable status shifts). The approach taken in *Martinez Sala* (see Chapter Three) may present a way forward and a new impetus for a wider definition of citizenship, perhaps underpinned by developments in legal competency under Article 13. Fries and Shaw (1998) have argued that the Court's judgement in *Martinez Sala* may indicate a general right to social welfare for all EU migrants based on legal residency, whether or not they are economically active. It remains to be seen, however, if this judgement marks a significant step towards the development of a less exclusive form of citizenship (Ackers, 1998).

The limitations of formal equality and rights

Achieving a broad equality of formal status for all Community nationals would undoubtedly promote inclusivity and remove some of the discriminatory aspects of Community law. However, as a piece of socio-legal research, this project has attempted to go beyond this to consider the relationship between citizenship as formal rights and citizenship as experience and practice. Chapter Two referred to the importance of studying the interface of formal legal status with other sources of social and economic status. This argument engages with the developing critique of rights as the vehicle for social advancement. Lister talks, for example, of the problems of 'minting' new rights, which may simply obscure "fundamental economic and social class divisions behind a veneer of equality" (1997, p 17). Rights, in some contexts, may be counterproductive. Discussion around the possibility of removing statutory retirement ages, while removing the discrimination implied in linking compulsory retirement to chronological age, may also effectively remove the right to retire, especially for those without private or occupational pensions (Mann, 2002).

The notion of choice implied in this gesture may itself compound social inequalities as some people are in a stronger position both materially and in terms of employment relations to exercise this new right. In that sense removal of age-related compulsory retirement ages might amount to a 'levelling down' of protection. In another sense, the removal of the right to retire is potentially at odds with Community measures designed to promote the 'work–life' balance, increasing the pressure on people to undertake paid work over the life course and well into the third age.

On an individual or private basis, rights may mean little to those persons who are able to insulate themselves from social risks. Indeed, many of our retired migrants positively choose not to use statutory services in some contexts, preferring instead to purchase their own support. In another sense, rights mean nothing if they are not implemented, if people are unaware of their existence or, if for other reasons, there is no service. This latter concern, about the interface of legal rights with domestic social policy forms a key focus of the work in Chapters Four to Seven, with important implications in terms of the potential of citizenship to promote social equality. It is perhaps in this context that Faist's (2001) notion of 'nested citizenship' presents a useful conceptual tool illustrating the relationship between what are often predominantly regulatory or 'negative' rights at Community level with the forms of redistributive and distributive social policies associated with domestic welfare systems. Faist uses the concept of 'nested citizenship' to describe the evolution of social citizenship in the European Union and the peculiar engagement of EU and national rights. European social citizenship, he argues:

> ... is sited in various governance levels; membership of the EU has multiple sites and there is an interactive system of politics, policies and social rights between the sub-state, state, interstate and supra-state levels. (2001, p 47)

Arguing that:

> ... the web of governance networks allows for enshrining a few new rights at the supra-national level, these interconnect with and re-adapt social rights and institutions in existing welfare states. (2001, p 46)

Faist suggests that the sovereignty of member states in terms of formal and 'full' citizenship remains uncontested. He is, however, less pessimistic about the consequences of this, for while there is not necessarily an "upward ratcheting of rights at the EU level", neither is there any evidence of an "automatic downgrading" (p 49) or the 'race to the bottom' as is often suggested. Nevertheless, this research has emphasised the importance of member state sovereignty in terms of the ability of the European Union to promote a more inclusive citizenship; formal rights in the context of significant spatial inequalities cannot translate into a universal experience. In that context Warnes suggests that, given the failure of 'social Europe' to deliver inclusive citizenship:

> The best course is to continue with the half-century-long process of elaborating bilateral agreement and administrative arrangements between the national social security agencies. (2002, p 14)

Arguably, the development of such bilateral approaches adds to Faist's notion of nesting.

While this multi-level approach might be seen as a reflection of the evolutionary and dynamic quality of European citizenship, the notion of nested citizenship would also seem to be based on the idea that EU and domestic policy fulfil different and complementary functions; that they do not stand in conflict. Faist thus refers to the distinction between market-making and market-correcting policies. The EU he suggests is not so much involved in the latter area, which implies the formation of redistributive rights and policies and, as such, demands a significant extension of the EU's revenue generation capacity. This smacks of a more sophisticated enunciation of the social/economic policy distinction.

The discussion in Chapter Two argued that citizenship as substantive equality involved the combination of formal rights and substantive provision. Together these form the basis for the exercise of human agency, which constitutes the cornerstone of citizenship. As Oldfield suggests, "For activity of any kind, including that involved in the practice of citizenship, people need certain resources" (1990, p 27). The empirical work has examined, through a grounded approach, how retired migrants respond to legal (Chapter Three) and policy frameworks and how these shape migration behaviour. In addition we have presented evidence of the processes through which retired migrants negotiate resource frameworks in order to maximise their own well-being and citizenship (see Chapters Five to Seven).

The findings indicate tensions both within and between dimensions of social policy and present a powerful case for more 'joined-up' policy making and evaluation (an issue already referred to previously in the context of the concept of 'worker' under the free movement and equality provisions). Eurolink Age (a European NGO working to promote the interests of older citizens in the EU) identifies the need for a more comprehensive policy audit or 'mainstreaming' in the context of the impact of EU policy on older people:

> The Commission and the Member States routinely assess the likely impact of EU policies according to many criteria. For example, each Commission proposal contains a detailed assessment of its likely impact on Small and Medium-Sized enterprises, on employment, and on how it accords with the principles of subsidiarity and proportionality. Over and above this, law requires assessment of the likely impact of EU policy on the environment and on sustainable growth, on health protection and on the welfare of animals. Yet the impact of such policies on elderly [sic] people remains conspicuously absent from such assessments. (1996b, p 16)

At present policies pursued under one head of action, such as free movement policy, for example, with the emphasis on the removal of barriers to migration and 'facilitating mobility' would seem to conflict with other Community initiatives. On the one hand, the Single Market strategy and its extension through European Monetary Union has imposed serious constraints on the weaker economies of southern Europe adding to other pressures (including demographic trends, for example) for a general 'levelling-down' of social provision, retrenchment and residualisation. Indeed, the comparative analysis of social security and care policies for senior citizens presented in Chapters

Five and Six suggests that a reduction of public provision is an element of recent reforms in the six countries that we considered and is, implicitly, also part of wider policy initiatives (CEC, 1999; OECD, 2000). The knock-on effect of such policies goes far beyond the often incremental reduction of this or that element of public provision. As Blomberg et al (2000) argue there is no such thing as a neutral reduction in public welfare services. On one level social rights can be seen as citizens' institutionalised expectations about types and scope of welfare services that they expect to be provided by the state. As less becomes universally available from the state as a 'right' and a more selective service ensues, citizens' expectations generally become lower while the wealthy increasingly opt out of public provision. Such changes exacerbate differences between various groups and in time the legitimacy of social rights is undermined.

Subsidiarity and spatial inequality

We have seen in Chapter Three that access to substantive social rights, on the basis of Citizenship of the Union, depends on the principle of non-discrimination. As such, there is no guarantee in terms of the level or quality of provision between member states and no requirement for member states to achieve a certain level of social protection. That said, we also noted in Chapter Three how the social rights attached to interstate mobility can open up domestic welfare systems to Community migrants in a very meaningful and tangible way. The 'cradle-to-grave' protection conferred on Community migrant workers (Allen, 1999) is certainly a right worth having in a very practical sense. On that basis we would question the interpretation, often presented, of European citizenship as mere symbolism. Kleinman presents a fairly typical, if dismissive view, suggesting that:

> While no one would argue that European citizenship possesses any substantive nature in 2001, others argue that a gradual and dynamic process can build on the largely symbolic nature of European citizenship in the future.... Citizenship of the Union is more political rhetoric than legal or social reality. (2002, pp 198 and 201)

If that were the case then evidence of discrimination in formal entitlement would translate to very little in terms of substantive rights. For those who fall within the privileged status of Community worker, European citizenship constitutes the basis of important welfare claims in the host state. Weighing up the costs and benefits of moving, in terms of welfare entitlement, however, demands consideration of the specific geography of the move and the social policy infrastructure in the respective member states.

It is at this level that important additional dimensions of inequality and discrimination arise, in particular, the compatibility of regional inequality or territorial injustice with free movement policy and the promotion of citizenship. The persistence of welfare diversity and the interpretation of subsidiarity as a brake on social harmonisation seriously limit the ability of Union citizenship to facilitate mobility and promote social equality. In principle, the argument (in support of a substantive equality approach) could be used to challenge the preservation of member state autonomy in relation to social policy in a more general sense on the grounds that it constitutes a barrier to mobility.

The discussion above, in the context of gender equality policy, illustrates the fundamental tension that exists between formal equality and substantive equality and the limitations of rights in the face of material inequality. In the context of the current project, the tension lies not only in measures to support carers (such as day care or leave schemes) but, more generally, in the persistence of wide variations in social provision between member states. Formal rights might provide access to welfare systems in the receiving country, but cannot ensure any level of minimum provision or well-being in those countries. Persistent differences in the level and scope of state welfare services available across the EU can have an important part to play in the migratory decisions of retired migrants and particularly in relation to return migration (see Chapters Four and Five; Dwyer, 2000a, 2001).

To the extent that the European Union has recognised the indivisibility of social and economic policy and the importance of social and family policy to wider economic objectives, progress has been incremental in teasing away at the parameters of Community competence. We have seen, for example, how the facilitating mobility test has been used to justify incursion into areas of family policy previously considered to fall outside the strict competence of Community law. While the logic of this approach would extend to measures to promote a progressive harmonisation of social policy, however, the principle of subsidiarity has acted as a brake on this process, restricting the ability of the European Union to 'interfere' in domestic social policy, and particularly in the regulation of the private dimensions of family life. Arguments in favour of a more direct and interventionist social policy role for the European Union might be countered with the 'defence' of the subsidiarity principle restricting Community competence in this field. Chapter Two referred to the grounds on which Community action might be justified in areas of concurrent competence. Arguably the scale or effects of the proposed action could shape the case for an extension of Community competency on the grounds that, in the context of facilitating mobility, the Community could better achieve sufficient achievement, on one hand argue for developing EU competence – justification for action on grounds that cross-border effects are so significant that national states can no longer contain citizenship.

Steiner (1994) argues that the effectiveness test must set aside the original meaning of the principle which guards against the abuse of power in order to both protect individual liberty and promote social responsibility. In that context she cites the words of Pope Pius XI:

> It is an injustice, a grave civil and disturbance of right order for a larger and higher association to arrogate to itself functions, which can be performed efficiently by smaller and lower societies. (p 124)

The concept has been interpreted in the context of UK social policy during the Thatcherite 'New Right' era as meaning that intervention by the state can only be justified when 'lower order' interventions (by the individual, family or voluntary organisations) are unable to provide support. Family care is thus considered to be both qualitatively better and morally superior. This raises some interesting questions in the context of mobility. Mobility is by definition a 'cross-border' phenomenon and case law has already recognised the need to develop family rights in order to promote mobility (Ackers, 1998; McGlynn, 2000). In other areas explicit recognition of Community responsibility for cross-border consequences of migration has resulted in new legislation and an extension of competency. The impact of migration in the case of family breakdown has thus recently formed the basis of a new Regulation shaping custody and maintenance issues. Migration inevitably results in a dislocation of family relationships and caring obligations across space. As such it disrupts in a very fundamental sense the relationships inferred in the words of Pope Pius XI. We have noted, in Chapter Seven and in previous work (Ackers, 1998) the problems of exercising legal rights in terms of moving elderly disabled family members to sources of family care (under the right to join provisions). Migrant citizens and their families are thus increasingly likely to look to 'higher' level actors – in the forms of more formal provision as the means by which to support their well-being. Family and voluntary care might be simply out of the question. Szyszczak and Moebius (1998) further argue that use of the subsidiarity principle as a means by which to restrict competency might fall foul of competition policy as diversity in provision may distort location decisions (in a similar vein to concerns expressed over 'social dumping').

Citizenship of the Union: the 'concealed multiplier of occupational success'?

In taking a broad and grounded view of the collection of resources constitutive of well-being the research has identified some key challenges to the European Union's ability to deliver a more inclusive and egalitarian form of citizenship. Many of the rights we have referred to concern claims against welfare systems for Income Support, health and social services. Measures designed to promote distributive justice in relation to these resources may, however, fail to reduce inequality and exclusion as new forms of social polarisation emerge. We have alluded to the limitations of rights-based approaches to equality in the face of differential access to private resources. Chapter Two referred to the work of Titmuss (1958) and the increasing salience of his concerns around the developing contribution of occupational and fiscal welfare to well-being and social inequality. The explicit promotion of insurance-based and occupational schemes, particularly as measures to promote mobility through the aggregation and transportation of benefits, represents another example of policy conflict. In a more general sense, this policy coupled with the pressure brought to bear on welfare systems is likely to exacerbate existing inequalities and promote new forms of social polarisation as those who lack the ability to contribute to these types of schemes are disadvantaged both materially and in terms of their mobility. In privileging paid work above other forms of contribution it can also be seen as enhancing them and at worst appears to reinforce the advantages of certain well placed groups relative to others.

Titmuss (1958), writing in the context of UK social policy in the post-war period was concerned that occupational welfare added a new tier to the pool of social resources available to those persons with already advantageous employment status. Those persons in forms of employment that did not deliver such 'perks' or those not engaged in paid work at all were forced to rely on the typically less beneficial and less transportable forms of social welfare provision. As Irwin notes, "... the social ordering of claims and obligations and the ways in which certain groups secure or maintain an advantaged position so that work-life advantage is later translated into retirement advantage" (1999, p 711) are crucially important in defining individual well-being in retirement. The privileging of paid work as the basis of social contribution in Community law, together with the attention to occupational and insurance-based schemes in EU policy adds a new dimension to Titmuss's consideration of the advantages of occupational and fiscal welfare. Citizenship of the Union extends the ability to access domestic welfare systems (Titmuss's 'social welfare' sector) only to those persons who have previously achieved the status of Community migrant worker (in other words they have worked in the host state for a period of time prior to retirement). In that sense, the 'modicum of social security' available can only be accessed by those who have worked in and contributed to the host state: paid work becomes the trigger to citizenship. Occupational welfare for the EU migrant worker, as we saw in Chapter Three, extends well beyond personal material rights to encompass aspects of family and immigration law. The migrant EU worker thus has the right to be accompanied by his or her family who then derive benefit by virtue of their relationship with the citizen-worker. In that sense, the social entitlement of families becomes a further extension of occupational status (to the extent that in the absence of the relationship with the citizen-worker they would not be entitled under the social advantages formula).

In terms of accessing (in a host country) what Titmuss (1958) referred to as 'social' welfare rights, past employment contribution in the home state cannot be transferred and those that have resided in but not undertaken paid work in the host state (including housewives and carers, for example) do not derive independent personal entitlement. Community citizenship thus operates as an extension of occupational entitlement. Not only does it provide access to a second tier of benefits, it also determines access to basic social citizenship in the host state. In that sense, the multiplier effect referred to by Titmuss assumes an even greater significance.

While the broad distinction between the role of the EU as primarily involving market regulation and the generation of 'negative' rights and the member states as the guardians of 'positive' rights to welfare remains true, it is not correct to suggest, as many authors imply (cf Faist, 2001; Kleinman, 2002), that the EU does not play a significant role in social redistribution. For sure, it lacks the kind of revenue generating capacity to underwrite large-scale social expenditure and target excluded groups (although its structural funds do have some impact in this respect). The privileging of certain forms of contribution and relationships, however, and the strengthening of the relationship between work and social entitlement on the one hand, and marriage on the other, undoubtedly constitutes a form of social redistribution. The articulation of citizenship rights at Community level with social resources at national level, implied in the nested citizenship concept, suggests the genuine material impact of Community law and, in that context, its redistributional potential and effect.

Welfare tourists or active agents?

Gough defines one of the basic elements of human need as being the "autonomy of agency – the capacity to make informed choices about what should be done and how to go about doing it" (1992, p 9). Mobility, we have argued, is a resource in its own right. It also constitutes a vehicle for the exercise of agency in a wider sense, however, and plays a determining role in access to other forms of social resource. The ability to exercise mobility thus provides access to climate, for example, or lower heating or housing costs or more beneficial fiscal regimes. It opens up enormous opportunities to negotiate, across a wider resource framework, access to an individually tailored citizenship package across transnational space. Differential formal rights thus shape the exercise of autonomy and agency.

We have already considered the problems of derived rights in this context and the extent to which they enforce dependency within families and personal relationships. These effects take on a temporal and spatial dimension as life course 'decisions' reverberate into retirement. This represents a restriction on personal autonomy and the ability to exercise agency, particularly affecting those people who are in a caring or dependency role. In other contexts, the research has evidenced the ways in which people engage with their formal rights to tailor a package best able to maximise their command of social resources. Many retired migrants are actively seeking to maximise the enjoyment of their later years by relocating in retirement. Putting together a package of welfare services that meets what they consider to be their personal requirements and needs is an important element in their migratory decisions and subsequent movements. Many are resourceful in negotiating and renegotiating the best welfare deal for themselves. If detrimental changes to their medical or financial circumstances indicate that further movement will enable them to better meet their changed circumstances they will pursue their goal single-mindedly. In the words of one respondent:

> "When you move abroad, you have to be curious and daring, but when it comes to returning to your home country you have to be very calculating and well organised. It's a kind of conflict I suppose." (R220; Swedish returnee)

While, to some extent respondents such as R220 are operating in the 'shadows' of the law, the divide between 'benefit shopping/welfare tourism' and 'reflexive/active citizenship' of the kind envisaged by Giddens (1994) would seem to be finely drawn. The research suggests that migration poses some increasingly serious challenges to the future of social citizenship and social institutions. The first of these concerns the role and ability of welfare systems at both national and supranational level to promote social justice and undermine social exclusion. The evidence presented in Chapters Five and Six, suggest that the ability to engage in this form of negotiation and manage your rights package to maximum effect is unevenly distributed and depends on a number of factors:

- Formal legal rights in Community law reflecting nationality, work status, family roles, and so on.
- The different availability and quality of social infrastructures at national and regional level.
- Employment histories and the relative balance of reliance on contributory and non-contributory benefits (reflecting both the quantity and quality [transportability] of benefits).
- Access to wealth (in particular to support second home ownership as the basis of retaining residency-based entitlements in two or more locations).
- Knowledge of options and awareness of rights and how to exercise them.
- Individual health and family status at any point in time. The unpredictability of life courses and the consequence of long-term chronic illnesses and bereavement may rapidly exhaust even considerable resources.

In this context, mobility presents increasing potential for the emergence of new forms of stratification and status differentiation. The second issue concerns the impact of 'status management' on the fiscal basis of welfare systems themselves. Migration decisions are not shaped by access to rights and resources alone (in that sense the notion of benefits shopping is far too narrow) but also encompass important dimensions of contribution, in particular, management of fiscal status. This raises serious questions about the ability of welfare systems (at national and EU level) to maintain their autonomy and insulate themselves from the ability of a highly sophisticated group of citizens negotiating for themselves, within a global resource framework, a personalised 'package' of benefits and privileges while minimising the contributions they have to make. This poses a fundamental threat to the financial assumptions underlying social planning. The prospect of increased mobility and the spread of awareness indicate the emergence of an increasingly complex and polarised hierarchy of social privilege and inequality, coupled with a reduction in the potential of domestic systems to respond to the genuine needs of those unable to operate at this level.

Mobility thus poses many challenges to the future of the nation state. Citing Horsman and Marshall (1994), Lister suggests that the "dawn of the age of migration and 'globalisation' is being heralded by some, such as marking the dusk of the age of the nation-state" (1997, p 55). To some extent European integration and the prospect of further harmonisation in fiscal and social regimes may address some of the imbalances so attractive to would-be migrants. In that sense it may, as one of our respondents suggested, "be more difficult for dodgers in the future due to the European Union" (R217, Chapter Six). On the other hand, the management of citizenship across global, social and financial space may test the very boundaries of the European Union itself: would-be migrants might simply take a broader view of the potential locations on offer.

This study has taken the concept of citizenship and attempted to redefine it through a broad socio-legal and grounded approach. We have sought to understand the relationship between formal, legal rights, social policy infrastructures in the participant countries and citizenship practice. As such it has evidenced the forms of status differentiation that exist and also the processes by which retired migrants engage with these and practice citizenship in their own lives. On another level, the work has provided an opportunity, in a specific context, to appraise the value of citizenship as a tool for the evaluation of the impact of legal and policy frameworks on retired migrants and as a vehicle for the promotion of a more inclusive and egalitarian European social model. Its specific definition and operationalisation in this research suggests that the concept is capable of capturing important dimensions of inequality and distributive justice both in terms of spatial or territorial inequality and also in individual or personal status and the impact of these upon agency and autonomy in retirement planning. As such the project has been able to say something meaningful about the capacity of 'Citizenship of the Union' to deliver a more egalitarian and inclusive European social space. In the process the book has identified some of the key challenges migration poses to the future of social policy. In summary, five key themes have emerged from the research. First, the level and nature of formal *status differentiation* within the population of retired migrants significantly restrict the inclusive potential of 'Citizenship of the Union'. Second, 'Citizenship of the Union', as it stands, serves to amplify the *advantages attached to occupational welfare*, compounding the relationship between the social division of labour and well-being. These processes are gendered. Third, in addition to distinctions in formal rights, the citizenship status and well-being of migrants reflects the diversity of social policy infrastructures and welfare systems across the European Union, raising serious questions about *distributive justice*. Fourth, people are not passive spectators of formal rights and policies; legal rights although important do not have a determinative effect. They are but one dimension of the wider resource framework. Both the quality and quantity of social resources is an issue here and the population of retired migrants show considerable skill in managing their individual status. The ability to maximise well-being is, however, unevenly distributed. Fifth, this evidence of agency, that is, the willingness to negotiate contributions and rights, and manipulate advantage across geographical and social space raises serious challenges for European and domestic welfare systems in the future.

Notes

[1] Warnes (2002) has recently written a paper on migration in 'social Europe' which addresses some of these issues.

[2] Community law utilises concepts of disability and dependency, which have been widely criticised by academics and activists concerned to promote the 'social' model of disability (for example, Barnes, 1991; Oliver and Barnes, 1998).

[3] Just as remittances have been shown to contribute significantly to local economies (King, 1986).

[4] This project will be directed by Professor Ackers at the University of Leeds and will commence in 2002.

Bibliography

Ackers, H.L. (1998) *Shifting spaces: Women, citizenship and migration within the EU,* Bristol: The Policy Press.

Ackers, H.L. (1999) 'Context, culture and values in migration research with children within the European Union', *International Journal of Social Research Methodology,* vol 2, no 2, pp 171-83.

Ackers, H.L. (2001) *The participation of women researchers in the TMR programme of the European Commission: An evaluation,* Brussels: European Commission (DG Research).

Ackers, H.L. and Stalford, H. (1999) 'Children migration and citizenship in the European Union: intra-Community mobility and the status of children in EC law', *Children and Youth Services Review,* vol 21, nos 11/12, pp 987-1010.

Ackers, H.L. and Stalford, H. (2002) *A community for children? Children, citizenship and internal migration in the EU,* Aldershot: Ashgate.

Ahn, S. and Olsson Hort, S.E. (1999) 'The politics of old age in Sweden', in A. Walker and G. Naegele (eds) *The politics of old age in Europe,* Buckingham: Open University Press, pp 135-51.

Alcock, P. and Craig, G. (eds) (2001) *International social policy,* Basingstoke: Palgrave.

Allen, R. (1999) 'Equal treatment, social advantages and obstacles: in search of coherence in freedom and dignity', in E. Guild (ed) *The legal framework and social consequences of free movement of persons in the European Union,* London: Kluwer Law, pp 31-49.

Andrietti, V. (2001) 'Portability of supplementary pensions rights in the European Union', *International Social Security Review,* vol 54, no 1, pp 59-84.

Araki, H. (2000) 'Ideas and welfare: the Conservative transformation of the British pension regime', *Journal of Social Policy,* vol 29, no 4, pp 599-621.

Ascoli, U. (1996) 'Retirement system reform: is Italy moving toward an increasingly minimal welfare state?', in E. Reynaud (ed) *Supplementary pensions: Actors, issues and the future,* London: Quarum (collection of conference papers), pp 114-26.

Atkinson, R. and Flint, J. (2001) *Accessing hidden and hard-to reach populations: snowball research strategies,* Issue 33, Social Research Update, Guildford: University of Surrey.

Augusztinovics, M. (1999) 'Pension systems and reforms – Britain, Hungary, Italy, Poland and Sweden', *European Journal of Social Security,* vol 1, no 4, pp 351-82.

Baldock, J. (1997) 'Social care in old age: more than a funding problem', *Social Policy and Administration*, vol 31, no 1, pp 73-89.

Baptista, I. (1999) 'Growing older, growing poorer: transition into old age in Portuguese society', Paper for the International Conference on the 'Status of the Older Population: Prelude to the 21st Century', Sion, 15-19 December.

Barnard, C. (1999) 'Gender equality in the EU: A balance sheet', in P. Alston (ed) *The EU and human rights*, Oxford: Oxford University Press, pp 215-279.

Barnes, C. (1991) *Disabled people in Britain and discrimination: A case for anti-discrimination legislation*, London: Hurst/British Council of Organisations of Disabled People.

Barton, L. (1993) 'The struggle for citizenship: the case of disabled people', *Disability, Handicap and Society*, vol 8, no 3, pp 235-48.

Betty, C. and Cahill, M. (1999) 'British ex-patriate's experience of health and social services on the Costa del Sol', in F. Anthias and G. Lazaridis (eds) *Into the margins: Migration and social exclusion in Southern Europe*, Aldershot: Avebury, pp 83-113.

Blackman, T. (2000a) 'Defining responsibility for care: approaches to the care of elder people in six European countries', *International Journal of Social Welfare*, vol 9, pp 181-90.

Blackman, T. (2000b) 'Social care and complexity: cross national comparisons', Paper presented to the SPA Annual Conference, Roehampton Institute, July.

Blair, T. (1997) 'The 21st century welfare state', Speech to the 'Social Policy and Economic Performance' Conference, Amsterdam, London: Labour Party.

Blair, T. (1999) 'Beveridge revisited: a welfare state for the 21st century', in R. Walker (ed) *Ending child poverty: Popular welfare for the 21st century?*, Bristol: The Policy Press, pp 7-20.

Blake, N. (1999) 'Family life in community law: the limits of freedom and dignity', in E. Guild (ed) *The legal framework and social consequences of free movement of persons in the European Union*, London: Kluwer Law, pp 7-19.

Blomberg, S., Edebalk, P.G. and Petersen, J. (2000) 'The withdrawal of the welfare state: elderly care in Sweden in the 1990s', *European Journal of Social Work*, vol 3, no 2, pp 151-63.

Bonoli, G. (1997) 'Classifying welfare states: a two dimension approach', *Journal of Social Policy*, vol 26, no 3, pp 351-72.

Bonoli, G. (2000) *The politics of pension reform: Institutions and policy change in western Europe*, Cambridge: Cambridge University Press.

Bottomore, T. (1992) 'Citizenship and social class forty years on', in T.H. Marshall and T. Bottomore, *Citizenship and social class*, London: Pluto Press, pp 55-92.

Boyle, G. (1997) 'Community care for older people in Ireland: a conceptual critique of the literature', *Administration*, vol 45, no 2, pp 44-58.

Brown, S. (1996) 'Developments in community care for elderly people', *Administration*, vol 44, no 3, pp 70-86.

Browne, A. (2000) 'Private care bonanza as sick spurn NHS', *The Observer* 19 March, p 1.

Brugiaviani, A. (1998) 'Social security and retirement in Italy', in J. Gruber and D.A. Wise (eds) *Social security and retirement round the world*, Chicago, IL: Chicago Press, pp 181-238.

Bruto da Costa, A., Cardoso, A. and Baptista, I. (1997) *National survey report working paper on ageing and welfare in Portugal*, Lisbon: CESIS Working Paper for 'Family structure, labour market participation and the dynamics of social exclusion' project, University of Bath.

Bussemaker, J. and van Kersbergen, K. (1994) 'Gender and welfare states: some theoretical reflections', in D. Sainsbury (ed) *Gendering welfare states*, London: Sage Publications, pp 8-25.

Cahill, M. (1994) *The new social policy*, Oxford: Blackwell.

Cardoso, A., Baptista, I. and Perista, P. (1999) *Ageing and welfare in Portugal: Policies and public debate updated report*, Lisbon: CESIS Working Paper for 'Family structure, labour market participation and the dynamics of social exclusion' project, University of Bath.

Carroll, D. (1999) 'Cross-cutting initiatives in public policy: some Irish examples', in G. Kiely, A. O'Donnell, P. Kennedy and S. Quin (eds) *Irish social policy in context*, Dublin: University College Dublin Press, pp 293-316.

CEC (Commission of the European Communities) (1990) *The Community charter of the fundamental social rights of workers*, Luxembourg: Office for Official Publications of the European Communities.

CEC (1993) *First report on citizenship of the Union*, COM (93) 702, Brussels: European Commission.

CEC (1995) *The demographic situation in the European Union*, Luxembourg: Office for Official Publications of the European Communities.

CEC (1997a) *Second report on citizenship of the Union*, COM (97) 230, Brussels: European Commission.

CEC (1997b) *Social Europe: The outlook on supplementary pensions in the context of demographic, economic and social change*, Supplement 7/96, Luxembourg: Office for Official Publications of the European Community.

CEC (1997c) *Supplementary pensions in the single market: A green paper*, COM (97) 283, Brussels: European Commission.

CEC (1999) *Towards a Europe for all ages: Promoting prosperity and intergenerational solidarity*, COM (1999) 221 final, Brussels: European Commission.

CEC (2000) *MISSOC: Social protection in the member states, situation on 1 January 1999 and evolution*, Luxembourg: Office for Official Publications of the European Communities.

CEC (2001) *The social situation in the European Union*, Luxembourg: Office for Official Publications of the European Communities.

Chalmers, D. and Szyszczak, E. (1998) *European Union law, volume two: Towards a European polity?*, Aldershot: Dartmouth.

Cheal, D. (1987) 'Inter-generational transfers and life course management: towards a socio-economic perspective', in A. Bryman, P. Allatt, T. Keill (eds) *Rethinking the life-cycle*, London: Macmillan, p 141.

Closa, C. (1992) 'The concept of citizenship in the treaty on European Union', *Common Market Law Review*, vol 29, p 1137.

Closa, C. (1995) 'Citizenship of the Union and nationality of member states', *Common Market Law Review*, vol 32, pp 487-518.

Comhairle (2001a) 'Health: entitlements to health services for the elderly' (now 'Retirement: Health services and older people: health services' at www.oasis.gov.ie/retirement/health_and_older_people/health_services_and_older_people.html).

Comhairle (2001b) 'Health: medical card' (now at www.oasis.gov.ie/health/medical_card.html).

Comhairle (2001c) 'Health: nursing homes subventions – fact sheet 2' (now 'Retirement: Health services and older people: long-term institutional care' at www.oasis.gov.ie/retirement/health_and_older_people/institutional_care.html).

Connell, P. and Stewart, J. (1997) 'Demographic projections and population ageing in Ireland', Seminar paper for the European Network for Research on Supplementary Pensions, session on 'Rebalancing supplementary and state pensions in the EU and the US: the role of the state in pension provision; employer, regulator, provider', Dublin.

Convery, J. (1998) 'Social work with vulnerable older people in the Republic of Ireland: factors influencing policy and practice', *Personal Social Services in Northern Ireland*, vol 57, pp 159-68.

Cousins, M. (1997) 'Ireland's place in the worlds of welfare capitalism', *Journal of European Social Policy*, vol 7, no 3, pp 223-35.

Coutinho, M. (1998) *Guaranteed minimum income in Portugal and social projects*, Social Services Research Papers, no 2, Birmingham: University of Birmingham.

CPAG (Child Poverty Action Group) (1997) *Migration and social security handbook. A rights guide for people entering and leaving the UK* (2nd edn), London: CPAG.

CPAG (1998) *National welfare benefits handbook* (28th edn), London: CPAG.

Craig, P. and de Búrca, G. (1998) *EU law: Text, cases and materials* (2nd edn), Oxford: Oxford University Press.

Dalley, G. (2000) 'Long-term care in the United Kingdom: community or institutional care? Individual, family or state responsibility?', *Journal of Ageing and Social Policy*, vol 12, no 1, pp 1-5.

Daykin, C. (1998) 'Complementary pensions in the European Union', *Economic Affairs*, March, London: Institute of Economic Affairs, pp 18-23.

Denman, M. (2000) *Pension schemes in the EU member states: Similarities and differences*, London: Eurolink Age.

D'Oliveira, J. (1995) 'Union citizenship: pie in the sky?', in A. Rosas and E. Antola (eds) *A citizen's Europe. In search of a new order*, London: Sage Publications.

DSS (Department of Social Security) (1998a) *A new contract for welfare partnership in pensions*, London: DSS.

DSS (1998b) *New ambitions for our country: A new contract for welfare*, Green Paper, Cmnd 3805, London: DSS.

DSS (1999) 'Habitual Residence Test reforms provide fairer access to income-related social security benefits', Press Release 1999/132, 14 June (www.dss.gov.uk/mediacentre/pressreleases/1999/jun/99132.htm).

DSS (2001) *Pensioners' guide: Making the most of government help and advice*, London: DSS.

Dwyer, P. (1998) 'Conditional citizens? Welfare rights and responsibilities in the late 1990s', *Critical Social Policy*, vol 18, no 4, pp 519-43.

Dwyer, P. (2000a) 'Movements to some purpose? An exploration of international retirement migration in the European Union', *Education and Ageing*, vol 15, no 3, pp 352-77.

Dwyer, P. (2000b) *Welfare rights and responsibilities: Contesting social citizenship*, Bristol: The Policy Press.

Dwyer, P. (2001) 'Retired EU migrants, healthcare rights and European social citizenship', *Journal of Social Welfare and Family Law*, vol 23, no 3, pp 311-27.

Esping-Andersen, G. (1990) *The three worlds of welfare capitalism*, Cambridge: Polity Press.

Eurolink Age (1995a) *Caring for older people: A European issue*, London: Eurolink Age.

Eurolink Age (1995b) *European Community law relating to older people*, London: Eurolink Age.

Eurolink Age (1996a) *Eurolink Age position paper on the free movement of older people within the EU*, no 08/1996, London: Eurolink Age.

Eurolink Age (1996b) Position paper for the 1996 Intergovernmental Conference 'Raising the profile of older people at EU level: the case for change' (www.europa.eu.int/en/agenda/igchome/instdoc/ngo/eurlink1.htm), p 3.

Eurolink Age (1999) *Pensions: The European dimension*, fact sheet 2, London: Eurolink Age.

Eurostat (1999) *Regional population ageing of the EU at different speeds up to 2025*, Statistics in Focus theme 1-4/1999, Brussels: Eurostat.

Faist, T. (2001) 'Social citizenship in the European Union: nested membership', *Journal of Common Market Studies*, vol 39, no 1, pp 37-58.

Fanning, B. (1999) 'The mixed economy of welfare', in G. Kiely, A. O'Donnell, P. Kennedy and S. Quin (eds) *Irish social policy in context*, Dublin: University College Dublin Press, pp 51-69.

Farigon, V. (1996) 'Social assistance and the North South cleavage in Italy', in M. Rhodes (ed) *South European Society and Politics*, vol 1, no 3, Special Issue on southern European welfare states, pp 135-54.

Faulkes, K. (1998) *Citizenship in modern Britain*, Edinburgh: Edinburgh University Press.

Featherstone, K., Kazamias, G. and Papadimitriou, D. (2001) 'The limits of external empowerment: EMU, technocracy and reform in the Greek pension system', *Political Studies*, vol 49, pp 462-80.

Ferge, Z. (1979) *A society in the making; Hungarian social and societal policy 1945-75*, Hammondsworth: Penguin.

Ferreira, C. (1997) 'Portugal', in Commission of the European Communities *Social Europe: The outlook on supplementary pensions in the context of demographic, economic and social change*, Supplement 7/96, Luxembourg: Office for Official Publications of the European Community, pp 174-81.

Ferrera, M. (1996) 'The "southern model" of welfare in social Europe', *Journal of European Social Policy*, vol 6, no 1, pp 17-37.

Ferrera, M. and Gualmini, E. (2000) 'Reforms guided by consensus. The welfare state in the Italian transition', in M. Ferrera and M. Rhodes (eds) *West European Politics*, vol 23, no 2, Special Issue 'Recasting European welfare states', pp 187-208.

Finch, J. and Mason, J. (1990) 'Decision taking in the fieldwork process: theoretical sampling and collaborative working', in R.G. Burgess (ed) *Studies in qualitative methodology*, vol 2, London: JAI Press, pp 25-50.

Finkelstein, V. (1980) *Attitudes and disabled people: Issues for discussion*, New York, NY: World Rehabilitation Fund, monograph 5.

Finucane, K.G. and Kelly, K.F. (1998) 'Securing retirement income in the Republic of Ireland', *Benefits and Compensation International*, vol 28, no 1, pp 28-32.

Fisher, M. (1998) 'Older male carers and community care', in J. Bornat, J. Johnson, C. Pereira, D. Pilrim and F. Williams (eds) *Community care: a reader*, Basingstoke: Macmillan, pp 134-44.

Fitzgerald, E. (2000) 'Community services for independence in old age – rhetoric and reality – follow the money trail', *Administration*, Autumn, vol 48, no 3, pp 75-89.

Freeman, R. (1999) 'Institutions, states and cultures: health policy and politics in Europe', in J. Clasen (ed) *Comparative social policy: Concepts, theories and methods*, Oxford: Blackwell Publishers Limited, pp 80-95.

Fries, S. and Shaw, J. (1998) 'Citizenship of the Union: first steps in the European Court of Justice', *European Public Law*, vol 4, issue 4, pp 533-59.

Gardner, J.P. (ed) (1994) *Hallmarks of citizenship: A green paper*, London: British Institute of International and Comparative Law.

George, V. and Taylor-Gooby, P. (eds) (1996) *European welfare policy: Squaring the welfare circle*, Basingstoke: Macmillan.

George, V. and Wilding, P. (1994) *Welfare and ideology*, London: Harvester and Wheatsheaf.

Geyer, R.R. (2000) *Exploring European social policy*, Cambridge: Polity Press.

Giarchi, G.G. (1996) *Caring for older Europeans: Comparative studies in 29 countries*, Aldershot: Arena/Ashgate Publishing Limited.

Giddens, A. (1994) *Beyond left and right: The future of radical politics*, Cambridge: Polity Press.

Ginn, J. and Arber, S. (1994) 'Gender and pensions in Europe: current trends in women's pension acquisition', in P. Brown and R. Crompton (eds) *Economic restructuring and social exclusion*, London: University College London Press, pp 58-85.

Ginn, J., Daly, M. and Street, D. (2001) 'Engendering pensions: a comparative framework', in J. Ginn, D. Street and S. Arber (eds) *Women, work and pensions: International issues and prospects*, Buckingham: Open University Press, pp 1-10.

Ginn, J., Street, D. and Arber, S. (eds) (2001) *Women, work and pensions: International issues and prospects*, Buckingham: Open University Press.

Glaser, B.G. and Strauss, A.L. (1970) 'Theoretical sampling', in N.K. Denzin (ed) *Sociological methods: A source book*, London: Butterworths, pp 105-14.

Glendinning, C. (1998) 'Health and social care services for frail older people in the UK: changing responsibilities and new developments', in C. Glendinning (ed) *Rights and realities: Comparing new developments in long-term care for older people*, Bristol: The Policy Press, pp 11-28.

Gori, C. (1999) 'Care allowances for the elderly in Italy: new features and challenges', Paper presented to the Social Policy Association Annual Conference, Roehampton Institution, July.

Gough, I. (1992) 'What are human needs?', in J. Percy-Smith and I. Sanderson, *Understanding local needs*, London: Institute of Public Policy Research.

Gough, I. (2001) 'Social assistance regimes: a cluster analysis', *Journal of European Social Policy*, vol 11, no 2, pp 165-70.

Gough, I., Eardley, T., Bradshaw, J., Ditch, J. and Whiteford, P. (1997) 'Social assistance in OECD countries', *Journal of European Social Policy*, vol 7, no 1, pp 17-43.

Gould, A. (1996) 'Sweden: the last bastion of social democracy', in V. George and P. Taylor-Gooby (eds) *European welfare policy: Squaring the welfare circle*, Basingstoke: Macmillan, pp 72-94.

Gould, A. (2001) *Developments in Swedish social policy*, London: Palgrave.

Granaglia, E. (1996) 'The Italian national health service and the challenge of privatisation', in M. Rhodes (ed) *South European Society and Politics*, vol 1, no 3, Special Issue on southern European welfare states, pp 155-72.

Guibentif, P. (1996) 'The transformation of the Portuguese social security system', in M. Rhodes (ed) *South European Society and Politics*, vol 1, no 3, Special Issue on southern European welfare states, pp 219-39.

Guillén, A.M. and Matsaganis, M. (2000) 'Testing the "social dumping" hypothesis in southern Europe: welfare policies in Greece and Spain during the last 20 years', *Journal of European Social Policy*, vol 10, no 2, pp 120-45.

Hall, S. (2001) 'Ministers to scrap retirement age', *The Guardian*, 14 February, p 10.

Hampson, J. (1997a) 'Social policy in the Latin rim: the case of Portugal', in M. May, E. Brunsdon and G. Craig (eds) *Social Policy Review 9*, London: SPA/London Guildhall University, pp 317-36.

Hampson, J. (1997b) 'Social protection and social insurance in Portugal', in J. Clasen (ed) *Social insurance in Europe*, Bristol: The Policy Press, pp 151-76.

Hantrais, L. (1999) 'Contextualisation in cross-national comparative research', *International Journal of Social Research Methodology*, vol 2, no 2, pp 93-109.

Hantrais, L. (2000) *Social policy in the European Union*, Basingstoke: Macmillan.

Hantrais, L. and Mangen, S. (eds) (1996) *Cross-national research methods*, London: Pinter.

Harrison, M.L. (1995) *Housing, 'race', social policy and empowerment*, Aldershot: Avebury.

Herlitz, C. (1997) 'Distribution of informal and formal home help services for elderly people in Sweden', *The Gerontologist*, vol 37, no 1, pp 117-24.

Hervey, T.K. (1995) 'Migrant workers and their families in the European Union: the pervasive market ideology of Community law', in J. Shaw and G. Moore (eds) *New legal dynamics of European Union*, Oxford: Clarendon Press, pp 91-111.

Hervey, T.K. and Shaw, J. (1998) 'Women, work and care: women's dual role and double burden in EC sex equality law', *Journal of European Social Policy*, vol 8, no 1, pp 43-63.

Horsman, M. and Marshall, A. (1994) *After the welfare state*, London: Harper Collins.

Hunt, P. (ed) (1966) *Stigma*, London: Chapman.

Irwin, S. (1999) 'Later life, inequality and social theory', *Ageing and Society*, vol 19, issue 6, pp 691-715.

Johnson, P. and Rake, K. (1999) 'Five country case studies: Britain', in M. Augusztinovics, 'Pension systems and reforms – Britain, Hungary, Italy, Poland and Sweden', *European Journal of Social Security*, vol 1, no 4, pp 351-82.

Journal of Ethnic and Migration Studies (2000) Reviews Section, July, vol 26, no 3, pp 553-67.

Katrougalos, G.S. (1996) 'The south European welfare model: the Greek welfare state in search of an identity', *Journal of European Social Policy*, vol 6, no 1, pp 39-60.

Kiely, G., O'Donnell, A., Kennedy, P. and Quin, S. (eds) (1999) *Irish social policy in context*, Dublin: University College Dublin Press.

Kiernan, K. (2001) 'The rise of cohabitation and childbearing outside marriage in Western Europe', *International Journal of Law, Policy and the Family*, vol 15, no 1, pp 1-21.

King, R. (ed) (1986) *Return migration and regional economic problems*, London: Croom Helm.

King, R. (1994) 'Migration and the single market for labour: an issue in regional Development', in M. Blacksell and A.M. Williams (eds) *The European challenge: Geography and development in the European Community*, Oxford: Oxford University Press, pp 218-41.

King, R. and Patterson, G. (1998) 'Diverse paths: the elderly British in Tuscany', *International Journal of Population Geography*, vol 4, pp 157-82.

King, R., Warnes, A.M. and Williams, A.M. (1998) 'International retirement migration in Europe', *International Journal of Population Geography*, vol 4, pp 91-111.

King, R., Warnes, A.M. and Williams, A.M. (2000) *Sunset lives: British retirement migration to the Mediterranean*, Oxford: Berg.

Kleinman, M. (2002) *A European welfare state? European Union social policy in context*, Basingstoke: Palgrave.

Knodel, J. (1993) 'The design and analysis of focus groups: a practical guide', in D.L. Morgan (ed) *Successful focus groups, advancing the state of the art*, London: Sage Publications, pp 35-50.

Korpi, W. (1995) 'The position of the elderly in the welfare state: comparative perspectives on old age care in Sweden', *Social Service Review*, vol 69, pp 242-73.

Kuhnle, S. (2000) 'The Scandinavian welfare state in the 1990's: challenged but viable', in M. Ferrera and M. Rhodes (eds) *West European Politics*, vol 23, no 2 Special Issue 'Recasting European welfare states', pp 209-28.

Laffan, B. (1995) 'The politics of identity and political order in Europe', *Journal of Common Market Studies*, vol 34, p 81-98.

Larragy, J.F. (1993) 'Formal service provision and the care of the elderly at home in Ireland', *Journal of Cross Cultural Gerontology*, vol 8, no 4, pp 361-74.

Lasch, C. (1995) *The revolt of the elite and the betrayal of democracy*, New York, NY: W.W. Norton.

Laslett, P. (1989) *A fresh map of life: The emergence of the third age*, London: Weidenfield and Nicholson.

Leece, J. (2001) 'Directing support: direct payments and older people', *Generations Review*, vol 11, no 3, pp 23-6.

Le Grand, J. (1987) 'The middle-class use of the British social services', in J. Le Grand and R. Goodin (eds) *Not only the poor: The middle classes and the welfare state*, London: Allen and Unwin.

Leibfried, S. (2000) 'Towards a European welfare state?', in C. Pierson and F.G. Castles (eds) *The welfare state reader*, Cambridge: Polity Press, pp 190-206.

Leira, A. (1992) *Welfare states and working mothers*, Cambridge: Cambridge University Press.

Leitner, S. (2001) 'Sex and gender discrimination within EU pension systems', *Journal of European Social Policy*, vol 11, no 2, pp 99-115.

Lewis, J. (1992) 'Gender and the development of welfare regimes', *Journal of European Social Policy*, vol 2, no 3, pp 159-73.

Lister, R. (1990) 'Women, economic dependency and citizenship', *Journal of Social Policy*, vol 19, no 4, pp 445-69.

Lister, R. (1996) 'Citizenship, agency and rights: feminist perspectives', Paper to the DIOTIMA Conference, 'The Gendering of Rights, Power and Citizenship', Athens, 9-10 February.

Lister, R. (1997) *Citizenship: feminist perspectives*, Basingstoke: Macmillan.

Litwak, E. and Longino, C. (1987) 'Migration patterns among the elderly: a developmental perspective', *The Gerontologist*, vol 27, pp 266-72.

Lødemel, I. and Trickey, H. (2000) *'An offer you can't refuse': Workfare in international perspective*, Bristol: The Policy Press.

McGlynn, C. (2000) 'A family law for the European Union?', in J. Shaw (ed) *Social law and policy in an evolving European Union*, Oxford: Hart Publishing.

McKie, L., Bowlby, S. and Gregory, S. (2001) 'Gender, caring and employment in Britain', *Journal of Social Policy*, vol 30, no 2, pp 233-58.

Malcolm, E. (1996) *Elderly return migration from Britain to Ireland: A preliminary study*, Report No 44, Dublin: National Council for the Elderly.

Mann, K. (1992) *The making of an English 'underclass'*, Buckingham: Open University Press.

Mann, K. (2002) *Approaching retirement: Social divisions, welfare and exclusion*, Bristol: The Policy Press.

Marquand, D. (1991) 'Civic republicans and liberal individualists: the case of Britain', *Archive Europèene de Sociologie* (XXXII), pp 329-44.

Marshall, T.H. (1992 [1949]) 'Citizenship and social class', Part 1 in T.H. Marshall and T. Bottomore, *Citizenship and social class*, London: Pluto Press.

Mason, J. (1998) 'Living away from kin: kinship and geographical reasoning', Working Paper No 7, Leeds: Centre for Research on Family, Kinship and Childhood, University of Leeds.

Matsaganis, M. (2000) 'Social assistance in southern Europe: the case of Greece revisited', *Journal of European Social Policy*, vol 10, no 1, pp 68-80.

Meehan, E. (1993) *Citizenship and the European Community*, London: Sage Publications.

Mirabile, M.L. (1999) 'The politics of old age in Italy', in A. Walker and G. Naegele (eds) *The politics of old age in Europe*, Buckingham: Open University Press, pp 110-22.

Niero, M. (1996) 'Italy: right turn for the welfare state?', in V. George and P. Taylor-Gooby (eds) *European welfare policy: Squaring the welfare circle*, Basingstoke: Macmillan, pp 117-35.

O'Callaghan, M. (1998) 'Defusing the bomb', *Pensions World*, July, p 16.

O'Carroll, G. (1998) 'National pensions policy initiative', *Irish Banking Review*, Autumn, pp 15-26.

O'Donnell, A. (1999) 'Comparing welfare states: considering the case of Ireland', in G. Kiely, A. O'Donnell, P. Kennedy and S. Quin (eds) *Irish social policy in context*, Dublin: University College Dublin Press.

OECD (Organisation for Economic Co-operation and Development) (2000) *Reforms for an ageing society*, Paris: OECD.

O'Keeffe, D. (1985) 'Equal rights for migrants: the concept of social advantage in Article 7 (2), Regulation 1612/68', *Yearbook of European Law*, vol 5, p 93.

O'Keeffe, D. (1994) 'Union citizenship', in D. O'Keeffe and P.M. Twomey (eds) *Legal issues of the Maastricht Treaty*, Chichester: Wiley Chancery, pp 87-109.

O'Keeffe, D. and Twomey, P.M. (1995) *Legal issues of the Maastricht Treaty*, London: Wiley Chancery Law, part 2.

Oldfield, A. (1990) *Citizenship and community, civic republicanism and the modern world*, London: Routledge.

O'Leary, G.G. (1999) 'Developing the pension system in Ireland', *Administration*, vol 37, no 3, pp 59-69.

O'Leary, S. (1992) 'Nationality law and Community citizenship: a tale of two uneasy bedfellows', *Yearbook of European Law*, vol 12, p 353.

O'Leary, S. (1998) 'Resolution by the Court of Justice of disputes affecting family life', in T.K. Hervey and D. O'Keeffe (eds) *Sex equality law in the European Union*, Chichester: John Wiley and Sons, pp 253-67.

O'Leary, S. (1999) 'Putting flesh on the bones of European Union citizenship', *European Law Review*, vol 24, p 68.

Oliver, M. (1996) *Understanding disability: From theory to practice*, Basingstoke: Macmillan.

Oliver, M. and Barnes, C. (1991) 'Discrimination, disability and welfare: from needs to rights', in I. Byneo, M. Oliver and C. Barnes, *Equal opportunities for disabled people: The case for a new law*, London: IPPR.

Oliver, M. and Barnes, C. (1998) *Disabled people and social policy: From exclusion to inclusion*, London: Longman.

O'Reilly, K. (2000a) 'New Europe, old boundaries: British migrants in Spain', European section, *Journal of Social Welfare and Family Law*, vol 22, no 4, pp 477-91.

O'Reilly, K. (2000b) *The British on the Costa del Sol. Transnational identities and local communities*, London: Routledge.

O'Shea, E. and Hughes, J. (1998) 'Funding long-term care in Ireland', *Administration*, vol 46, no 1, pp 55-70.

O'Sullivan, T. (2000) 'Learning by comparing health services', *Administration*, Summer, vol 48, no 2, pp 43-56.

Pacolet, J., Bouten, R., Lanoye, H. and Versieck, K. (2000) *Social protection for dependency in old age: A study of fifteen member states and Norway*, Aldershot: Ashgate.

Papadopoulos, T.N. (1997) 'Social insurance and the crisis of statism in Greece', in J. Clasen (ed) *Social insurance in Europe*, Bristol: The Policy Press, pp 177-204.

Parker, G. and Clarke, H. (1997) 'Will you still need me will you still feed me? – Paying for care in old age', *Social Policy and Administration*, vol 31, no 2, pp 119-35.

Pascall, G. (1997) *Social policy: A new feminist analysis*, London: Routledge.

Pateman, C. (1992) 'Patriarchal welfare state', in L. McDowell and R. Pringle (eds) *Defining women. Social institutions, gender and difference*, Cambridge: Polity Press/Buckingham: Open University Press, pp 223-45.

Paton, C. (1999) 'New Labour's health policy: the new healthcare state', in M. Powell (ed) *New Labour, new welfare state? The third way in British social policy*, Bristol: The Policy Press, pp 51-76.

Perista, H. (1999) 'Caring for older women in Portugal: a family matter or a woman's role?', Paper presented to the International Conference on the 'Status of the Older Population: Prelude to the 21st Century', Sion, 13-15 December.

Phillipson, C. (1996) 'Intergenerational conflict and the welfare state: American and British perspectives', in A. Walker (ed) *The new generational contract. Intergenerational relations, old age and welfare*, London: University College London Press, pp 206-37.

Pierson, P. (1995) *Dismantling the welfare state*, Cambridge: Cambridge University Press.

Ploug, N. and Kvist, J. (1996) 'Welfare states and old-age pensions', in N. Ploug and J. Kvist, *Social security in Europe: Development or dismantlement?*, The Hague: Kluwer Law International, pp 75-89.

Priestley, M. (2002: forthcoming) 'Whose voices? Representing the claims of older disabled people under New Labour', *Policy & Politics*, vol 30, no 3.

Pringle, K. (1998) *Children and social welfare in Europe*, Buckingham: Open University Press.

Pringle, R. (ed) (1992) *Defining women: Social institutions and gender difference*, Cambridge: Polity Press/Buckingham: Open University Press.

Rake, K., Falkingham, J. and Evans, M. (2000) 'British pension policy in the 21st century: a partnership in pensions or a marriage to the means test', *Social Policy and Administration*, vol 34, no 3, pp 296-317.

RFV (The National Insurance Board) (1999) *Social insurance in Sweden 1999*, Stockholm: RFV.

Rodriguez, V., Fernández-Mayoralas, G. and Rojo, F. (1998) 'European retirees on the Costa del Sol: a cross European comparison', *International Journal of Population Geography*, vol 4, pp 183-200.

Rogerson, P.A., Burr, J.A. and Lin, G. (1997) 'Changes in geographic proximity between parents and their adult children', *International Journal of Population Geography*, vol 3, pp 121-36.

Rose, H. (1981) 'Rereading Titmuss: the sexual division of welfare', *Journal of Social Policy*, vol 10, no 4, pp 477-502.

Rose, H. and Bruce, E. (1995) 'Mutual care but differential esteem: caring between older couples', in S. Arber and J. Ginn (eds) *Connecting gender and ageing*, Buckingham: Open University Press, pp 114-29.

Ruxton, S. (1996) *Children in Europe*, London: NCH Action for Children.

Santana, P. (2000) 'Ageing in Portugal: regional iniquities in health and health care', *Social Science and Medicine*, vol 50, pp 1025-36.

Saraceno, C. and Negri, N. (1994) 'The changing Italian welfare state', *Journal of European Social Policy*, vol 4, no 1, pp 19-34.

Scheiwe, K. (1994) 'EC law's unequal treatment of the family; the case law of the European Court of Justice on rules prohibiting discrimination on grounds of sex and nationality', *Social and Legal Studies*, vol 3, p 243.

Sinfield, A. (1978) 'Analyses in the social division of welfare', *Journal of Social Policy*, vol 7, no 2, pp 129-56.

Singleton, A. (2000) 'Combining quantitative and qualitative research methods in the study of international migration', *International Journal of Social Research Methodology*, vol 2, no 2, pp 151-59.

Ståhlberg, A.C. (1995) 'Pension reform in Sweden', *Scandinavian Journal of Social Welfare*, vol 4, pp 267-73.

Stalford, H. (2000) 'Retirement and the EU: some legal issues', unpublished research paper, Leeds University.

Steele, L. (2001) 'Long-term care for the elderly: the issue explained', *The Guardian Unlimited*, 19 March (society.guardian.co.uk/longtermcare/story/0,8150,459332,00.html).

Steiner, J. (1994) *Textbook on EC law* (4th edn), London: Blackstone Press Ltd.

Sundström, G. and Malmberg, B. (1996) 'The long arm of the welfare state shortened: home help in Sweden', *Scandinavian Journal of Social Welfare*, vol 5, pp 69-75.

Sutherland, S. (1999) *With respect to old age: Long-term care – rights and responsibilities: A report by the Royal Commission on Long-Term Care*, Cm 4192-I, London: The Stationery Office.

Symeonidou, H. (1996) 'Social protection in contemporary Greece', in M. Rhodes (ed) *South European Society and Politics*, vol 1, no 3, Special Issue on southern European welfare states, pp 67–86.

Szyszczak, E. (2000) *EC labour law*, London: Longman.

Szyszczak, E. and Moebius, I. (1998) *Yearbook of European Law*, vol 18, pp 125-56.

Taylor-Gooby, P. (1996) 'The response of government: fragile convergence?', in V. George and P. Taylor-Gooby (eds) *European welfare policy: Squaring the welfare circle*, Basingstoke: Macmillan, pp 119-219.

Taylor-Gooby, P. (1999) 'Policy change at a time of retrenchment: recent pension reform in France, Germany, Italy and the UK', *Social Policy and Administration*, vol 33, no 1, pp 1-19.

Titmuss, R.M. (1958) 'The social division of welfare', in *Essays on the welfare state*, London: Allen and Unwin, now reprinted in P. Alcock, H. Glennester, A. Oakley and A. Sinfield (eds) (2001) *Welfare and well-being: Richard Titmuss's contribution to social policy*, Bristol: The Policy Press, pp 34-55.

Turner, B.S. (1993) 'Outline a theory of human rights', in B.S. Turner (ed) *Citizenship and social theory*, London: Sage Publications, pp 162-90.

Twine, F. (1992) 'Citizenship: opportunities, rights and routes to welfare in old age', *Journal of Social Policy*, vol 21, no 2, pp 165-75.

Twine, F. (1994) *Citizenship and social rights: The interdependence of self and society*, London: Sage Publications.

Ungerson, C. (1999) 'Personal assistants and disabled people: an examination of a hybrid form of work and care', *Work, Employment and Society*, vol 13, no 4, pp 583-600.

Ungerson, C. (2000) 'Thinking about the production and consumption of long-term care in Britain: does gender still matter?', *Journal of Social Policy*, vol 29, no 4, pp 623-43.

UPIAS (Union of Physically Impaired Against Segregation/Disability Alliance) (1976) *Fundamental principles of disability*, London: UPIAS.

Veniopoulou, K. (1988) *Nuclear norms and extended networks. Ideology and reality in welfare provisions*, Athens: mimeo.

Walby, S. (1994) 'Is citizenship gendered?', *Sociology*, vol 28, no 3, pp 379-95.

Walker, A. (ed) (1996) *The new generational contract*, London: UCL Press.

Walker, A. and Maltby, T. (1997) *Ageing Europe*, Buckingham: Open University Press.

Ward, I. (1997) 'Law and the other Europeans', *Journal of Common Market Studies*, vol 35.

Warnes, A.M. (1986) 'The residential mobility histories of parents and children, and relationships to present proximity and social integration', *Environment and Planning A*, vol 13, pp 1581-94.

Warnes, A.M. (1993) 'The development of retirement migration in Great Britain', *Espace, Populations, Societes*, no 3, pp 451-64.

Warnes, A.M. (2002) 'The challenge of intra-union migration to social Europe', *Journal of Ethnic and Migration Studies*, vol 28, no 1, pp 135-52.

Warnes, A.M., King, R., Williams, A.M. and Patterson, G. (1999) 'The well being of expatriate retirees in southern Europe, *Ageing and Society*, vol 19, pp 717-40.

Weatherill, S. (2000) *Cases and materials on EC law* (5th edn), London: Blackstone Press.

Weekers, S. and Pijl, M. (1998) *Home care and care allowances in the European Union*, Utrecht: Netherlands Institute of Care and Welfare.

Wilk, L. (2000) 'Intergenerational relationships: grandparents and grandchildren', in *Family issues between gender and generations*, European observatory on Family Matters, Directorate-General for Employment and Social Affairs, European Commission.

Williams, A.M. and Patterson, G. (1998) 'An empire lost but a province gained: a cohort analysis of British international retirement in the Algarve, *International Journal of Population Geography*, vol 4, pp 135-55.

Williams, A.M., King, R. and Warnes, T. (1997) 'A place in the sun: international retirement migration from northern to southern Europe', *European Urban and Regional Studies*, vol 4, no 2, pp 115-34.

Williams, F. (2001) 'In and beyond New Labour: towards a new political ethic of care', *Critical Social Policy*, vol 21, no 4, pp 467-93.

Wilson, G. (2000) *Understanding old age*, London: Sage Publications.

Wistow, G. (1997) 'Funding long-term care', in M. May, E. Brunsdon and G. Craig (eds) (1997) *Social Policy Review 9*, London: SPA/London Guildhall University, pp 105-23.

Yeates, N. (1997) 'Familialism and selectivism in community care for the elderly: a comparison of the Republic of Ireland and the UK', in M. May, E. Brunsdon and G. Craig (eds) (1997) *Social Policy Review 9*, London: SPA/London Guildhall University, pp 290-316.

Appendix: Methods outline

A qualitative approach

The study adopted a research approach utilised successfully in previous comparative work on gender and migration (Ackers, 1998). A particular feature of this lay in the combination of legal and policy analysis with the development of qualitative approaches centred on life history interviews as the basis of investigation. While there is nothing unique about the use of qualitative methods in this kind of research, their application across six countries is relatively novel and raises some real challenges in maintaining effective research partnerships and meaningful collaboration. The success of this approach was very much facilitated by the continuing use of established partnerships[1].

The research sought to examine a range of issues using qualitative approaches. These included: reasons for the selection of particular destinations; an assessment of the reasons for migration or (any) return; and the experiences of moving to, and residing in, a particular region in terms of access to welfare services and healthcare. They also considered the impact of migration on family networks and caring resources. As such the book can be seen in part as an exploration of transnational kinship.

The interviews thus focused on:

- the characteristics of the population of retirement migrants including financial, marital and family status;
- migration motivations and factors affecting mobility and future plans;
- post-migration experiences in terms of access to, and experiences of, health and welfare services including informal family-based care.

The sample

The research objectives of this study demanded a broad approach encapsulating the experiences of the range of retirement migrants (post-retirement migrants, returning workers, and returning retirees) from across the EU. Unlike a number of recent British studies of IRM, this study was not solely concerned with the population of retired British expatriates in southern Europe. The sample thus included a number of southern European locations, a Scandinavian country and the UK. We had also originally included the Netherlands in order to capture an example of continental Europe. A decision was taken, however, to replace this country with Ireland. This change reflected recent interest in Ireland as a retirement location.

Generally speaking the population of post-retirement migrants is highly clustered, suggesting a focus on certain countries and regions (often coastal and tourist locations). Research partnerships were established in Greece, Portugal and Italy reflecting the movement of northern Europeans to these areas and the incidence of labour migration from these areas and subsequent return. A conscious decision was taken to avoid fieldwork in Spanish locations for the simple reason that this area formed the focus of a number of other concurrent studies of retired British expatriates (Betty and Cahill, 1999; King et al, 2000; O'Reilly, 2000a, 2000b). Within Portugal we also decided to avoid the Algarve as this had received some research attention and we were aware of other locations, close to Lisbon, which attracted retirement migrants. For similar reasons we avoided working in Tuscany (Italy).

Given that the fieldwork aimed to explore the respondents' own accounts and understandings of motivational factors and behaviour in relation to migratory movements in retirement, a purposive non-random sampling technique was adopted (Glaser and Strauss, 1970; Finch and Mason, 1990). Furthermore, the lack of coherent and reliable statistical data on international retirement migration ruled out the possibility of recruiting a representative sample. Practical considerations also had an influence in the choice of particular locations. It was important to seek out post-retirement migrants, returning workers and also a number of returning retirees. The areas chosen bore this objective in mind. Ultimately, our sampling strategy was guided by the knowledge and investigations of the research partners in the participant countries. Preliminary interviews took place with key informants in the chosen locations who then assisted project partners in the identification of the sample. Snowballing techniques were then used[2]. Locations for the work were as follows:

- Greece: mainly Athens and the island of Corfu with a small number from Macedonia in northern Greece;
- Italy: Trieste and the surrounding rural area, also around Lake Garda;
- Portugal: Lisbon and the municipalities of Sintra and Caiscais, which is an historic resort area south of Lisbon;
- Sweden: the whole country;
- The UK: England and Wales;
- Ireland: Dublin and County Roscommon.

The bulk of interviews were carried out during 1998-99. For practical reasons the population of returnees in the three southern European locations and Ireland were located in broadly the same area as the other post-retirement migrants. The UK and Swedish samples consisted entirely of returnees (both returning workers and returning retirees). Returnees are, almost by definition, harder to identify as their more dispersed residence and reintegration in the home area, together with their common nationality render them relatively 'hidden'. It was, therefore, necessary to recruit respondents from a wider geographical area.

In all, a total 210 semi-structured qualitative interviews were held with retired EU migrants; 100 with post-retirement migrants living in host EU countries and 110 with returnees who were resident in their country of origin. These interviews generated a total of 260 respondents who were either post-retirement

Table 6: Numbers, nationality and last previous location of returnees

Nationality/interview location	Numbers and last previous location of returnees	
UK	SP (13) P (5) GK (1) F (2) G (2) D (2)	25
Italy	F (4) G (9) UK (4) L (4) B (4) S (2)	27
Sweden	SP (8) F (8) UK (7) I (2) A (1) SW (1)	26
Portugal	F (15) G (1) D (1) B (2)	19
Greece	G (19)	19
Ireland	UK (15) (+US 4)	19 (135)

A = Austria, B = Belgium, D = Netherlands, DN = Dual Nationality, G = Germany, F = France, GK = Greece, I = Italy, L = Luxembourg, P = Portugal, S = Sweden, SP = Spain, SW = Switzerland, UK = United Kingdom

Table 7: Numbers, nationality and location of post-retirement migrants

Interview location	Numbers and nationality of retired migrants										
Italy	A (3)		UK (1)		F (1)	G (18)	I (5)			DN (3)	31
Portugal	A (1)	B (5)	UK (2)	D (16)	F (2)	G (1)	I (1)	SW (2)	S (1)	DN (2)	33
Greece			UK (28)	D (5)	F (1)	G (3)			S (1)		38
Ireland			UK (22)							DN (1)	23
Totals	4	5	53	21	4	22	6	2	2	6	125

Table 8: Age profile of respondents

Age of respondents	Post-retirement migrants	Returnees
<65	63	36
66-76	50	74
77+	12	17
Unknown	0	8

Table 9: Gender profile of interviews

Interviews by gender	Post-retirement migrants	Returnees
Male	33	43
Female	42	42
Couples (male/female)	25	25

migrants (125) or returnees (135). It was originally intended that respondents be interviewed alone, however, on a number of occasions couples were interviewed together. Tables 6 to 9 give a more comprehensive outline of the respondents in terms of gender, age, nationality and location.

Data handling and analysis

Interviews were conducted in the language most appropriate to the respondent and were generally recorded on audiotape. Transcripts were then translated into English as necessary and interviews relayed by e-mail to the research fellow in Leeds where the data was systematically coded. The texts were then analysed using basic grid analysis and thematic coding techniques. Overview grids (adapted from Knodel, 1993) provided a summary of the range of opinions (and the justifications for those views) across all the respondents in relation to a specific area of fieldwork enquiry. The development of these tables, and an accompanying percentage count of the respondents' various responses, provided an indication of the level of support for a particular view in terms of actual numbers of respondents. In this way the researcher was restrained from relaying an account based merely on the views of one or two particularly forceful, articulate respondents and/or a personal opinion on the matter under investigation. Overview grids also proved helpful in illuminating the full range of opinions offered.

In order to ensure that the thematic coding was systematic, consistent and flexible the data was first coded according to a number of general relevant categories. Further investigation of the transcripts enabled the generation of grounded subcategories that more sensitively reflected the views of the respondents. The use of a Nud*ist software package allowed the data to be retrieved in any combination according to various base characteristics, specific questions and themes, and so on. In this way a rigorous and systematic analysis of the data generated was achieved.

A note on the citation of interview material

Where material from the interviews is cited in the book an interview number is provided in the text. The prefix to this number reflects the category of respondent. All of those with a prefix 'R' are returnees; 'L' refers to interviews with key informants some of whom were retirees themselves. Those without a prefix are post-retirement migrants resident in a host country at the time of interview. The location in which an interview took place is indicated by the first digit of the respondent's number as cited in the text. Zero (0) indicates UK; 1 denotes Italy; 2, Sweden; 3, Portugal; 4, Greece; and 5, Ireland.

On occasion, the research partners summarised contextual material relating to cases. Where this material has been used to supplement the translation of the respondents' own statements, it is presented in square brackets to distinguish it from the narrative. The variability in this approach reflects one of the problems of undertaking collaborative research where the problems of transcription are compounded by the need to translate material or interview in a second language. This perhaps reflects one dimension of what Hantrais and Mangen (1996, p 10) refer to as the "greater compromises in method" inherent in comparative research[3].

Notes

[1] These existed in Greece, Italy and Portugal. A research partnership was established in Sweden for this project and a research fellow was employed in Leeds to undertake the empirical work in the UK and Ireland.

[2] The use of snowball sampling in accessing 'concealed' populations and in using key informants as a route into the target population are discussed in Atkinson and Flint (2001).

[3] For a more detailed discussion of the importance of contextualisation to comparative research see Ackers (1999) and Hantrais (1999).

Index

Page references for figures and tables are in *italics*; those for notes are followed by n

Also available from The Policy Press

Shifting spaces
Women, citizenship and migration within the European Union
Edited by Louise Ackers, Centre for the Study of Law in Europe, University of Leeds

"... a very good book for academics and students in the fields of politics and law, as well as policy-makers at national and European level. This book not only provides an important review of citizenship literature and law, it also fills a substantial gap in academic and policy-making literature." Journal of Social Welfare and Family Law

£18.99 ISBN 1 86134 038 9
HB £45.00 ISBN 1 86134 127 X

Welfare rights and responsibilities
Contesting social citizenship
Peter Dwyer, Department of Sociology and Social Policy, University of Leeds

"... a very accessible introduction to a variety of perspectives on social welfare citizenship." Work, Employment & Society

"... deserves a wider audience than most academic texts." SCOLAG Legal Journal

PB £17.99 ISBN 1 86134 204 7

Approaching retirement
Social divisions, welfare and exclusion
Kirk Mann, Department of Sociology and Social Policy, University of *Leeds*

"... a lively review of the ideological contests surrounding retirement and pension policies." Jay Ginn, School of Human Sciences, University of Surrey

This book assesses different approaches to retirement pensions policy, highlighting their relative strengths and weakenesses. An invaluable resource for social science students at all levels and for those who teach them.

PB £17.99 ISBN 1 86134 282 9
HB £45.00 ISBN 1 86134 283 7

MORE ▶

The gender dimension of social change
The contribution of dynamic research to the study of women's life courses

Edited by Elisabetta Ruspini, Department of Sociology and Social Research, University of Milano Bicocca, Italy and Angela Dale, Faculty of Economic and Social Studies, University of Manchester

"... an impressive book that brings gender into a central position within longitudinal studies." Enzio Mingione, Faculty of Sociology, University of Milano-Bicocca, Italy

HB £35.00 ISBN 1 86134 332 9

Social assistance dynamics in Europe
National and local poverty regimes

Edited by Chiara Saraceno, Faculty of Political Sciences and Department of Social Sciences, University of Torino, Italy

"... an original contribution to the understanding of comparative social assistance." Stewart Miller, School of Social Policy, Sociology and Social Research, University of Kent at Canterbury

PB £17.99 ISBN 1 86134 314 0
HB £45.00 ISBN 1 86134 315 9

What future for social security?
Debates and reforms in national and cross-national perspective

Jochen Clasen, Department of Applied Social Science, University of Stirling

"This collection contains important reflections on emerging themes in social security. Anyone concerned with how welfare provision is being shaped for the future would be well advised to invest in this book." Katherine Rake, London School of Economics and Political Science

PB £18.99 ISBN 1 86134 410 4

For further information about these and other titles published by The Policy Press, please visit our website at: www.policypress.org.uk or telephone +44 (0)117 954 6800

To order, please contact:
Marston Book Services
PO Box 269
Abingdon
Oxon OX14 4YN
UK
Tel: +44 (0)1235 465500
Fax: +44 (0)1235 465556
E-mail: direct-orders@marston.co.uk

The POLICY

P~P

P R E S S